GW00733994

SUMMER 2015

MEANJIN

VOLUME 74, ISSUE 4

QUARTERLY

EDITOR Jonathan Green
meanjin@unimelb.edu.au

DEPUTY EDITOR Catherine McInnis

POETRY EDITOR Judith Beveridge

POETRY CRITIC Martin Langford

LAYOUT Patrick Cannon

COVER DESIGN Design by Committee

COPYEDITOR Richard McGregor

PROOFREADER Richard McGregor

WEBSITE DESIGNER Madeleine Egan

INTERNS Will Abbey, Melanie Basta,
Jared Catchpoole, Zoe Papageorgiou,
Ella Shi, Ellen Spooner

PATRON Chris Wallace-Crabbe

EDITORIAL ADVISORY BOARD
Louise Adler, Alison Croggon, Kate Darian-Smith,
Richard Glover, Jenny Grigg, Brian Johns,
Hilary McPhee, David Malouf and Lindsay Tanner

FOUNDING EDITOR
Clem Christesen (1911–2003; editor 1940–74).
Meanjin was founded in 1940. The name, pronounced
mee-an-jin, is derived from an Aboriginal word for the
spike of land on which Brisbane sits. The magazine
moved to Melbourne in 1945 at the invitation of
the University of Melbourne, which continues to be
Meanjin's principal sponsor. In 2008 *Meanjin* became
an imprint of Melbourne University Publishing Ltd.

SUBSCRIPTIONS
Contact the *Meanjin* office or subscribe online
at our website.

WHERE TO FIND US
Postal address: *Meanjin*, Level 1, 11–15 Argyle
Place South, Carlton, Victoria 3053 Australia
Telephone: (+61 3) 9342 0317
Fax: (+61 3) 9342 0399

Email: meanjin@unimelb.edu.au
Website: www.meanjin.com.au
Twitter: www.twitter.com/Meanjin
Facebook: www.facebook.com/Meanjin

Printed and bound by McPherson's Printing Group
Distributed by Penguin Random House
Print Post Approved PP341403 0002
AU ISSN 0025-6293

MEANJIN

VOLUME 74, ISSUE 4 QUARTERLY

EDITORIAL

Jonathan Green

THE TRADITIONAL *Meanjin* editorial combines a string of nostalgia-tinged observations on Queensland, poetry and 1940 in more or less that order. So there's tradition served. Here in the summer of 2015 we should probably consider our present, but marvel too at the consistency and longevity of this magazine and the kind of conversation on Australian culture, literature and ideas it has sought to nurture and expand for 75 years. Like the shark, as once described by Woody Allen, the magazine must move through the water to survive. So, some changes here at *Meanjin*. A new editor, me (the eleventh in uninterrupted sequence), and a remodelling of the object you are now holding: a new typographic feel, a new size and hopefully enhanced readability.

Judith Beveridge has unflappingly edited *Meanjin*'s poetry for ten years. That is a contribution to this magazine and to Australian letters that should not be underestimated. This issue holds Judy's last selection. She has decided to concentrate on her own writing and academic work. We owe her more than simple thanks. Stepping into this considerable breach will be Bronwyn Lea. Brownyn is a poet and teaches writing at the University of Queensland. She was poetry editor at the University of Queensland Press, and inaugural editor of *Australian Poetry Journal*. There's more: for the first time in some years *Meanjin* now has a fiction editor. He is Peter Pierce, a respected critic and editor of *The Cambridge History of Australian Literature*.

Enough said. Please, read on …

The *Meanjin* Dorothy Porter Prize for Poetry 2015

Once again it was a pleasure for us to judge the prize for 2015. We made a shortlist of six poems. While it was not our intention, this shortlist aptly represents the diversity of poems published in *Meanjin* in 2015.

The shortlisted poems
Louise Carter, 'Amaranthine'
Russell Erwin, 'And Still' (*for Emmelise*)
Barry Hill, 'The Glove' *For Ronald Farren-Price*
Penny O'Hara, 'Wiradjuri Country' *For my anthropology teacher*
Christopher Palmer, 'On the Death of the Past'
Omar Sakr, 'Election Day'

The winners
First Prize of $1200 to Russell Erwin for his poem 'And Still'. This is an elegant poem that pits unemotional logic against the intense suffering of loss. There's an understated argument threading through the stanzas that has an unexpectedly profound effect on the reader.

Second Prize of $500 to Penny O'Hara for 'Wiradjuri Country'. With some stunning imagery, O'Hara provides a vivid picture of the country. There's a quiet narrative to this poem guiding the reader towards the teacher we all long for but few are fortunate to find.

Third Prize of $300 to Barry Hill for 'The Glove', dedicated to the great Australian pianist Ronald Farren-Price. This poem reminds us that not everything can be expressed in words—not even by poets. There are some wonders that approach the sacred.

Congratulations to all the poets from us both.

Andrea Goldsmith and Kristin Henry

NATIONAL ACCOUNTS

December Quarter

Robyn Williams

M Y FRIENDS IN England are puzzled. Again. They look at Australia as they would stare sorrowfully at a teenage relative, off the rails. Such promise, such disappointment. Why isn't their lad from Oz as steady and confident as that other young blood from New Zealand?

I came to this magnificent country with its long history and huge promise back in 1964. I knew no-one here and explored in innocence. I had been given a romantic vision of the Land Down Under by my Aussie friends in London. They were always welcoming visitors, from Oz—uniformly cultured and relaxed folk who all seemed to be natural athletes and who by right knew British intellectual superstars such as Bertrand Russell and J.B. Priestley personally. They enjoyed a jar with the informality that contrasted sweetly with London swank,

Yet here I was, in 1964, at a country town in New South Wales, lying by yet another of those vast Olympic pools reading a novel when the man with the whistle arrived. 'You

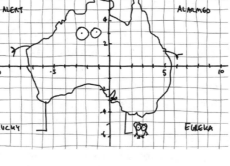

can't wear those in here,' he announced, pointing at my speedos, 'you must wear shorts. You should cover up. Now leave the baths.'

I was so dumbfounded I complied. Today speedos seem to be the required apparel of those in charge; but in 1964, despite the Beatles revolution and a swinging Northern Hemisphere I appeared to have landed in Erewhon— everything was back to front. Where was the larrikin spirit, the anti-authoritarian chutzpah that I'd been promised before I got on that ten-quid ship from England? I knew that Samuel Butler's novel *Erewhon* was modelled on New Zealand rather than Oz, featuring a land where criminals went to hospital and the sick were sent to jail, but the Topsy Turvy Land I'd encountered in those first few months looked very much like Butler's satire. Yes, there were rebellious spirits, but when the man with the whistle turned up they all fell into line, looking down at their boots. Years later I joined the ABC and witnessed its

JACK

frequent compliance to finger wagging from Canberra and I learned the precious and ever so appropriate phrase 'The Pre-emptive Buckle'.

On this last visit to Britain in September 2015, the puzzlement was tinged by sadness. 'What *is happening* in Australia? Why all this crap about climate change? Why are you being so cruel to refugees? Why are you claiming to be impoverished? Why are you still digging holes in the landscape instead of innovating and *investing* in new technologies?' It seemed to be a Brit take on Barry Jones' 1980s entreaty that *Sleepers Wake!*

This is, of course, a comment on *political* culture, not the wisdom of our crowds. Our crowds are doing fine. Science in Australia is a triumph, with the world's youngest ever scientific Nobel Prize winner, Lawrence Bragg, laureates Elizabeth Blackburn, Brian Schmidt, Barry Marshall, Robin Warren, Jack Eccles, Mac Burnet, Howard Florey and more to come. Young scientists are brighter than ever and their ideas are simply thrilling. In the arts we are triumphant and, in September the West End was enraptured by Nicole Kidman's performance in *Photograph 51*. Sport is fine, especially if you are female. And, as I told my interlocutors, if you look at the goodwill of communities Australia is up there with the best as public reactions to the Lindt café siege and the recent Rozelle

convenience store horror demonstrated. The people were golden and in the words of Malcolm Turnbull showed genuine 'love' following the tragedies in their town.

No, our dire reputation abroad has been, in recent years, a problem of tribes: political tribes. We had lost a generation of leaders when Labor was stupid enough to sack Kim Beazley and the Liberals allowed Peter Costello to slide away. The *ingénus* filled the vacuum and fought tribally. It was ugly. Its aftermath still is.

Once more Australia was ignoring the future and looking backwards. The land that had invented social welfare, votes for women and an open door for various (white) nationals, was now looking back to Mother England and taking out its disciplinary whistle (in the name of freedom!), while Labor played mad faction games and fought like hyenas: Mad Max, once more.

It was as if democracy and political parties were still too immature to cope. The party of Menzies remains quite young. As for Labor, its first PM (the world's first national labour head of government?), Chris Watson, was from New Zealand via Chile, and may have been 'illegal' during the four fragile months in 1904 he did the top job. Ever messy.

Have we turned the corner in late 2015? There is hope, as two distinguished intellectual Lords in London who admire Australia told me before I left. They were hoping that the public spirit of enlightenment would return, as it often does. They know Australians and want the words of new PM Malcolm Turnbull to be realised: that 'we should respect the intelligence of the people'. If we do we'll have grown up. •

Robyn Williams has been the presenter of ABC RN's *Science Show* for 40 years. He is a visiting professor at UNSW, was visiting fellow of Balliol College, Oxford, in 1995–96, and is a fellow of the Australian Academy of Science.

ONDAATJE IN SOMERSET

Geoff Lemon

THIS IS NOT about cricket. That's a disclaimer for those who would glance at a landscape's principal feature and decide the route is not for them. It's not about cricket in the way that *The Lion King* is not about lions, *Buffy the Vampire Slayer* is not about vampires, *A League of Their Own* is not about baseball. They are about love and friendship and fragility, the things we can't escape from. It's also true that this is about cricket, in the way that *Buffy the Vampire Slayer* is about vampires. You can't have the rest without a context.

It's the northern summer of 2015, and the middle of an Ashes tour. Between the outsized hype of the men's series is a more measured contest between women. Their first meeting is a one-day game in Taunton. Driving through Somerset county, England unfolds towards the south-west like a sleepy arm towards a nightstand. London's clotted sky separates into watery sunlight, rippled across the country's storied green. Down countless lanes of motorway, surfing traffic by shunting the snout of a rental car fancier than any you will ever own into the channels that appear, you sense your ribcage open a little and feel something lift.

> I'm the prow
> on an ancient vessel,
> this afternoon
> I'm going down to Peru
> soul between my teeth

England's county cricket grounds are legion, each a castle of modest pride. Low pavilions in twentieth-century brick, dim tea rooms with ageing carpet, grass banks or rows of creaky scaffold for the scattered hundreds who might attend an average day. Corridors crammed with photos or honour boards of past players with reputations grander than the surroundings, their achievements available for rote recital by elderly members shuffling by.

In these locales many a correspondingly mediocre cricketer gets something named after him, whether for local service or a modicum of international achievement. Marcus Trescothick has a stand. Andy Caddick has a stand. Graeme Hick has a stand. Basil d'Oliveira deserves one, but it's a bleak and jerry-rigged affair. Eric Hollies gets a featureless terrace. Ian Botham has a stand at Taunton and a restaurant at Southampton and a knighthood at Buckingham Palace and a television job for life, despite a public dedication to being personally objectionable. Even Britain's supposed elite are not immune to populism.

Somerset is famous less for Botham than for his departure. When the unglamorous, bespectacled captain Peter Roebuck backed the sacking of West Indies imports Viv Richards and Joel Garner, Botham walked too. All three stars were in decline, but still. Imagine Bob Marley, Jimi Hendrix and Mick Jagger (another embarrassing knight, as it happens) being kicked out of a supergroup by the obscure classicist who wrote the arrangements. Botham carried an unedifying hatred of Roebuck to the latter's death and beyond.

There is one Somerset dedication from beyond the cricketing parade. The Ondaatje Stand brings to mind the Sri Lankan–Canadian poet who famously became a novelist and wrote *The English Patient*, after years of less famously practising his original form. But while Michael Ondaatje wrote the verse quoted earlier, the building is named for his older brother Christopher, leader of his own peripatetic existence as a businessman, Olympic athlete and the kind of nostalgic philanthropist who gives large sums of money to small cricket clubs.

On this day, the arena between the dedications plays host to a culmination. The English Cricket Board has accelerated its backing for women's cricket over several years. Now a heavily promoted series begins with a sell-out, a big chase and a win for the home side. From a distance the crowd is a bubbling backdrop

Old Father Time, weather vane at Lord's Cricket Ground

to flecks of blue and green moving on the field. This complex, articulate choreography could be described by the younger Ondaatje: 'friends / whose minds and bodies / shift like acrobats to each other'.

The bar of Taunton's stone hotel that night is a world of vested interests pressed together in celebration. Of the commentators, reporters, ex-players and administrators, most hold at least two of those roles and some all four. Each is a women's cricket advocate. But it's hard to see this as corrupt: having the big names in one place also shows how small the circuit is, and how populated by people sincerely trying to build something. Their welcome is strong. The hotel requires drinks to be charged to a room, so those of us more likely to be sleeping in our rental cars than within its august walls trade damp wads of forgotten cash while inflating the accounts of broadcasters and athletes. The men's tour would never be so collegial. (Some weeks later on the same system, former England captain Mike Gatting will accept two payments for the same round, fleecing a Wisden Young Journalist of the Year of 30 pounds. Beware.)

Before we join this scene though, I wander down the main street with a BBC television duo in search of dinner. A woman greets us from a laneway. 'Hey. Do you know if Zinc is open tonight?' Patrick or I would have fired off a negative and kept walking, but Chris the cameraman is medically incapable of being unfriendly. 'Where is it?' he asks in his practical London syllables, and she's away.

There's clearly something amiss. She has a blank face, unresponsive even to her own tumbling monologue. Her tone is unsettling: a singsong that is part public address system, part small girl blaming a doll for the grim fate of a childhood pet. Pigtails, hoody, she could be 25 or 40. 'I'll walk up with you,' she says. We pass her nightclub, as dark and quiet as you'd expect at ten on a Tuesday night in Taunton. The main street runs an empty cobbled curve into the evening gloom. The only thing open is a chain pub, so she follows us there, nursing a Diet Coke and eventually being talked into accepting a solitary onion ring as she watches us eat dinner.

She says she's from somewhere different each time we ask. She changes her name. She says she has a fiancé called Marshall whom she's met twice. That the two purses she's carrying are to separate her French and English money, necessary after her mother moved to Limoges and changed her name. She says unprompted things like 'Have you ever had a godly experience?' or 'I don't like Jeremy Kyle. David Cameron's a good bloke. I think David Cameron's Polish.' Between each discursion, she'll ask again what we do and where we're from.

'What's your game then?'

'I'm a journalist, like I said.'

'You're another one!'

'I'm … the same one.'

'You must be so intelligent. Did you go to college?'

'University.'

'Which one?'

'Bristol.'

'Clifton? I could tell you a few stories about Clifton. There was this church near Clifton and it just went on and on and on.'

'What does that mean? Never mind. Bristol's all right. It's very arty.'

'What about Banksy, Banksy's my brother.'

'That's not real, is it? Is that street talk?'

For a while this seems funny—we have to talk to anyway, so we ask questions to provoke her strange answers. Then there's an unspoken moment where all three of us realise we're making sport of a damaged person. Laughter curls to nothing like an insect in a flame. Soon she is casually assigning her parents the names of the Moors murderers, or impassively mentioning serial killer boyfriends and dungeon imprisonment. Of course nothing's true—a half-chewed mash of tabloid crime reporting from the last 20 years—but the sadness is palpable.

She says she'll take a taxi home, but when the time comes she'll have none of it. 'I'm staying out all night, to three in the morning.'

'What's going to be open?'

'I'll find somewhere.'

When further negotiations fail we leave her, that melancholy face atop blocky shoulders in pastel pink, two purses on the table, the scene reflected in the shiny fake timber ranked row on row by the drinking barn that we're leaving. Back at the hotel bar, none of us are able to explain the story.

Much later, commentator Daniel Norcross and I are the human detritus left at the night's high-water mark. The only other stayers are two strangers sitting quietly at the bar. They turn to us. The Gowler brothers are a marketing dream: Cambridgeshire farmers in town for junior cricket, who watched the women's match on a whim and were surprised to be impressed. Having ascertained our line of work they pump us for gossip, disappointed to learn that we don't often find ourselves on the lash with Warnie and KP.

Christopher is the avuncular sibling, Edward darker of expression and temperament. His face lights up though when he speaks of his son: Will Gowler is lining up for Cambridgeshire Under 13s the next day. A fast bowler. Tall and wiry. Whippy wrists, proper pace for his age. There is talk of an international future, a seam of belief running through the bravado. We must come to the tournament tomorrow, says Edward, buying whiskies. We'll see the future of English cricket.

I have no reason not to. The day is warm and sticky, early rain leaving an atmosphere like flypaper. The grounds of King's College are a cricketing champagne fountain: as you skirt the perimeter of one match, the slope drops away to reveal another, then another, each oval populated by a further set of teenagers in whites. Near the edge of the school's domain I take an orbital slingshot back around the dozenth boundary to find the Gowlers on camp chairs by the rope.

Edward hands me a beer, but the mood is not high. Yorkshire have chewed through Cambridgeshire's top order, and when the tiny wicketkeeper gives his innings away, young Will Gowler comes out at number eight. I ask how his batting is. 'He's not bad,' says Edward, with the constipated preoccupation of a man who knows he's fudging but doesn't want to give it away.

Will sees out a few deliveries but is soon bowled. His father looks queasy. There's no disappointment *in* his boy, just disappointment *for* him. Yorkshire are set 100 to win. Will sends down seven tight overs but the chase skips on around him. On the boundary, able to watch but never intervene, is Edward Gowler, aching, living every ball his son bowls. We worry twice as hard for other people, worry like Ondaatje for 'children wise / as tough shrubs'. How hard it must be raising teenagers, fearing for them, a fervent and endless prayer for their fortune as they tear themselves further away from you each month.

Sometimes you are so busy
discovering your friends
I ache with loss
—but that is greed.

I do not know this yet, but a week later my friend Kat will be dead. I will get a shaky long-distance phone call. There will be uncertainly of circumstance, though intent seems irrelevant beside the result. In the minutes beforehand I'll be on top of the world: a lived dream of working on a Test series for the ABC with one of my commentary heroes. We will be in the middle of a video shoot. I will accept the call but not its contents. The news will be impossible, colliding before sliding from view like a bird down glass. We will hang up and I will keep working, because there is no other possible thing to do.

Some days later it will sink in with the suddenness of a horseshoe through a mile of ocean. In a late-night Birmingham pub I will book a flight home to Melbourne and go straight from the bar to a bus to a hungover airport to a day in midair suspension to a midweek funeral on the greyest and bitterest day of winter, where the rain comes in sideways and the people fold back inside the blank church before the hearse has even gone from view. A friend will hold onto me in an empty corridor like we're mutual flotation devices. The hall will be too featureless for any real person but especially this one. The mourners will raise their massed grief to a collective animal pitch. Her family so staunch that day, facing an unthinkable absence in all that follow.

Was that woman in Taunton ever cared for like that? Most of us are once, at least as children. The questions pile up: whether she ever had anyone; when they drifted away; how she resorted to hailing strangers to talk out the relationships in her head. 'Where the bloody hell is Marshall, that's what I want to know,' Chris had muttered with frustration when we were trying to get her home.

'Marshall is hanging out,' she had said, pronouncing the last two words as if she'd just found them at the back of a cupboard and couldn't remember what they were for.

'What's he up to? That crazy cat.'

'He kicks it, here and there.'

'Do you live with him?'

'I don't live with him at the moment, but it's going to be … it's gonna be soon. I just go round mostly on my own.'

Fuck. I will return to England after the funeral. The Australian men's team will have subsided, the women will be fighting back. All of it will be irrelevant. I will run into Chris at a match. He will tell me that he's thought of her every day, and confirm that a heaviness has stayed with us all.

We have this religion about hardship. How it makes us stronger. How each setback increases the distance we can travel, each swing of the axe pares us back to something sleeker. Scars fuse into a carapace, misfortune begets wisdom as though bad luck were a vaccination. This has the same provenance as all religious belief: a fear of how to get through life if suffering serves no purpose.

In 1976 Jeff Thomson busted his bowling shoulder by crashing into a teammate. He was probably the fastest ever, but he was never as fast again. The perfect machine of youth was dented. We are injured and told it will heal, not conceiving that healing is partial, that we will carry the dull memory of that damage with every step. Enough scar tissue and a joint can't move.

We're not all going to make it. Some of us crash up against life so hard we break, or part of the mechanism does. Tip over a grandfather clock and see what is knocked out of true. Some of us limp on, some only get so far. There are those so alone they live in their own world among ghosts; those who despite any amount of love can't find a way to carry on. Many live the fear and joy of having children, knowing those kids can't be guarded or recalled.

You step delicately
into the wild world
and your real prize will be
the frantic search.
Want everything. If you break
break going out not in.

But the real message of that missive is: don't break. Please. Let probability's burden fall on someone else's child. We are brutal in our computing of the numbers but we cannot do it differently. We raise our loved ones up then send them into that wildness. We carry model ships down to the docks and regard the ocean. The water is treacherous, the expanse unthinkable. All we want is to keep safe what we love. But there is nothing for it. We push our fragile craft out to sea, and scour dockside markets for amulets against storms. •

Geoff Lemon is a writer, radio broadcaster, and editor of *Going Down Swinging.*

HIROSHIMA 70

Kumi Taguchi

M Y DAD WAS hidden away in the mountains outside Tokyo when the bombs fell and the war ended. He didn't see the horrors of burned skin and ash shadows. He'd hear about them later when he returned home.

He'd been living in the mountains for two years, since he was ten. At that time the Japanese government decided that it needed to preserve the next generation if Tokyo was obliterated. So kids were sent on their own, with nuns to look after them, into green, serene havens of nature.

He told me many years later that he remembered being handed a sheet of paper with hand-drawn pictures on it: sketches of the edible and poisonous plants in the area. What he should forage for and what he shouldn't. His mother, my beautiful grand-mother—whom I remember as an elderly, elegant woman who smiled and made us tea—visited her sons once in those two years. My daughter is about the same age as my dad was when he grew up much earlier than any parent would wish. My daughter still asks us to remove spiders from her room.

Each day, the kids had to practise escape drills. This included walking in a line, each child with their left hand on the left shoulder of the friend in front of them. There were B-52 bombers flying overhead, on their way to Tokyo. The war was far but near.

One day dad and his best friend were in a line together for their daily drill. Dad's friend was behind, his left hand resting on dad's shoulder. They walked along together, learning to survive together. There wasn't much sound but dad tells me there was a bomb and shrapnel. And then he remembers the hand resting on his shoulder slipping away. I find it hard to imagine what a young boy must think when he turns around and sees his best friend, his comfort, lying lifeless on the ground. You wonder what experiences shape a child.

When he was on the cusp of adolescence, the war, in its physical form, ended. A revela-tion in the mountains, dad told me. Because he remembers a radio. And on that radio, the voice of a man who, until then, was per-ceived as nearly god-like, unreal. The voice of emperor Hirohito telling his people that the war was over. No-one had heard him speak before.

Fast-forward to dad as a man in his prime. At 40 he is offered a job at the Australian Broadcasting Commission, to work at Radio Australia. With leather satchel in hand, he leaves behind his home country and makes a blue-skied land of opportunity his home. The memory of that war was still raw here, too. And dad found himself talking to veterans, many of whom had been brutally treated by the Japanese. Dad deliberately went to RSL clubs so he could talk over what it all meant with those who'd fought for the other side. Over a scotch and a beer. RSL diplomacy.

When he was 55 he moved into a retirement village in suburban Melbourne. He was still self-sufficient and healthy but that's what he wanted. I reckon he loved being the young man on the block, too. With most of his fellow residents at least 20 years older than him, he took on the role of cooking the weekly village barbecue. With tongs in hand turning sausages, still speaking broken English and still smoking.

He's now very frail. Everything takes a lot longer now: putting on shoes, getting into the car, walking to the local mall for a meal. He loves it when I visit, although he'd never say so. Having a cappuccino together is the highlight and I'm pretty sure he only goes to a café when I'm there.

Last time I saw him, he pulled out an old photo album. He's not a very sentimental person, but he does think about life and he wants to figure it out. He showed me a photo of his best friend at university. There is an old black and white photo of them in fitted, military-style uniforms. They look handsome and cool. A few days before graduation, dad's friend was found hanging in his college room. No-one knew why he decided to take his own life.

You wonder what experiences shape a man. •

Kumi Taguchi was born in Melbourne to an Australian mother and Japanese father. Her first media job was at the *7.30 Report*, answering phones and collecting dry-cleaning. Kumi spent six years reporting in Hong Kong before returning to Sydney as a journalist and news anchor for the ABC.

CHECK YOUR ENTITLEMENT

Damon Young

You're all gonna wonder how you ever thought you could live so large and leave so little for the rest of us
—Selina Kyle, *The Dark Knight Rises*

Society is God
—Pierre Bourdieu, *Pascalian Meditations*

WE ARRIVE IN the world screaming, smeared in blood and shit. Small animals, abject and abraded by things. The inch between animation and termination is a few days warmth. And life is chiefly sleep anyway: a blur, a craving, then oblivion again. Our divinity is *Ananke*: necessity.

Then before long, this goddess bloats. We spend more than four times the average weekly wage on a single, short helicopter flight ('because of … concern for the country'). We become belligerent when an RAAF trip fails to offer our special meal, then offer a weak apology ('all of us are human'). We lament free international business-class travel ('No edible food. No airline pyjamas … I lie in my tailored suit').

The 'we' here provides a nice rhetorical intimacy between infantile simplicity and adult sophistication. But we ordinary citizens do not command the perks of Bronwyn

Bishop, Kevin Rudd or Bob Carr, or become livid or whiny when these are missing. We certainly do not spend more than the median price of a unit in Melbourne ... on Australian flags. These are the priorities of an elite clique of privileged politicians.

Everyone begins life as a flimsy, clumsy animal, but soon expectations vary. Some get used to the commonwealth of averageness, while others are special: they need more money, security, kudos and power. And not simply need—they *deserve*. The word for this in English is 'entitlement', which has a double meaning. On the one hand, it refers to the rights we can legitimately claim. This is its positive or neutral gist: those goods that law or custom guarantee. On the other hand, it suggests demands that are excessive. This is its negative connotation: those goods that are luxurious, superfluous or *verboten*, and the outlook of those who grab them.

Importantly, the second definition requires the first. When someone falls into a tantrum because her macadamias are served in a packet and not on a plate, it is because she believes she has a *right* to spiffily presented nuts. By humiliating the steward and putting out her fellow passengers, Cho Hyun-ah, daughter of the Air Korea chairman, demonstrated her belief: her status entitled her to exacting snack etiquette. Her own public shaming revealed otherwise: she had no such right. This was just more 'imperial abuse of an owner family', as one Korean newspaper put it.

These embarrassing episodes point to another part of entitlement: passion. Those scorned for this vice respond badly to privation. Shaken by their sense of loss, they mock, chastise and attack others. Trivially, this includes the wealthy suburban café patrons who yell at waitresses because their coffee is tepid—and then because the milk is burnt.

More horrifying are those who abuse, assault and murder women who dare to say 'no'. For these men, women are not human beings, with their own physical and existential autonomy. They are things: the means to male ends; the equipment claimed as a boy's birthright of pleasure and status. ('You cannot rape your spouse,' said Donald Trump's special counsel, Michael Cohen.)

The point is not that hospitality rudeness and male brutality are equal, but that both involve more than simple belief. For good or ill, entitlement involves profound emotional ties, and a violent response when these ties are cut—even if the rage or grief is hidden by public contrition, as it is by professionally groomed politicians and celebrities.

Aristotle, writing in the fourth century BC, discussed entitlement in his *Nicomachean Ethics*. He examined the vice of vanity, which involves a pathological need for glory. These preening men do not simply pretend to be better than they are—vanity is not deceit. They genuinely believe they deserve plaudits and are, said Aristotle, 'fools and ignorant of themselves'. Just as importantly, they long for applause and wreaths, so their cognitive error goes hand-in-hand with desire: too much, or for the wrong thing.

The Aristotelian outlook is helpful, because it emphasises the complexity of entitlement: not simply an idea, or an emotion, but a whole human orientation to the world. This is what Aristotle called a *hexis*, and in English we might say disposition. Politicians face-first in the trough are not simply canny—their entire bent is towards a certain quantum of luxury.

Missing in Aristotle's theory are the social origins of hexis. The Greek thinker argued that 'man is by nature a political animal', and rightly so. But by this he meant that human potential is only ever actualised in a community; that the laissez-faire vision of aloof individuals is false. He was not arguing against social hierarchies and the virtues and vices they encourage. Put another way, Aristotle criticised vain citizens who got above their station—he had no issues with the station itself. He was, in many ways, a conservative with aristocratic sympathies.

As French sociologist Pierre Bourdieu notes, the hexis—what he calls a *habitus*—is profoundly political. It arises from the social hierarchy and helps to maintain it. There are countless positions to take up in any society: differences in class, status, gender. The hexis is what aligns these: unthinkingly, spontaneously, in a matter-of-fact way. '[T]he habitus makes possible the free production', Bourdieu writes in *The Logic of Practice*, 'of all the thoughts, perceptions and actions inherent in the particular conditions of its production—and only those.' From accent, fashion and gait to music and food, to party political membership (or not), the hexis is a bundle of tendencies that are produced by, and themselves produce, the social order.

The right hexis brings cash, mates and leverage; the right old boys' tie, ideological mania or selective amnesia. Shimmying up the slick pole of politics is a game, but this does not make it false—any more than the competition in school, academia or business. Bourdieu has a neat word for the commitment this requires: *illusio*, our investment in the sport of social success. The currency of success varies: money for some, celebrity for others, bohemian 'opting out' for others still (which is itself a kind of opting-in, with all its handed-down symbols and signs of iconoclasm). But no-one is outside society's snakes and ladders play. The game is real.

Which brings us back to those newborns, mucky but seemingly pure. While they begin life as bundles of rightly needy egotism and solipsism, the world soon coopts their instincts. Their urges, cravings and appetites are incorporated into some social milieu. They still get to reward themselves, but only through *this* family, *that* primary school, *this* office, *that* party. They sacrifice immediate contentment for institutional love.

In this light it is foolish to expect that politicians or senior executives will willingly forgo their absurd expenses—in their world the flights, chauffeurs and allowances are ordinary. The perks are not banal or common, since they distinguish the elite from the hoi polloi. But they are the normal recompense for a certain kind of ambition and sacrifice; the payoff for the negotiations, compromises and cruelties of their game. In many cases they are raised, schooled, trained and managed to expect more: cash, real estate acreage and clout. This is all part of their illusio.

One problem is that this elite usually legislates or lobbies to increase their portion of the pot, and decrease everyone else's. The same politicians siphoning commonwealth dollars for party fundraising also introduce policies that give corporations tax breaks, while vilifying and punishing struggling welfare recipients. They declare that 'the age of entitlement is over' while helping themselves to generous expense accounts, and continuing state sponsorship of middle-class real-estate investment. Their entitlement is corrosive.

But this logic of inequality works globally. Those 'progressives' who tinker with redistribution usually have a stake in capitalism itself, which requires a large cohort of poor, precarious employees. Without cheap labour—often in areas with lax environmental and safety laws, and anti-union thuggery—profits decline and capital stops circulating. The current economy *needs* millions to go without. Their pitifully low wages prevent under-consumption and recession. Their toil, raw resources and energy enrich and enhance our communities, just as ours develop those of the world's financial capitals. And these disparities often worsen existing gender and ethnic divides.

Most Australians take for granted a standard of living unthinkable for much of the world's population—and we benefit from their privation. When one of my daughter's school friends visits our two-bedroom unit and pronounces it 'very small', she is revealing her privilege. But our rented 'dog box' dwarfs the seven-by-seven hut, home to a Bangladeshi garment worker's family of five. My household now hovers just above Australia's poverty line, and this changes week to week. But we are hardly subsisting on 20 cents an hour like those who sew our jeans.

It is glib to pronounce entitlement relative and end it there. Politicians licking the nation's plate ought to be censured. Corporates jostling for handouts ought to be stopped. We should recognise that these mandarins are only ordinary in their doorstop performances, or glossy weekender profiles. And we can legislate ethically, in the interests of a fairer society (there is such a thing). But it is hard not to conclude that what shrivels Australia's discussion of entitlement to a few partisan idiocies is itself entitlement. •

Damon Young is a philosopher and author. His next nonfiction book is *The Art of Reading* (MUP, 2016). See <www.damonyoung.com.au>.

WHITE'S BROWN WOMAN

Denise Varney

I'M READING Patrick White's play *A Cheery Soul*, first published in *Four Plays by Patrick White* in 1965 and first staged at the Union Theatre, University of Melbourne, in 1963. It is built around a misogynist construct, the difficult woman, here the aged Miss Docker, a woman who is difficult to like, difficult to be around and makes difficulties for others. She is also, ironically, cheerful and good, the cheery soul of

the title, and oblivious to the disparagement but not the condescension of others. This is apparent early in the play when the respectable Mrs Custance, who is moved to perform an act of kindness towards the less fortunate, invites the homeless Miss Docker to move into their 'little glassed-in veranda room'. Mrs Custance refers to her as 'a dedicated soul' but tends to agree when Mr Custance, a man with a 'Nietzschean moustache', likens it to 'the soul of a bulldozer'; others such as the Vicar denounce her '*militant* virtue'.

To read the play according to the majority view of its characters is to accept that Miss Docker is a difficult woman, a wrecker, a nuisance, a meddler and self-centred in her selflessness. But another possibility emerges. Readers of the text will note the stage directions at her first appearance:

> Miss Docker is about 60. Although not particularly large, she gives the impression of being over lifesize. She is dressed up. Beige powder and plenty of purple lipstick. Probably a dark brown woman underneath. (p. 189)

The beige powder and purple lipstick are appropriately theatricalist for a Patrick White play, but the ascription of 'a dark brown woman underneath' opens up an intriguing line of possibility for the character, with implications for our broader understanding of White's 1960s plays. The 'dark brown' underneath is at least ambiguous. It refers to sun-baked or to racially or ethnically marked skin. Later she is described as sounding 'so … brown', as in earthy, perhaps, but also different from the white-skinned speakers. And there is a reference aimed at her about a 'piebald cat'. The ambiguity adds unexpected racialised layers to the play that to my knowledge have not previously been considered. Miss Docker to date has been played by light-skinned or white actors. Yet there it is. Reading it some 50 years after it was written, the 'dark brown woman' cannot but be noticed. More critically, the brown skin shifts the way in which the play must be read, without resorting to presentism. Written in 1963, the dark brown woman could well be a member of the stolen generations, the light-skinned—brown, not black—children removed from their families and taken into religious and state institutions or adopted by white families. She could also be a woman who has slipped through the racist White Australia policy that was not repealed until 1972.

The suggestion of Miss Docker's racial identity is carried over into people's reactions to her. Confronted by Miss Docker's thick beige powder and purple lipstick, Mrs Custance is immediately uncomfortable. She is flustered and ill at ease, defensive and irritated. She finds Miss Docker difficult to be around, wanting tea at the wrong time, listening to music and spilling things. Mrs Custance's reaction might be said to be affective, not cognitive, so much as an instant sensation. Would she have the same reaction to a woman who was below her in social class? Not likely. The logic of the scene is that Miss Docker is poor and is hence given a room. A more likely explanation is that Miss Docker's skin generates a set of racist responses. Mrs Custance's reaction is of skin to skin. Sarah Ahmed writes that how 'feelings feel in the first place may be tied to a past history of readings, in the sense that the process of recognition (of this feeling or that feeling) is bound up with what we already know'.[1] Mrs Custance knows about Indigenous peoples. She lives on the land of the Dharug people, whose country stretches west of Sydney and up to the Hawkesbury River. Her reaction is bound up with a past history or readings of fringe dwellers, dark-skinned servants in big houses, the missions and the women in Kings Cross, Sydney. She feels deeply uneasy.

The ambiguity surrounding the racial identity of Miss Docker makes it possible that the play presents an antithetical proposition. Instead of the woman as a wrecker, she is a woman subjected to life as an outsider. That she has neither the homely nor soulful characteristics of her implied character indicates that she might be read against the grain to reflect the wider social malaise of misogyny and racism. By now, the pattern of White's approach to character is taking shape. She is marked as vulnerable in the face of normative social values. Her circumstances are more materially than spiritually or temperamentally determined, and she keeps her desolation to herself. If Miss Docker is indeed Indigenous Australian, or has other unspecified non-white heritage, then her alienation accrues a greater unspoken significance in the dramatic world of the play. As an older single woman in 1960s Australia, without a home of her own or an income, keeping busy and being cheerful is quite plausibly an acquired strategy for survival, which is not to say that the play presents this as productive or effective.

This reading of *A Cheery Soul* suggests a lot more prescience on the part of its notoriously difficult author. •

Denise Varney is Professor of Theatre Studies and co-director of the Australian Centre in the School of Culture and Communication at the University of Melbourne. She is working on a research project on Patrick White's theatre 1962–2015.

---

1   Sarah Ahmed, *The Cultural Politics of Emotion*, Routledge, New York, 2004.

AUSTRALIA IN THREE BOOKS

Peter Pierce

For Love Alone,
by Christina Stead

Waiting for the Past,
by Les Murray

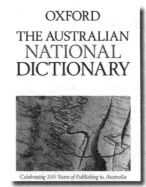

The Australian National
Dictionary

S OME OF THE finest works of Australian fiction were written by women who had left the country long before, yet whose memories of it were the strongest inspiration. Aged eighteen, Henry Handel Richardson left Australia in 1888 to study music at Leipzig. Her trilogy *The Fortunes of Richard Mahony* (published in one volume in 1930) was written and researched in London, save for a two-month visit to Australia in 1912. Christina Stead, whose childhood was spent at Watsons Bay in Sydney before the Great War, dreamed passionately of a world elsewhere. Savings from teaching and office work enabled her to take ship for London in 1928. Hers would be one of the most fabled expatriate careers in Australian literature. While her novels remained unpublished here until the 1960s, she forged a reputation in Britain and the United States, before

coming back in 1974 to a strange place that was in some ways still home. Her novel *For Love Alone* (1944) draws to rich effect on her young adult years of struggle in Sydney and then in London, as it tells the story of the indomitable Teresa Hawkins.

The book's ecstatic Preface, 'The Sea People', declares that Australia, 'the island continent in the water hemisphere', populated as it was from 'the old world, the land hemisphere', is 'a fruitful island of the sea-world, a great Ithaca, there parched and stony and here trodden by flocks and curly-headed bulls and heavy with thick-set grain'. Nevertheless it is a place from which Teresa, who 'smelled, heard, saw, guessed faster, longed more than others', feels bound to leave. For all the disappointments that mean-spirited men cause her, this is a triumphant feminist odyssey. Stead draws on her own dreaming, long walks at night, intense yearning to depict the force that animates Teresa to set out, not only—as the title has it—*For Love Alone*—but in quest of a keener understanding of self and of the prejudices that seek to trammel her. This is one of the greatest Australian novels of the last century.

Think first of the titles of some of Les Murray's books of poetry: *The Boys who Stole the Funeral*, *Poems against Economics*, *The Vernacular Republic*, *Lunch and Counter Lunch*. We are already dared and on the way to being engrossed by the sprawl of Murray's imagination, wit and a seldom equalled

The International Prototype
Benjamin Dodds

The kilogram is the unit of mass; it is equal to the mass of the International Prototype of the Kilogram.
—the Third General Conference on Weights and Measures, 1901

Her polished body does not
weigh a kilogram. She *is* the kilogram,
definitive artefact (nine parts platinum,
one part iridium) that rests
in a darkened Paris vault
beneath three nested bell jars.

She does not weigh fifty-three
millionths of the total steel
used to erect the Sydney Harbour Bridge,
nor does she weigh three times as much
as the average human heart—
these and all else take their measure
from her cylindrical precision.

Metrological scripture
declares her eternal,
immutable arbiter of mass
that shall never know the indignity
of any gain or loss.
Unbreakable law gives her the right
to remain the kilo
even should she fluctuate—
a laughable prospect
on the day she was set
so immaculately in place.

But very real is the minute
yet significant decline
proclaimed by the balance
at scheduled unveilings
(perhaps the very source
of her deterioration)
when she's weighed against
six true and perfect daughters
cast in gleaming exactitude
for this task alone.

Lost across a life of more than a century
is only a dust-speck's amount of her matter,
so little of something as to be nothing.
But as she diminishes by any degree,
the universe puts on weight.

poetic ear. His has been one of the greatest careers of any Australian poet and it now spans half a century. Few others have come from apparently less privileged backgrounds. Murray is the son of a widowed dairy farmer from northern New South Wales, a dropout from Sydney University, sometime public servant and translator (adept in half a dozen languages), an unrelenting and unbowed controversialist in the acrid arena of Australian letters. After a gap of several years comes another volume dedicated 'to the glory of God'—*Waiting for the Past* (2015). The titles tantalise as they astonish: 'When Two Percent Were Students', 'Diabetica', 'The Privacy of Typewriters', 'Big Rabbit at the Verandah', 'The Glory and Decline of Bread'.

To read the book is to be moved by the plenitude of subject and form of Murray's poetry. Here he remarks 'the oaten seethe / of thoroughbred horses in single stalls / across a twilit cabin', or 'verandah shops with history / up roads like dry-gully bends'. His own body demands attention, whether from vertigo attacks and falls or the difficulty of cutting one's toenails as an old man. Murray sympathises with carers who 'have learned the bad-smelling / jobs, and soak things as they chat'. With resolute defiance of fashion he declares 'I am an old book troglodyte / one who composes on paper'. Now he thanks his spouse Valerie, 'dear pardoner, kindest wife', then overhears the sound of a rifle: 'clear-shack! Pea-shack!' In the sectarian world in which Murray grew up, 'unpreached help / has long been the message'. There is much more, from the loved world where 'tiny spinnakers / of blue wrens wag among waves / of uncut lawn grass'. Murray was 50/1 for this year's Nobel Prize in Literature; he ought nearly to have been favourite.

It is no surprise that Murray was the most astute reviewer of the first edition of *The Australian National Dictionary*. This 'dictionary of Australianisms on Historical Principles', modelled on the *Oxford English Dictionary* and edited by W.S. Ramson, was perhaps the finest publication of the bicentennial year. To sample it is to be plunged back into Australia's history, learning of the first usages of words still current, or those whose meaning has changed, or others that but for this book would be lost to memory. Ramson and his colleagues drew on the pioneering work of Sidney Baker (*The Australian Language*, 1945) and such specialised compendiums as Bruce Moore's book of scabrous Duntroon cadet slang, the collection of underworld argot by Gary Simes and *The Barracker's Bible* compiled by Garrie Hutchinson and playwright Jack Hibberd. To browse in the *AND* is a delightful immersion from which one wants no early release.

Take the letter 'N'. There are nearly ten pages on 'native', whose primary meaning (as instanced by Cook in 1770) is 'An Aboriginal'. 'Negrohead' refers to a kind of coral reef named by Flinders in 1802, while 'Nelly' for 'a cheap wine. Also Nelly's Death' is a colourful remnant of a now-vanished vernacular culture. 'Never-never' for 'the far interior of Australia' dates back to 1833 and only recently has lost common currency. The words tumble enticingly in succession: 'new chum', 'New Hollander' (Dampier, 1697), 'night parrot' (first named in 1913 and now thought extinct), 'ning nong' for a fool, with thanks to Nino Cullota's *They're a Weird Mob* (1957—actually by John O'Grady and first published as a serial in the *Sporting Globe*), 'no-hoper', initially used of racehorses and then of people, 'nudge', nowadays perhaps a too-polite usage for drinking to excess. These linguistic resources are among the lost treasures of Australian life, but the *AND* is a sure and amply satisfying path back to them. •

Peter Pierce is an adjunct professor at Monash University; editor of *The Cambridge History of Australian Literature* and has been a book reviewer for 40 years.

THE POLITICS WE DESERVE

Can Malcolm Turnbull save us from our political funk? That's up to all of us

Katharine Murphy

REAMS, WE KNOW, can be fleeting, disappearing with the dawn. Small moments of insight are equally evanescent, best to jot them down when they happen.

There have been two small epiphanies for me in this political year. The first happened when, for a whole afternoon, the heavily contested universe I inhabit didn't turn the full force of its scorn on Tony Abbott. Peace broke out on the day Abbott announced that 12,000 displaced Syrians would come to our shores to find refuge from unimaginable horror. For several hours the nation absorbed the unexpected news that something rational had emerged from Canberra. The flow of information was orderly, measured and proportionate, as was the reaction. It had been so long since I'd felt peace and stillness in my world, the harmony of the moment resonated. I'd been on the deepest of dives, pressure pounding in my ears, then, suddenly: surface, light, sky, release.

But the peace wasn't going to last. Even in that pause, momentum coiled. Tumult, once unleashed, is pervasive. The combat culture Tony Abbott had promulgated was about to take him out.

My second moment came on the evening Malcolm Turnbull took back the Liberal Party leadership. I was at home when news of the challenge broke, and felt the stress of a parent absorbing a work-related hiccup at short notice. There was a frantic hour of domestic sorting, but from the moment my backside hit my parliament office chair I felt perfectly calm. Given the bedlam, and the self-evident fact we were about to endure several punishing days of waterfall reporting, that calm was a strange sensation to feel.

There was none of that surge of adrenalin that makes you feel ill, only that little pulse of anticipation that every journalist feels when they step up to contribute to a major news event. I pounded the keyboard with ten-minute updates, and wondered what on earth was going on with me.

Was it the nature of this particular contest, which ran with no ragged edges, no outbursts of emotion—a Christopher Nolan coup: stylised violence with no blood spatter, like a dance, almost restful to watch? No. Not that. It felt bigger than that. Eventually I twigged that this world—the rolling Canberra crisis—was no longer an exotic development. There had been many nights like this since 2010, delivering them to our readers had become routine.

When Kevin Rudd was taken out in the dead winter of 2010, the whole building

Malcolm Turnbull in parliament
Image courtesy Mike Bowers (@mpbowers)

erupted. It was chaos. Half the Labor Caucus didn't know what was happening. In between pounding the keyboard I ran from office to office when people stopped answering their phones. It was new, and visceral. It was raw and bizarre: a first-term prime minister cut down before facing re-election.

But five years later we'd lived through the change from Rudd to Gillard then back to Rudd, the inevitable change of government, then Tony Abbott's stumbles and missteps, and a different cycle of self-destruction: one of arrogance rather than nihilism and despair. Then came the precipitous crash triggered by handing a knighthood to the Queen's oxygen thief of a husband, which generated the February vote on a leadership spill. Abbott pleaded for his political life and was given six months grace. In late September, time was up.

To arrive here felt inevitable—about as dislocating as a scheduled stop on a commuter train. Another new Australian prime minister, then home before midnight.

This time we even managed a bite of pizza in the office. We who inhabit the world of national politics have adjusted to high-velocity chaos. It's our new normal. Some reporters in my corridor have known only this, and possibly can't imagine the alternative: a reporting life where years pass and a government just governs.

I'm not saying I'm desensitised, that I'm blasé, that I don't care. It's just that my heart no longer thumps, even if my head constantly aches. And what does that mean, when little by little we all adjust to this new normal? Does it mean that this is all there is, that things can't change?

. . .

Malcolm Turnbull's prime ministership bloomed early in the Canberra spring. We were all still in a protective huddle, backs to the wind. The winter had been punishing and the ground was yet to thaw.

At an early Turnbull public event, over at the Australian War Memorial, Thucydides loomed out of the smoking ruin of Tony Abbott's discarded death cult and his budget emergency, a little Turnbull speech bubble that felt weightier than just some rhetorical frippery. The Athenian general waged war and then wrote about it, producing a history with sufficient resonance to span the rise and fall of civilisations. Turnbull's invocation felt like a statement of intent: here was a character happy to own such a reference without apologising to the editor of the *Daily Telegraph* for being up himself.

As David Marr noted with typical precision in *Guardian Australia*, Abbott was already fading, fading very fast from our memories. Abbott would press back of course, surfing and showering and bromancing with Hadley-the-Heartbroken in the reinforcing warmth of the 2GB studio, then with soul brother Mitchell at 3AW, both places of testosterone and monochrome, more front bar than womb.

Abbott was clutching at our fleeing heels and the media will welcome him. As my first bureau chief said to me 20 years ago, 'That story needs conflict, and no lower than the third paragraph.' But the real people were already in another place. The polls had bounced. In the spring at least, it was done.

Turnbull has the self-belief to think he could be a modern Thucydides. The mind of Malcolm is hard-wired to dream big, to fancy himself both of the fray and above it. Our new leader wants politics to be an adventure worthy of his talents. We must all rise beyond 'rule in/rule out' games, lift our eyes from the still-steaming entrails of leadership challenges—deals, numbers, undisclosed promises, treacheries—and look to the future.

Turnbull is banking on us wanting to do that, assuming, that, like him, we lacked the collective stamina to live a moment longer in the strange, quarrelsome, reductive, vacant universe of Abbottland. The early signs suggest he's onto a winner with that impulse, but Abbott's assertive lingering does not bode well. Turnbull is also trapped inside a cage constructed from all the undertakings and commitments he doesn't want us talking about.

He knows full well the Liberal Party has veered too far right, and is out of step with the default national consciousness. He also knows he leads a party whose tribes considered two options: dying with Abbott and living with Turnbull. Not everyone chose to live. Not everyone will choose to let him live either.

Turnbull knows he has to carry the government back towards the political centre, but how, when, how fast—and what, exactly, will reason cost? How, too, to avoid becoming overweening in the reset, to avoid defaulting too heavily to 'the rightness of all things seen by Malcolm'—a recurrent tic that has brought him undone more than once. Thucydides saw hubris in the downfall of Athens. Turnbull was born ready to lead, but people have to consent to being led.

Given the scale of the task, it's impossible to say how long the initial national catharsis will last. Beginnings in politics matter. It's largely forgotten now, but when Abbott first took office he thought he could call time on the madness. He thought that by withdrawing from the fray he could end the frenzy of the rolling news cycle and the very state of permanent panic he had engendered in politics in order to destroy his opponents. His first instinct wasn't fight, it was actually flight.

There was a moment when Abbott could have gone either way: become a leader with the imagination and self-belief to be more than the script handed to him by his victory machine, to lean into events and new experiences and let them temper him; or default to the leader he ultimately became, a mouthpiece for boosters and backers, the peddler of grim formulations, conforming to the scripts and prognostications of the modern-day witches of *Macbeth*: Jones, Hadley, Bolt (double, double, toil and trouble).

Perhaps if his flight experiment had worked, Abbott would have approached his time in power differently. Politics is full of sliding-door moments: roads not taken, opportunities that once lost can never be recouped. Turnbull isn't hesitating at the door of his prime ministership. He is unfurling wings in the hope the headwinds will lift him beyond the confines of all the grand bargains he doesn't want to talk about; hoping too they don't become a dead weight at the moment of flight.

A ceasefire is in order before we adjust permanently to the strangeness of the world we inhabit and mindlessly replicate the essential conditions because we've turned failure into a production line. It truly would be a disaster to discover that we had commodified dysfunction within the media–political eco system and conspired somehow, unwittingly, to turn politics into the worst reality television program anyone had ever seen.

Turnbull's call for a new politics is both entirely self-interested and completely necessary. The idea that toxicity can be consigned to the past is compelling enough to put us all on the cliff, unfurling wings, waiting for that westerly. Even if he fails, it is time for the rest of us to think big, and perhaps succeed.

. . .

Political scientist Gerry Stoker tells us democracy is designed to disappoint, and he's absolutely right. Politics is a deeply flawed business. We want our politics simple, clean and conflict free, when inherently it is none of those things. Democratic politics isn't a panacea, it is simply a mechanism to synthesise societal conflict without resort to violence. Democracy is about 'the tough

Backbench Insurrection

JACK

process of squeezing collective decisions out of multiple and competing interests and opinions', Stoker writes in *Why Politics Matters: Making Democracy Work*. 'Politics is designed to disappoint—that's the way that the process of compromise and recon-ciliation works. Its outcomes are often messy, ambiguous and never final.'

Stoker also notes one of the great paradoxes of our age: 'Democracy is more dominant as a form of governance than ever before, but within both established and newer democracies there appears to be a considerable disenchantment with politics.'

In all Western democracies, this is the age of disruption and of disenchantment. In our consumerist and on-demand societies, we think we can trade up to a better model of politics. Disenchantment is powerful enough to have swept Jeremy Corbyn to the leadership of the British Labour Party, despite the surfeit of punditry suggesting a leftist of such unfashionable persistence is entirely unelectable as British prime minis-ter. Corbyn, in parliament since the 1980s, is the insider's outsider. The consistency of his dissent is, apparently, a beacon for support-ers tired of endless compromise and reposi-tioning and tough love for the greater good.

Disenchantment is also the drumbeat of the presidential race in the United States. Americans are flirting with political 'outsiders'—the most voluble being billionaire Donald Trump, who is busily creating a universe where things don't have to make sense as long as they generate a headline. Elaine Kamarck, writing for the Brookings Institution, considers the current phenomenon of non-politicians:

> There is a lot of speculation as to why non-politicians are so popular this time around. Most of it centres on voters' distrust and disappointment in traditional politicians and on polarisation among the two political parties. The political system is not working very well at all. You have to go all the way back to 2009 in the Real Clear Politics averages of polls to find a point where the same number of Americans thought the country was going in the right direction as thought the country was going in the wrong direction—a time when America was still in the honeymoon phase with their new president, a political newcomer himself. Since then many more Americans have thought the country was on the wrong track.

Kamarck counsels against defaulting to the easy conclusion:

> The logic that seems to be pushing forward the Trumps … of the world is the belief that politics and politicians are the problem. But what if the problem with our politics is just the opposite? Not enough politicians who are good at politics?

She contends that politics once worked to sift out its own show ponies. The backroom process of securing major-party nomination for the presidency—a system that prevailed until the 1980s—might have lacked showbiz, but it worked to test core skills:

> Would-be presidents had to wheel and deal their way to the nomination of their party. Those who won had generally shown some ability to put together coalitions and to win the respect of their peers. As the process changed and primaries replaced those awful smoke-filled rooms, a critical element of the nomination process got lost.

This is an interesting thought to inject into the Australian political scene. Julia Gillard's failure to secure a working majority in either chamber at the 2010 election could have delivered paralysis: a do-nothing parliament. In fact it delivered the opposite. During that period the Australian Parliament passed more than 400 bills, some of them major reforms, including a carbon pricing scheme, the mining tax, plain packaging laws for cigarettes, parental leave and a Murray–Darling Basin plan.

Gillard as prime minister struggled to project competence in public. She lacked the default arrogant entitlement of the 'great men of history'. Her private self got lost in the expanse of bitterly contested public space. She also failed to soothe or reassure, her mere presence being an affront to harmony for critics who crouched contentedly in the comfort of her flaws and missteps, the better to justify their more bizarre misogynistic impulses.

But while the writhing and the discontent thundered outside, and the reverse treachery seethed inside, Gillard proceeded, grittily in the circumstances, with governing and legacy-building. Gillard was a flawed prime minister in many respects, an enigmatic character who failed to inspire confidence, but she proved a master of the head down, bum up, getting it done approach. Ezra Klein recently reflected in *Vox* on this public–private phenomenon:

> The inside game—courting donors, winning endorsements, influencing the primary calendar, securing key committee assignments, luring top staffers, working with interest groups—makes up the bulk of politics. Mastery of the inside game is hard to assess and so is frequently undervalued, but it's also determinative—it's why wooden campaigners like Mitt Romney and Al Gore win primaries, and why no current leader of either party's congressional wing can deliver an exciting speech. The media often scratches its head over how such weak politicians prove so successful at politics, but the answer is they're not weak politicians—they're excellent politicians, but the part of politics they excel at is largely hidden.

When Abbott succeeded in replacing the riven Labor government, he quickly demonstrated he possessed none of Gillard's supple backroom arts. He achieved the demolition of some of Labor's policies—carbon pricing, the mining tax—but his wheels spun on his own agenda. He arrived in government asserting entitlement and mandate, including, bizarrely, for things he had neglected to tell the public about prior to winning the 2013 election. Abbott hectored the non-government parties in the parliament, eschewing courtship. As a consequence, the government's agenda failed to progress. Delivering neither a coherent agenda nor certainty in the polls, Abbott was torn down by his own side.

While the United States flirts with outsiders as the antidote to its malaise, Australian politics is imposing a short shelf life on leaders. We've developed a vicious coup culture. Kevin Rudd and Tony Abbott were deposed during their first terms. Julia Gillard was denied the chance to campaign for a second. It looks corrosive and highly unstable, and perhaps it is. Perhaps in two decades we'll say with certainty that Australian politics veered into zero-sum chaos in mid 2010 and never recovered. It is entirely possible. But I'm not prepared to call that yet.

Every event of the past five years is connected to every other event. There's nothing random about the sequence. Treachery is nothing new in politics, nor is turbulence a new condition. There were five prime ministers between 1967 and 1972. Gough Whitlam could probably tell Abbott and Turnbull what winner-takes-all hyper partisanship and a hostile press look like, having experienced both in his tumultuous period in office.

A feeling of semi-permanent chaos and crisis has visited us before, and politics being a cyclical business, the national parliament has stabilised to deliver the voters more productive times. Malcolm Fraser stabilised after Whitlam by talking big but sitting tight, and Bob Hawke stabilised after the vacancy of the Fraser years by jolting Australia into modernity.

There's one constant in politics: success breeds success. The question is, what will Turnbull do? Can he find his own circuit breaker, and more importantly, will we let him?

• • •

This is big dreaming territory. Australia is again having a debate about reform. This would be a promising development, an automatic stabiliser on a febrile political culture, if the debate didn't so often ignore fundamentals. The first and most important fundamental is politics has to first strengthen its own foundations before it can engage in the worthy business of fixing the country. Politician, heal thyself.

The second is we really have to stop banging on about the death of reform, as if this phrase means something. It sounds portentous, but it's actually fatuous. The 'death of reform' discussion is a proxy for the slow death of mansplaining. It's a respectable-looking concept that allows querulous outrage to substitute for analysis.

> Politics has never before had the power it now possesses to publish and broadcast to a mass audience without filters.

Read the *Australian* newspaper and what you'll get most days is a cohort of white middle-aged men raising a collective fist at a universe with the temerity to tolerate dissent and interruption. Why can't things be as they were, in the days when power was a closed shop? Why must the system (whatever that is) be broken? To overcome its current challenges, Australian politics has to go back to its roots, and by that I mean back to people.

Standing between people and their parliament is a toxic swamp of self-interested rent seekers intent on making parliamentarians their puppets. The rent seekers move in at the first whiff of any 'reform' debate, eager to annihilate any grey area and safeguard their interests—stakeholder advancement first, broader public or national interest a distant second.

We've all seen the worst-case scenario: weak politicians folding at the first hint of grapeshot, or worse, folding in order to create a miniscule point of difference with their opponents for some ephemeral advantage. Media outlets parrot the various tired old wish lists and formulations from the usual suspects because it's too hard to break the cycle and think of something genuinely new; and then they compound the vacancy with race-call stories rather than ferreting down into detail.

No wonder people increasingly want to take back politics and the discussion around politics. Voters appear perplexed at the capacity of politics to prioritise things that seem to work against their best interests, and audiences are ropable about journalists standing inside the system and looking out rather than standing with them, on the outside, looking in.

Australian voters aren't sitting around their dining tables concluding something is horribly askew because the dynamics of 1985 don't seem to work in 2015. They are either disconnecting from the process in disgust or they are using the hyper-connected nature of modern life to make their voices heard. Grassroots activism abounds in the new digital town square. Politics has a real opportunity to harness this interest and work to buttress its civic connections. The power of many can offset the influence of the few. That's the point of democracy after all.

Australians have raised their voices on same-sex marriage, both for reform and for the status quo—revolutionising the terms of that debate in only ten years. Abbott in his dying days wilted on taking in more displaced people from Syria because the community rallied to their cause, and its voice carried into the Coalition party room. Earlier in 2015 the connectedness of social media had allowed a sizable protest to gather in Melbourne in the space of half an hour—an event that led to a ham-fisted Australian Border Force operation being cancelled.

Petitions fly around the internet like darting birds. At big national moments the community gathers around the digital campfire to pitch in on the conversation. People seek out their political representatives online, inserting their views in threads on social media, blogging and posting up a storm. There is energy and, sometimes, even hope, countering the disaffection. This energy suggests the appetite for reform persists, defying its own death notice. But the institutional processes long practised to achieve reform are in desperate need of a refresh.

Thirty years ago the community had sufficient trust in institutions to be able to sit back and watch the captains of industry sit down with the trade union movement and hammer out a broad reform consensus. But that era of reform has delivered losers as well as winners, missteps as well as landmark achievements. And the Zeitgeist has moved on.

Reform is no longer the exclusive activity of various elite power centres in the Australian economy. A well-intentioned reform 'summit' sponsored by two major newspapers and reprised by Malcolm Turnbull mainly served to underscore how tired that mechanism is for achieving a program that the community might go on to support—a bunch of people in a secured room, pumping out dot points before the lunch break, thinking relentlessly inside the square in order to manufacture a consensus.

An Australian political figure who wants to break that dispiriting cycle and take us into the territory of new politics has to be looking at mechanisms to bring the public in. I think a prime minister—such as our current incumbent—who exhibits a genuine curiosity about people, who is inherently social, who rides public transport because it gives him opportunities to have spontaneous conversations outside the bubble, is at least capable of conceiving a more community-centred politics. Whether he's capable of overcoming deep institutional resistance to such utopian notions is another question entirely—but there are some working examples to draw on internationally.

Locally, the citizens' assembly Gillard proposed in 2010 as a mechanism to build community consensus around the need to act on climate change—the one foolish journalists, including me, mocked mercilessly and sought to bury in the bin of crazy campaign notions—was an idea ahead of its time.

Perhaps if that mechanism had been permitted to run its course, if the public had been given time to consider evidence, to work though the various possibilities and policy options, it would have been harder for Abbott to play short-term politics with carbon pricing in a manner that was destructive to Australia's long-term interests. We'll never know.

A model like that could also put some structure around a national conversation about the urgent and necessary task of budget repair. I'm enough of an optimist to think that if you deliver facts and information to people they are capable of separating ideology and prejudice from substance. And if the media are a significant part of the problem, if we can't get out of our 'here comes the chaos' rut and our minds out of the platitudes rut, technology gives politics unprecedented opportunities to step around the filters and speak directly to the public.

Politics has never before had the power it now possesses to publish and broadcast to a mass audience without filters. Foolishly it has largely used the opening phase of this power to spam people with pap and propaganda rather than seek to connect and explain and listen in meaningful ways. Just as journalism is learning the new art of practising in a crowd, gradually having democracy and humility thrust upon it, so must politics.

Bringing people into a deliberative process does not in and of itself lessen the capacity of politics to lead. I'm not an advocate of mob rule. To my mind engagement is a strengthening activity that helps deliver politics a mandate to do its work. If politics is under siege from media bullies and sectional interests, it makes sense to go back to basics, to turn to the people at the bedrock of the system.

Perhaps a durable connection between politics and the citizenry might also help to restrain our collective worst impulses: the febrile outbursts of panic, restlessness, cynicism. 'My solution to the problem of disenchantment with politics is deceptively simple. It is to expand the opportunities for citizens to have a say in the issues they care about,' Stoker says.

> We need a politics that allows citizens to have a say over what is important to them, not what professional politicians, lobbyists or journalists or scientists tell them is important. Having a say does not mean, for most people, having a veto or being the final judge. As amateurs, citizens are cautious about claiming decision taking responsibility. Having a say means wanting to influence, but not having to decide.

· · ·

We also have to talk about money, and we have to talk about freedom. The two issues are connected. It's a most extraordinary state of affairs that a profession in the middle of an acute public crisis in its integrity can't act in its own interests and get the money out of politics. Money is killing politics in several ways at once. It's diverting resources from meaningful focus on the big issues facing the economy. Senior players have to chase the cash for their party organisations, and I would prefer they were working on policy solutions rather than tolerable seating plans at elite dinners for important cheque-writing people.

There is also a significant problem of perception that I can illustrate with a couple of examples. Abbott probably tried to kill the renewables industry during his two years as prime minister because he couldn't quite accept the science of climate change. The prospect of randomly inflicted catastrophe doubtless offended his deep belief in salvation for the chosen. But because the Liberal Party takes donations from the resources industry and mouths the industry's talking points to reassure somebody or other, it fuels the perception you can buy influence.

Labor faces a similar problem. Was the recent foot stamping about the China free trade agreement a function of a flawed text or a function of the fact the ALP relies on the union movement for money, for campaign workers, for predictable factional blocs at the national conference? Like Abbott and renewables, the FTA fuss is probably a function of questions about the text, but who could have any confidence that is the case? The major parties are too much in hock to their respective bases, and modern Australian society is a much more complex organism than a ritualised fight between capital and labour.

There are entirely viable alternatives to the current system of funding and disclosure, yet the major parties can't seem to come to terms on prescriptions that would strengthen their position at the expense of the puppet masters. In this obstinacy they are the ultimate boiling frogs. Increasing public funding, restricting donations to individuals at low thresholds and implementing a system of continuous disclosure wouldn't solve the influence and rent-seeking problem, but it would give the public some confidence that there are boundaries.

The other thing the party of Menzies could consider seriously is encouraging the culture of the free vote, rather than merely tolerating it. Too much freedom makes any country ungovernable. A bit more freedom oxygenates politics. It raises the stakes in any serious policy discussion, and experience shows it also raises the tone of big debates. The Australian Parliament's finest hours are always found during free votes.

Of course the Turnbull regime is thinking far more modestly about new politics. This opening phase is about drawing lines, of dialling down the clamour in an effort to be heard, and creating space to think and reflect between now and facing the voters some time in 2016. Such a compressed timeframe doesn't permit revolutions. It does allow time to deal with some obvious deficiencies. Turnbull has the opportunity to craft a different conversation. To do that he will have to maintain the courage of his independence, to be both of the system and, somehow, above it. He will have to be the man prepared to lose the leadership of the party over a principle, but a wiser man—one with the patience to build coalitions to get things done.

Does he have the patience? I don't know, quite possibly not. Does he have the intelligence? Yes, absolutely, with one caveat. The problem with being the smartest guy in the room is your company quickly confounds and disappoints. Will the government rally around him out of self-interest if not for any higher motivation? Possibly, but don't bet the house on it.

Can he pull us out of our collective funk? Left to his own devices, I believe he can. His record indicates his politics has purpose.

He's ambitious enough to want to be the man for the times, and pragmatic enough not to be a hostage to the constraints the moment will impose on him.

But how does anything change? Ultimately it changes with individual action. It can't all be left to one man sweeping up the debris of a period many of us would prefer to forget. It's about me stretching to serve readers every day with truth and clarity and focus, owning my deficiencies and limits. It's also about your decisions and actions, and the politics you are prepared to hope for. Change isn't about one man, it's about all of us, and it's about time we had the courage to raise our voices and ask for the politics we deserve. •

Katharine Murphy began her career in the Canberra parliamentary press gallery in 1996. She is deputy political editor of *Guardian Australia* and Adjunct Associate Professor of Journalism at the University of Canberra.

References

Elaine Kamarck, <http://www.brookings.edu/blogs/fixgov/posts/2015/09/16-republican-debate-appeal-of-the-non-politician-kamarck>, 16 September 2015.

Ezra Klein, <http://www.vox.com/2015/9/28/9407889/american-politics-changing>, 28 September 2015.

Gerry Stoker, *Why Politics Matters: Making Democracy Work*, Palgrave Macmillan, Basingstoke, UK, 2006.

Casuarina cunninghamiana—River She-oak
Russell Erwin

It must be midday: gathered to it like flood wrack is the dark.
The thatching of the cassowary's feathers has mothered shade
beneath its skirts. You know it will be cold there:
it will be matted with needles the colour of an Isa Brown hen,
white-flecked with fungi, must-thick in decay.
Beyond, light is pottery hard.

In their height, their shabbiness too, there is assurance, acceptance
— maybe from all they have withstood, have learned—
but as if a building had been exposed before completion
there is a construction site's confusion: of wire, matted
and complicated, thick as the tangle of a Pre-Raphaelite girl's hair,
the stiff necessity of cables, ugly, messy, blackened as if from work.
That chaos which needs demand and we ignore,
preferring beauty in the achieved form.

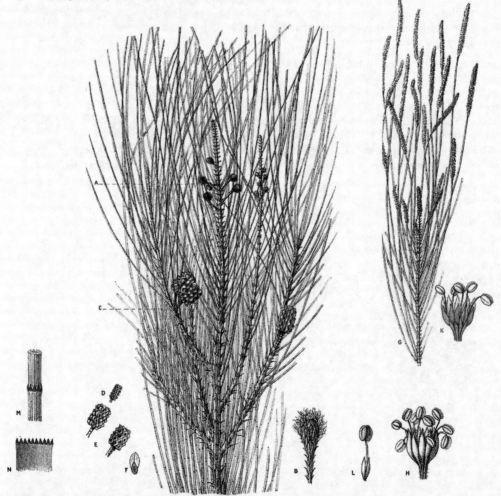

Self-sufficient, there is an air of indifference about them
like members of the upper class casually associating with their own.
The eye's interest drifts: off to the right a dense hedge of black,
a younger generation milling as young things do
and this you know means the glitter of water.
Out of these white-dry hills it is the music of this place,
a relief and balance, reassurance and laughter.

This fringe of deeply green seems like a refuge
for little noises: scurryings, scratchings, chips of song,
in the presence of all that steep concentration of silence,
solid in the summer heat. And so this valley is preserved
from the knowledge of any other place. Apart, that is,
from summer's catalyst—smoke's first pale whisper.

Being noon, it is permanent as Luxor.
Then, a shift of air and the needles, delicate,
fine enough to be Asian, release a sigh
as clear, as defined, as you remember
of the coolness of water after exertion.
We think it speaks of our sorrows, our grief
but it is simply acceptance, like that, say, of a widow
left minding the farm. Each day measured.
The air passing through, like the breath.

It is still. It is midday. It alters.
Subtly, the sun carves new shields, pins new maps
onto trunks. Patterns appear, disappear like tidal islands.
And shade adjusts, resettling the flounce of its skirt.
A breeze lifts. The river escapes.
Like us, it cannot endure the soughing
that even in summer seems like the muted suffering of Neapolitan women.

'THE LONG LETTER TO A SHORT LOVE, OR …'

In her love letter novella to Martin Amis, Germaine Greer bared her fragile heart and complex soul

Margaret Simons

'IT COULD BE worse. It has been worse. It will get worse. For the moment, though, it's not too bad.' Germaine Greer was sitting in the British Airways Monarch lounge at Heathrow Airport, 'for all the world as if I was rich and famous'. It was 1 March 1976, and she was one of the best-known people in the world.

Greer was on her way to the United States for a lecture tour she was dreading. The travel was forced upon her. The US lecture circuit was lucrative, and despite her fame she was in financial trouble, under pressure to pay tax on income received and spent years before. She had been writing letters to the bank, putting them off on the strength of her expected earnings from the US circuit. She hated the tours. They left her drained and exhausted. She took weeks to recover from them.

Sometime before she left for the airport she had spoken by phone to her lover. He had suggested she write to him, and so she had bought a hard-backed A5 notebook and in it, as she waited for the inevitably delayed departure, she wrote the first entries in what was to become an extraordinary diary and travelogue. On the first page, she gave the document a name: 'The Long Letter to a Short Love, or …' She never completed the alternative title.

The name was a pun. The love affair had only just begun and was already, so far as we can tell, nearly over. She hardly knew him. As well, the man she was addressing was notoriously sensitive about being short, and she was not above teasing him. He was a journalist, working for the *New Statesman*, and only just beginning to be well known, emerging from the shadow of his famous father. Her 'short love' was Martin Amis, who would become one of the defining literary voices of the late twentieth century.

But was she really writing to him or, as she began to suspect towards the end, to the man she wanted him to be, or thought he might become? Martin Amis became her imaginary friend, and company during the lonely ordeal of the tour. At the end of the document she called him a whore, albeit beloved, but by then she wasn't sure who she was talking to. She never sent the letter. Instead she packed the document, about 30,000 words long, into a manila folder, labelled it neatly, catalogued it and stowed it away. So far as I know, I am the first person to have read it other than Greer herself.

Greer sold her papers to the University of Melbourne archives in 2013. It is an enormous collection—478 archive boxes of documents chronicling six decades in the life of one of the world's most important thinkers. Greer said she would use the proceeds of the sale to finance the care and rehabilitation of her rainforest property at Cave Creek in south-east Queensland.

> What was it like to be Germaine Greer in the spring of 1976, when the storm you had helped unleash was enveloping the world, and everyone wanted to hear you talk about sex.

In her most recent book, *White Beech, The Rainforest Years*, Greer describes how she became 'the servant of the forest' after buying the land in 2001. Since then she has spent every spare cent on it.

The archive arrived in Australia in August 2014 and a few months ago was opened to scholars for the first time. It includes manuscripts of Greer's books, her diaries and correspondence. There are letters to Fellini and her lover Warren Beatty—the latter almost pastoral, with descriptions of a drive through Wales in spring, along with a critique of his role in the movie *Lilith*: 'You were so droll, mooching around like a method actor with your forehead carved into so many knots and furrows as are required of a serious actor under strain.' Greer did not spare her lovers. As for the spring:

> A warm mist like a spray of blood seems to hang over the hedges and within the copses. The imagery of spring is delicate and fresh but I find it violent and obscene. Everything seems to be pushing and bursting, swelling up and cracking open, oozing and sticky and murmuring. I saw the infant Wye

leaping down to the sea and lambs tottering drunkenly tit-wards and I thought of what I always think of these days, and so by association, my dear, of you.

What was she thinking of? Perhaps her longing for a child, which she had begun to confess to journalists, along with the fact that her fertility was compromised. The archive spans the years from her student life in Melbourne, Sydney and Cambridge to the present day. It includes early notes and a synopsis of her groundbreaking 1970 bestseller *The Female Eunuch*, a book with which she could truly claim to have changed the world. Many scholars are already at work upon her papers, and there will be new findings and fresh reflections as a result.

But this document, the hitherto undiscovered and private long letter, will in my opinion be one of the most remarkable finds. Composed in her round handwriting over four weeks of lonely travel, it contains writing as sharp, as sour and as funny as anything she has published since. Literary criticism is mixed with personal memoir and travelogue that, with its acid observation and mix of awe and horror, recalls the madcap travelogue of Nabokov.

She used part of the writing later. Her account of a meeting with Frank Zappa in Los Angeles' Beverley Wilshire Hotel is one of the highlights, and was expanded 30 years later, after his death, in a piece she wrote for the *Guardian*. There are also suggestions of material she made the focus of her 1990 book *Daddy We Hardly Knew You*—the miserable Melbourne school days, the thirst for adventure and affection in a loveless house, all glossed with rage and tears and transcended by her potent wit.

But for the most part the letter remained private, a companion over those few weeks, and today a moving memoir of what it was like to be Germaine Greer in the spring of 1976, when the storm you had helped unleash was enveloping the world, and everyone wanted to hear you talk about sex.

Greer opposes it being published in full—which was suggested to her by Melbourne University Publishing—and declined to be interviewed for this essay. She was offered the chance to read a draft of this essay and provide comment. This she also declined.

In his memoir *Experience*, published in 2000, Amis wrote about the loneliness of the touring writer: 'A writer's life is all anxiety and ambition—and ambition, here is not readily distinguishable from anxiety; it is a part of your desire to do right by what talent you have.' And elsewhere he commented:

> On such tours … you feel like 'the employee of a former self' because the book is now out there to be championed … while you have moved on … you arrive in each city and present yourself to its media; after that, in the evening, a mediated individual, you appear at the bookshop and perform.

He could have been writing about Greer in 1976.

• • •

Greer is not known for her lyricism, but this long short letter is lyrical in places, and it is sad. Archivists have a convention of attempting, so far as is consistent with keeping records safe, of boxing documents in the same order as they were kept by the person who collected them: the order in itself might be significant. So it is that this intensely personal document is stored alongside the press clippings generated during that four-week journey, in which Greer is recorded on the front pages of US newspapers as having addressed audiences of thousands who gave her standing ovations for her attacks on the 'Pill culture'. She encouraged women to 'hound' the manufacturers of

unsafe contraceptives and become 'enlightened consumers'. In Colorado she told an audience of 1200 that men were 'absolute monsters of fertility' and described the average ejaculation as a 'sacrilegious waste of life'. It made sense, she said, to control fertility in the female, but no satisfactory method had yet been devised.

Yet in the letter to Amis there is very little mention of these public outings. She records a 'better than usual' standing ovation in Las Vegas, after which she drove down the Sunset Strip hooting and waving at the picket lines of hospitality workers, who were on strike and 'making holiday in the rainbow light'. Las Vegas, she told him, was:

> Preposterously beautiful against the velvet black night of the desert, a panoply of words and pictures, stripes and stars. Imagine, then, my dearest, the mad pride of the Las Vegas culinary workers who last night at eight o'clock reduced the whole thing to hysterical emptiness by walking out of the hotels which house the thousands of suicidal moths brought in by the display.

She imagined 'Sammy Davis Junior, Ann Margret and Wayne Newton must spend the night warming TV dinners'. Greer herself had trouble finding food, and dined on salad, soy bean sausages and ice-cream with butterscotch sauce bought from a supermarket. The next day she wrote: 'I sit enveloped in a yellow miasma, produced by thunderous farting.'

Another time, having given a lecture in Victoria, British Columbia, she wrote to Amis about the pleasures of a good hotel in the British tradition:

> Soon the waiter will bring me my tea, tea served properly with really truly milk from cows tits, in a pot with hot water on the side … my lecture is done,

and a roaring success, except that a young swollen pallid person fainted with a crash when I was describing the atrocities which occasionally ensue from the IUD.

She segues. She has a pain in her right side. 'Ovulation, I suppose. Futile.'

Elsewhere in the document, she told Amis she suffered from neurasthenia—a term on which medical dictionaries are somewhat ambivalent. Does it even exist? The definition, when provided, describes chronic fatigue, moderate depression, insomnia and 'nervous prostration'. Nobody, watching her progress, criss-crossing the country in a tumble of words, could have guessed. Yet this was a very unhappy and difficult time for Greer, and the letter has to be read in this context. And yet, for large parts, it is simply sparkling with wit.

The Long Letter is a message in a bottle from the past—to borrow the cliché, from a foreign land. Greer and Amis, like all of us, were stuck in their present. The past was defining, the future shrouded in mist. They could not have known that the mid 1970s was the height of the sexual revolution of which Greer was progenitor, enthusiast and victim. They could not have known that when this document found an audience people would be campaigning for the right to marry rather than the right to remain unwed. Or that the Cold War would be over, without the world having self-destructed. Or that the times would be more liberal, yet also strangely more conservative, than their own. Nor would they have known that Greer had already written the book—*The Female Eunuch*, published in 1970—for which she would be best remembered. Although she was to be a public figure for the whole of the next 40 years, she would never again be quite so unquestionably at the centre of the storm of change.

Four years before beginning the Long Letter, Greer had completed a translation of Aristophanes' *Lysistrata*, in which women refuse to sleep with their husbands unless they stop the Peloponnesian war. She was not to know the work would not be performed until 1999. She was hoping it would be soon. Amis, on the other hand, had just published his second novel, *Dead Babies*. He had won a prize for his first, *The Rachel Papers*, and was beginning to be spoken of in his own right, rather than as the precocious son of his famous father and loving foil, rival and critic, Kingsley Amis, who then as now, was held to be the best English comic novelist of his generation.

Together Greer and Amis were part of a literary set that gathered around the *New Statesman*. This group ate together, argued together and sometimes slept together, building a network of broken hearts, powerful friendships and lasting enmities. Their friends included Julian Barnes, Clive James, Christopher Hitchens and Amis's boss at the *New Statesman*, Claire Tomalin. These were to become lions in their own right—all famous writers, journalists and intellectuals, but in 1976 they were just starting out, and Greer was easily more famous than any of them. *The Female Eunuch* had changed the times. It argued for a new, powerful, sexual emancipation. Greer was never merely correct line. She did not come from the established line of feminists, who argued for equality. She thought equality in the male mould was 'an incredibly conservative aim'. In part she blamed women themselves for their impotence, their eunuchdom, and it was potency that she wanted, and emancipation, including sexual.

In 1976 Amis was 26 years old, Greer ten years older. She was more than six feet tall. He was five foot four. Greer was carrying *Dead Babies* in her luggage, but had not, when she started the letter, read it. Perhaps Greer would have argued with the description of what she was writing as a love letter. In a news clipping from an interview done on her tour, she asserted: 'I don't fall in love. I don't get completely done in by one person. I'm always capable of infidelity. Obsession is all too likely, it happens all the time. But I don't like it and I wish it didn't happen.'

It is not a secret that Amis and Greer had an affair, although their relationship is not mentioned in Amis's *Experience*, nor in the biography of him written by Richard Bradford, nor in the Greer biography *Untamed Shrew*, written by the journalist Christine Wallace. Google Greer and Amis's names, however, and you will find the fact of their relationship recorded on sites that catalogue the personal lives of celebrities. It also got a tangential mention in a memoir Julie Kavanagh wrote in 2009 of her relationship with Amis.

At the time Greer was writing the letter to Amis, Kavanagh was his partner. Kavanagh wrote of those times: 'By the summer of 1975 Martin had become as famous as his father, and it seemed to me that everyone was after him, however unlikely, from Germaine Greer to [magazine editor] Mark Boxer.' Amis, she said, was discovering sexual success:

The feelings of profound unattractive-ness from which he claims to have suffered a couple of years before we met—feelings of short-arsed, physical inadequacy which he novelises time and again—had given way to Byronic magnetism. There was lost time to make up and no time for restraint.

Greer, too, had multiple lovers, and on this lonely trip was sometimes accompanied by a Detroit-based boyfriend, about whom she felt ambivalent, and who seems to have made her miss Amis all the more. On the plane to Boston from Heathrow, she wrote to Amis:

Last time we endured one of these meet-ings I advised him to try fucking first and talking later, but I suspect that he is no

less jittery than I am and the action will not follow the word. It's just the begin-ning that's crusty; when we get through that it's all smooth, like creme brulee … if I have to spend too long with [him] (ie a whole day) I get restive and irritated by his undemanding mind. It is better this way. Rather it is only possible this way. And this way it is only just possible.

At Heathrow, Greer had bought at the bookshop two books by Aleksandr Solzhenitsyn, the Nobel Prize–winning Russian dissident author who had been expelled from the Soviet Union in late 1974. From the perspective of the present day, Greer and Solzhenitsyn are an odd intellec-tual pairing. This was the Cold War, when the orthodoxy was to see Communist Russia as evil. Greer, being unorthodox, was sceptical. Solzhenitsyn had become something of a modern-day prophet of the right. Feted in the West, he had been asked to speak to then president Gerald Ford about the Soviet threat. At the same time he was criticising what he saw as the ugliness and vapidity of Western pop culture.

Predictably, Greer was not a fan. She wrote to Amis, as her plane flew over the frozen wastes of Newfoundland on the way to Boston from Heathrow, that she had bought *The First Circle* despite Solzhenitsyn's 'sanctimonious face on the cover, peeping athwart the title … To reward myself then for so egregious [a] decision to appal myself, I slipped the *Penguin Book of Sunday Times Crosswords* into my dilly bag.' In the air, she shared the crossword with Amis. Three clues had eluded her, including 'Figure of a parson with no alternative to fish (R-c-a---e)'. She was freezing in her exit-row seat, wrapped protectively in fox furs, and observing her fellow passengers with a sour eye:

In all planes there is one passenger who stands up and gazes about a lot, and addresses all who catch its eye. This time the exhibitionist is a girl with bright brown crusty eyes and bull-nosed breasts. She has long hollow buttocks in roomy belted jeans. I hate her almost more from behind than I did when evading the pertness of her scaly eyes. The captain says we have only one generator—I hope it will not be my fate to hold the creature afloat in the freezing Atlantic.

On descent into Boston, she felt:

Knives in the Eustachian tubes. Pain, pain, pain … the pain in my belly makes me think that the pressure in my Fallopian tubes isn't equalised either. …Jesus, Mary and Joseph I'd give you my heart and my soul not to have to do this again.

But she manages, partly because he is 'with' her:

Dearest interlocutor, you have a very good effect on me. My dream of loving better because loving others is coming true. Your eyes were upon me as I fell from the air bus yesterday and … I didn't mention the pain in my head. I didn't curse and stamp … because my first lecture was last night or because I was to sleep under the spent kerosene film of Logan airport.

She met her lover and then lectured at the exclusive women's college, Wellesley.

Off to Wellesley, all glossy with sex … and I lectured funny at first, till I got angry and laid it on the creamy women of Wellesley and they stood and cheered. Then home to the Hilton and [her lover] did imitations of my lecturing posture which I found very sexy.

Then after curling up around his silvery hairy brown body I thought of you … It astonishes me with that tobacco hair and those tangled black eyelashes that you do not have brown eyes. Your eyes … are cool colored, sort of air force blue-grey, and strangely unreflecting. You slide them away from most things and look at people through your thick eyelids, under your hair, your eyebrows and your lashes. You look at mouths more than eyes. Is it because you hate to look up? It is very shy and graceful and tantalising, as well you know.

She flew on. She had a nightmare hour at O'Hare airport, Chicago, where due to a late connection her luggage, containing *Dead Babies*, was left behind. 'Here I am again. God, how glad I am you're here … It is 10 o'clock in our night and I have miles to go before I sleep, and thousands of words to say.' Now she was 'in a long ghostly procession of dead white scorpions moseying down to take off from the world's most phantasmagoric airport' and her head had erupted in painful bumps. 'I explore my sore head like an old ape … the stewardess's perfume smells like rotting strawberries.'

She arrived in Kansas City 'sticky with sweat after tumbling down the sky in a rain of coffee cups and sick bags'. Again, Amis's imaginary presence gets her through:

Losing bags on a three week 10,000 mile tour is an ordeal, but because your eyes were upon me I was brave and funny about it, bought medicated shampoo, begged a dinner from the hotel, washed my sour and lousy head, sprang forth to lecture in a thorough good humour, all one hour and ten minutes. The idiot press demanded privileges, but I huffed and puffed a little and they blew away.

Later that night at the Kansas City Marriott

Hotel, 'a grey and sightless monolith by a leaden lake in a treeless landscape', her bag caught up with her. She had *Dead Babies* once again. And so it went. On 4 March she was in Detroit, where she suffered a near physical collapse:

I have eschewed coffee. My bowels boil so, that I have had no option. No alcohol, no cigarettes, now no coffee. Nothing but black pride in my entrails holding me up … my mirror tells me that I am thick with collapsed, unhappy breasts. My shanks are dry … Detroit spreads her vast desolation under scummy grey sky.

Solzhenitsyn was not a good travel companion. She struggled with the prose, the sententious tone and the political message. She said of *The First Circle*:

I suspect that I am expected to observe in this book the canonisation of the intellectual, which I am unlikely to tolerate. The whole campaign of support for S has been in terms similar to the campaign to liberate only that pornography which has artistic merit.

Taxiing to take off to Montana, via O'Hare, she watched the passengers in their boots and Stetsons.

My skull feels as it if it has suddenly got too small for my brain. Nothing gives. All is tight and hard and sore … You elude me. My brain feels too sore and tired to bring you out of the filing cabinet in any significant shape. I get as far as seeing you answering Richard King's questions about the *New Statesman*, smoking and swinging your leg, so bitter and so funny. I'm glad you're not actually implicated in this pain and squalor. I'm writing to you like

a shipwrecked sailor putting a note in a bottle. To whom it may concern. Why should my shipwreck concern you?

Solzhenitsyn was not radical, nor intellectual enough for her. She wrote that she was

slightly shocked by the caricature of Stalin. It verifies my suspicion that I cannot make out the right case against Soviet Communism. One is not inspired to fear Stalin so much as to despise him, which is too easy. We MUST see him as the successful exponent of a system which is the inevitable result of certain realities both economic and political. It must never be forgotten that only Stalin could wield enough power to stop Hitler. That is the real tragedy; the knowledge that has destroyed the innocence of the twentieth century.

But later her spirits were rising, and she wrote:

There is greatness in Solzhenitsyn, dammit. It would have been easier to deal with his very dreadfulness if he had been inconsiderable. His limitations stem from the same source as his greatness. Of course he knows … very little about Marxism in the context of the intellectual life of the free world. He reacts against socialism as I do to the Catholicism of my childhood. I reject God thereby losing baby with bathwater. He buys God for reasons just as ineradicably absurd … He is in other words a socialist novelist with his teeth sunk in the hand that has fed him.

Her spirits and her body recovered thanks to a sauna at the Holiday Inn, Bozeman, Montana, in which she had 'purged this old body of Detroit and all its poisons'. The bath had all but done for Solzhenitsyn who 'shed all his leaves as his cheap binding vapourised in the heat … My breasts seem to have climbed back to their usual position and the furrows in my face have shrunk away.' In the meantime, she had given another lecture and was watching the 1970s war movie *Kelly's Heroes* on the hotel television: 'Clint Eastwood and Telly Savalas in full battledress at the end of my bed, what more could a girl ask. (Yourself, my dearest, and the smoothness of your skin against my clean, clean limbs. I smell of birch branches.)'

Later in the trip she sees Solzhenitsyn interviewed on the television show *Panorama*, and she reflects more on communism:

When I was a little tiny girl, I used to embroil myself terribly over the issue of communism. Every day we were told that communism was the work of the devil. Consequently I every day became more and more convinced that the Church had reason to hate and fear the abolition of private property. Again and again I called the nuns to question. More and more I reflected glumly on the conviction that anti-communism was simply negative. Religion, having betrayed its own professed bosom, could only babble in terror at the demand for social justice which threatened to sweep away those representatives of God who had not only neglected to implement Christian principles in action upon earth, but had denied them by implication in the conduct of their own affairs. So I was driven out of my classroom. So my school friends said an Our Father and Hail Mary for my black rebellious soul.

Bozeman she found 'a collection of pasteboard and glass and words flung higgledy piggledy on to a low plateau surrounded by blazing white mountains'. She flew out, bound for Great Falls, and instead of reading Solzhenitsyn, 'now a terrible fagot of loose pages', she stared at the snow beneath.

It is noon here, seven o'clock in your night … what are you doing my dear? I know you so little that I can't even guess … You have the most delightful shirts and your neck is fifteen inches round. You make the cuffs less dirty than one would expect but perhaps you spend less time at your desk than one would expect. Try as I might I cannot remember anything about a tie. Perhaps I never saw you wearing one. I do after all perfectly recall your black jacket, your trousers (two pairs anyway) your boots, your socks and your unspeakable underpants.

The First Circle was finally deposited in the waste bin of the Holiday Inn in Phoenix, Arizona. She picked up two short novels by Solzenitsyn, which did not impress her either, and also read *Cancer Ward*, which provoked reflections on mortality and God, and memories of a horror period in a Sydney hospital while nurses suggested she repent. Greer wrote that she did not believe in God, nor approve of him. As for Solzhenitsyn:

I would give the whole oeuvre, so far, for any story by Chekov, which contains more compassion, more unpretentious virtuosity, and more understanding of the basic dilemma than Solzhenitsyn can ever identify in his theological wilderness. Come to think of it, I'll read *King Lear* before I give Solzhenitsyn any more of my time.

On she went, to Seattle and then to Vancouver and Calgary, where the restaurant of her hotel was 'full of skiers sporting pig skin faces and white necks'. She was squired to Calgary by Dr William Epstein, an expert on nuclear weapons and formerly of the UN disarmament division, 'nice, right minded if self-deceiving'. He told her cheerfully that the world was bent on destruction then, dropping her at the airport, kissed her four times 'rapturously'. There, she writes: 'I went to the bookshop and bought *By Grand Central Station I Sat Down and Wept*, if only because [literary editor] Francis Wyndham's comment was on the cover and the last time I saw him, you were in the same room. Gloom supervenes.'

By 7 March she was back in Phoenix, and at last had a couple of days break from her mediated, public self. She hired a Gran Torino and went on a two-day fast-paced tour of Arizona. She almost left Amis behind:

> I had meant not to write in this book this morning … but I got four paces beyond my door and had to scurry back and fetch it. It is as if I don't see without you: if I am not observing it for you I fall into traveler's catatonia and the outside world disappears.

In Jerome, Arizona, she observed for him the county's lady sheriff 'complete with hand tooled belt, silver and turquoise buckle, tear gas canister, revolver and handcuffs', but the

> wild west is not as interesting as it ought to be … all the signs in outback Arizona are lettered in old colonial characters on imitation split boards and painted red on phony creosote. Jerome is a dead mining town, hideously resuscitated for the tripper trade.

But she loved the landscape:

> Earth all acid colors … the sky is limitless … as you leave the valleys and climb into the hills the blueness swallows you up and turns into jostling mist and driving snow. It would be grand and empty if you could escape the realtors' cabins and cold beer stores. I came

around one bend with all the grace and precision of a legless dinosaur and beheld innumerable entreaties to buy myself some artificial logs and build me an 'air-lock cabin' in the wilderness.

Only Stalin could wield enough power to stop Hitler. That is the real tragedy; the knowledge that has destroyed the innocence of the twentieth century.

That night she wrote to Amis from a fake log cabin with a view of the Grand Canyon. She had dined badly, with Solzhenitsyn for company, and now could hear the sounds of a couple in the 'magic fingers' bed in the cabin next door, and 'bloodcurdling human cries indicate that the American nation disports itself nearby'. The Canyon, though, was beautiful. 'Kant would approve the use of the term sublime,' she wrote. The next day she rose to watch the sunrise but found herself 'Incapable of feeling the right sentiments in the right place':

> The use of the term 'rim' in reference to the Canyon's edges reveals the Founding Fathers, or at any rate the Naming Fathers, to have been struck by the Canyon not as a huge cunt, but as the biggest arse hole in the world … I was induced to laugh at the obvious when I came across a sign saying 'rim Worship site'.

When she returned her Grand Torino to the rental company, she had spent two days and driven a total of 820 miles, 'tearing around the back blocks, at high speed, shooting through pine forests and thundering over plateaux, struggling to drive my leviathan nicely around hairpin bends instead of wallowing in the accepted American Fashion'.

She had seen a road runner and laughed out loud: 'it looked so very much funnier than they do in cartoons'.

That evening she was depressed. Americans were disporting themselves 'in the heated waters of the Ramada Inn swimming pool like hippos' and she was imagining Amis pronouncing the name of the region she had just driven through. 'I think of your lips and teeth saying Tonto, nipping the T's. It's one word that even you cannot drawl.'

• • •

True to her intellectual roots as a Shakespeare scholar, Greer did indeed read *King Lear*, as she swooped up and down the coast of California, nearing exhaustion and in a kind of horror at the excess and soullessness of the cities. Her San Francisco hotel had been hosting the National Association of Recycling Industries. 'Competitors embrace, buy and sell to each other, cement a relationship by being drunk and uninhibited together.' 'It seems to my tired brain', she wrote between San Francisco and Los Angeles, 'that Lear was struggling against the same odds as America.'

> An opportunist, huckster society, unconcerned with truth, unaware of truth, innocent even of appetite, using all as mere manipulation. Lear, like any conman's victim, asks to be manipulated, begs for hard sell and brings chaos upon himself. 'What can you say to draw a third more opulent than your sisters. Speak.' The bosom that cannot profess is lost here too. Most of the people I meet alter truths as if they were falsehoods, for the function of all utterance in this word-stricken society is manipulation, not meaning.

Yet it was also Los Angeles, the heart of US awfulness and madness, as she saw it, that provided Greer with her most heart-warming encounter of the trip—getting to know Frank Zappa, one of the most innovative and versatile rock musicians of his generation, his wife Gail and their family. Greer gave an account of the meeting in her letter to Amis, but reprised it at greater length in 2005 when she wrote for the *Guardian*, after Zappa's death.

Their encounter began in the famous Beverley Wilshire Hotel, then the pinnacle of celebrity and luxury. Elizabeth Taylor was staying there at the same time as Greer, and she met 'dear Woody Allen' on the steps. She considered ringing Warren Beatty, her some-time lover, but decided not to. The reason was simple. The night before, 15 March, she had discovered that she had crabs. She assumed she had contracted them from her Detroit lover, but as she acknowledged there were many couplings in which they could have passed to her, or from her: 'The unspeakable question is could I by any con-catenation of adverse influences have given them to you? … I spent the evening hunting for them until I had two adults, a teenager and assorted eggs assembled in an ashtray.'

The next day she went down to breakfast. There were Zappa and his wife, who were staying in the hotel while their house was being decorated. They called her over, and she told them about the crabs. Zappa was almost pleased, and took charge of the situation. As she wrote later in the *Guardian*:

> 'Not a problem,' said Frank. His black Rolls-Royce with tinted windows was waiting in the hotel driveway; in no time we were at Schwob's drugstore, and Frank was yelling over the heads of the would-be Lana Turners twirling on the stools at the counter: 'Blue lotion, please, blue lotion for the crabs.' The words rang out like a triumphant fanfare.

She would describe the Zappas as the only sane people in Los Angeles. It was after this encounter, as Greer travelled to San Francisco for the second time, that she began to wonder if she was writing to Amis at all:

As the miles add up, I find this letter harder and harder to write. My style falters and whole paragraphs emerge as dry as powder. Yesterday I left this book in a taxi cab and would have lost it if the driver hadn't driven back … with it. As for you, my darling, I see you very rarely. Even in my dreams you send me only your handmaidens.

In Los Angeles she had encountered the American writer and socialite Anthony Haden-Guest.

I dragged you screaming into our conversation, which was a bad move for he asked at once about Julie [Kavanagh], and I was ravening for a glimpse of your dear self. Of you he said 'the oldest young man he had never known' and then 'Isn't it odd how the sons have fulfilled the ambitions of the fathers? Auberon Waugh is an upper class gentleman, and Martin Amis is small and sexy and cultured.' I was pleased with that because it implied a connection, if tenuous, between Waugh and your beloved self. He did say 'small' more or less in that position, in a way that made it sound like an achievement, and I liked that too. I think of your arms, your shoulders, your nipples, your soft thick skin. I cannot get you all in focus. The image of Frank Zappa drives you out. Frank Zappa staring at the swollen curve of my breast in my old blue t-shirt. 'Australian tits,' he says, and keep staring as only a 50s delinquent could stare. 'They have their ups and downs,' say I and they demonstrate by standing to attention. Odd. He is a really beautiful ugly man, with hair like curled black silk and legs no longer than his arms. His lips are dark brown, his nose, nobility. Would I? Yes, I would.

On to Missouri, and she read *By Grand Central Station I Sat Down and Wept*, the novel-length prose poem written by Canadian author Elizabeth Smart cataloguing a destructive love affair. The book was then a cult hit. Greer thought it 'Awful in the real sense of the word "awful"'. It was a 'vortex of egotism'. In this mood, Greer had no time for female victimhood:

The immense greed and insatiable narcissism of women is nowhere more arrestingly deployed. Any man appalled by the single mindedness of women's love ought to read it. We are all taught, you see, to value ourselves highly, to give great importance to the commerce of the body, to accept death rather than devaluation. Our love is as pure, classic and unreasonable as hatred.

And it was in this mood, with Zappa's image in part obscuring the memory of Amis, that she at last began to read *Dead Babies*. The experience dominated the last long, sad and angry movement of the letter.

• • •

Dead Babies has dated. It was a satire on its own times, an ink-black comedy peopled with the kind of comic grotesques that Amis was to make a feature of his fiction. Re-reading it is difficult. At times the fist fucking, the violence, the ghastly characters are so overwhelming that one loses the comedy and is left only with the disgust. Julian Barnes reviewed it when it was released, and wrote:

Sparkling might not be the first adjective that springs to mind to describe a novel packed with the concentrated disgust which *Dead Babies* contains. Nevertheless, Martin Amis's version of the bleak and wrecky future that awaits a sex-and-drug-addicted society is so fizzing with style, so busy with verbal inventiveness, that the adjective is impelled upon one.

Amis has said in recent years that he dislikes both his first novels. Today *Dead Babies* reads like a young man experimenting with horror and his ability to shock. In an arch dig at the format of an Agatha Christie, *Dead Babies* follows a group of people staying for a drug-addled weekend of awful sex and casual cruelty in a country house. At the centre are two characters that Greer, correctly, spotted as caricatures of Amis's blackest views of himself.

First there is Keith Whitehead, a man so short and ugly that people vomit when he takes his clothes off. He was to recur in later novels by Amis. Then there is Giles Coldstream, a man obsessed with his teeth. Amis has since described, in *Experience*, the decades of pain and worry he had over his woeful dental condition, resulting eventually in expensive and painful treatment over many months in the 1990s. But when he wrote this novel, his teeth were still a burden to him—one of the reasons, he was later to say, that he never smiled. *Dead Babies* opens with Giles Coldstream dreaming that he is spitting out his teeth.

Greer began to read the book on 23 March, in the Hilton Inn, Columbia. She was guffawing. 'I adore Keith Whitehead, the nadir of your own self image, and therefore dear to me.' But she didn't like the 'sixties coterie' that was creeping into this 'immaculate style'. The novel was meant to be set in the near future. His characters would not therefore 'express themselves in dated 60s slang, not if they are worth reading about anyway'.

Next she was in the Eastern International Hotel in Kennedy, then on a flight that made her bowels 'crawl with terror'. She was becoming irritated by his prose. 'If anything else "implodes" in this book I shall scream … Page 230. I scream.' She landed in Paducah, Kentucky, and informed Amis that the grass was no bluer than anywhere else, then she laid into him, a mix of love, punishment and psychoanalysis:

I believe it is my dearest author's design that I should not dislike Keith Whitehead. If suffering may make saints in Solzhenitsyn's mould it may well make Keith sympathetic, especially as he does not do any harm to anyone else … Keith plus Giles equals a cloacal view of Martin Amis, and everyone else riding the shit blast. Moreover the tall, affluent people whom Keith cannot succeed in joining are dull. It is not their hedonism that makes them so, but their inability to perceive beauty and experience pleasure. The author cannot manage his narrative for the same reason that he could not end *The Rachel Papers*. He is himself a victim of their crapulent culture, envious even as he is satiric, unable to achieve his own perspective or to safeguard his own utterance from the contamination of their style. My darling, your narrator is still a small boy undergoing petty humiliations at a public school. Coveting, adoring and hating his tormentors, devising for them a hellish punishment as fatuous as any poetic justice. The book resounds with your own fear of obesity, baldness, homosexuality and ridicule; if I did not love you before I should be hopelessly in love with you now. This nugget of disgust and confusion you lay before the public so trustingly. No wonder they were outraged. William Burroughs, William Golding, Hunter S Thompson, all the petrified froth of the [illegible] conjured up in this owl-ball of a book.

She wrote to him next from the 13th floor of the Nashville Holiday Inn ('a bad hotel'), with a view of a sandstone replica of the Parthenon. 'Small, squat and dull as a gas chamber … I draw back, concentrating my sick attention on your small hands and feet, your boots abandoned to the fifth position.' This time she began her critique of his book with an anecdote, recalling a day on Rhodes when she lunched with 'verminous hippies'. 'After lunch I asked if I might void my over-charged bowel anywhere.' She was directed towards a bridge, where she found neat rows of turds 'all singing loudly, accompanied by flies'. She added her 'steaming offering'. When she returned, her host hippie took himself off to the bridge and on return said, 'I hope you don't mind … I did mine on top of yours.' Greer comments: 'I could have murdered him.' She recounted the experience, she said, because of *Dead Babies*:

> You have voided in the public eye. You will not be thanked for it. It is not the unpleasantness of your vision that excites reproof but the vulnerability of the author, for once casually revealed. As for me, it makes me helpless with desire for you. Now I know that I shall never force this letter upon you. The thought of it makes my heart pound, as if we were to shit together.

Later she criticises the way he 'scatters its dramatic personae in a fairly callow manner'.

Amaranthine
Louise Carter

There's a tree branch pressed against your window:
leaves flexed up, muscular and persistent.
Roots sunk deep into the marshy clay
sucking fecundity upwards, persisting, *breathe.*

You've still juice; nature's sorcery agrees.
When I see you, cologne boils to steam
and we vibrate in harmony with bliss. Swollen
with major chords, a cacophonous deliciousness.

Enough to make a lugubrious old man giggle.
Swing-dancing into our allotted roles,
eerily synchronous as if we'd already rehearsed
the steps in another life, or in dreams.

Let's treat this like a memory we can walk
around in. The palace doors creak open onto
gilded wings; in every room an instrument.
We can stay forever. We are immortal here.

They achieve 'no identifying style', and in a reference to Kingsley Amis:

> Papa still il miglior fabri.' [Father still the better craftsman.] 'Nevertheless [*Dead Babies*] probably works out your relationship to the genie of the sixties. Now that those sterile traces are kicked over, what will you do. (Think not, my dear, that I am unaware that these observations are unpardonable, these questions brutal. After such, what forgiveness?)

> Must I despise all those whom I can have and adore the ones I cannot? These tears are shaken from the primal wound. Mother, I hate you.

In the next entry, Greer has returned home. She is exhausted, near physical and mental collapse. Bills have arrived that mean her earnings from the tour are spent before she has even received them. She is now quite certain that she will never send the letter:

> This despairing cry to someone who hardly exists will never be heard. The man I wrote to was the man who would have known how to finish *The Rachel Papers*, who would bear my criticisms of *Dead Babies* and even recognize it. I have not despaired of his eventual existence but I shall be too early to see it. Perhaps when he loses his battles with physical degeneration, he will understand, but understand is not what I want. It is better for him and for me that this book remains closed. I do not care as much as I wish I did, and he is not what I wish I cared for … For a month and from 6000 miles away I loved him well.

She is suffering from neurasthemia: 'hot rheum flowed from my eyes down my temples. I felt as if gallons more waited to drown the bed, swelling my eyes and garlanding the day with headaches.' And a few pages later:

> How can I dismiss you, my own darling? I have no choice. In the month that has passed since you telephoned and bade me begin my letter, I have come to rely upon you absolutely, but I have also made you in my own image, simply imposed my alter ego upon you, and with it all my passion, and alas all my loneliness. I dare not allow irrelevant reality to intrude upon this self indulgence. Behind the … haze of my darling, I see your real outlines as unnaturally meaningless and squalid, for I am tensed against information about you.

Greer confided her obsession with Amis to friends who 'roar with delight to discover anything so exciting as an infatuation … they remind me that I have been fond of other whores …' Another of her lovers calls to visit.

> I hate the skinlessness of the side he turns to me. Why can I not love those who love me? Is it still the deathliness of unloved childhood? Must I despise all those whom I can have and adore the ones I cannot? These tears are shaken from the primal wound. Mother, I hate you. Martin I love you. Actually I love Keith Whitehead. From henceforth this letter is addressed to Little Keith.

Those are the last words in the letter.

In preparation for writing this essay, I contacted both Greer and, through his agent, Martin Amis. Amis's agent said he was not available for interview, and a suggestion that he might consider emailed questions received no response. Greer engaged in some email correspondence, but made it clear she wanted nothing to do with the essay receiving public attention, largely out of concern for the many friends and lovers who are mentioned in it. Greer's second book was published in 1979. Titled *The Obstacle Race*, it was about female painters. In the same year she took a job at the University of Tulsa, which seems to have solved her financial problems. She went on to become a fellow of Newnham College, Cambridge. Greer was also a lecturer at the University of Warwick (1967–72) and Professor of English and Comparative Studies at the University of Warwick from 1998. She published many more books, including a sequel to *The Female Eunuch*, *The Whole Woman*, published in 1999, in which she argued there had been little progress in the feminist movement:

> When *The Female Eunuch* was written our daughters were not cutting or starving themselves. On every side speechless women endure endless hardship, grief and pain, in a world system that creates billions of losers for every handful of winners. It's time to get angry again.

Martin Amis's best-known novels were published in the 1980s and 1990s. They have put him unquestionably among the finest writers in English. But he has also become controversial, loved and hated by the critics and often in the media. *London Fields* was famously left off the shortlist for the Booker Prize because some of the judges thought it woman-hating. He has been accused in print and by his peers of egotism, narcissism, misogyny and greed. The barbs directed at him make Greer's loving criticism from 40 years ago look comparatively mild.

Meanwhile his best novels are glittering and savage.

As for the two of them, there are few records of their dealings with each other. In an interview published in 2009 Amis talked about his latest book and mentioned Greer tangentially. She had quoted him, he said, as saying that 'all men should be locked up until they're 28 … We're terrible, we can't help it!'

In 2009 Amis's 1984 novel *Money* was adapted for television by the BBC, and an interview Greer did with Amis about the book was released. A snippet of their encounter survives on YouTube. *Money* was a wonderfully tricksy book, narrated by a character called John Self, described by one reviewer as 'obese, junk-guzzling, alcoholic, chain-smoking, pill-popping, priapic, with rotting teeth, tinnitus and a dodgy heart'. The novel also features a minor character called Martin Amis.

In the snippet of the interview on YouTube, Greer is still giving Amis a hard time. She laughs at his assertion that television has caused a 'convulsion of stupidity'. She tells Amis that he is talking like the Martin Amis in the book, who is 'rather prissy really' and that 'in the Martin Amis that I know slightly there is a good slice of John Self'. Amis's response, if any, is not recorded. She accuses him of being 'a brilliant hater, with an eye for what is grotesque', but concludes that this talent is, in the end, 'profoundly moral'.

I like to think he would have paid her the same compliment. It is my own conclusion. •

Margaret Simons is a journalist of more than 35 years' experience, and director of the Centre for Advancing Journalism at the University of Melbourne. She has written two biographies, two novels and a number of books on media, politics and gardening.

Artwork by Ulrike Sturm

See that Gully: The Ghost I Have Become in a World of Asbestos

John Kinsella

Bird thou never wert
—Shelley

I TELL HIM, My name is Ghost. And at that very moment a kookaburra laughs. I find myself thinking that no-one owns the laugh of a kookaburra, not even the kookaburra. It's not copyright. And kookaburras have only been over here, here in the West, for a hundred or so years. People from t'other side often don't realise that, thinking their way is the normal way. Maybe lyrebirds can mimic a kookaburra's call where they come from. Wouldn't know—have to look it up. I can see from the blood in his cheeks, his scrunched eyes, the mild tremor taking hold of his limbs, that he thinks I am laughing at *him*. I'm not. I am simply saying, My name is Ghost.

See that gully, he says—yelling and grinding grit with yellow teeth, all incisors—if you don't shut your mouth, your *bloody lippy always goin' on about shit* mouth, I'll stuff you in it and cover you with dirt and no-one will ever find you. He says this with his boots pinning my boots to the ground, his face so close to mine that the spit arcs across, and he means it. I stare at him, and in the mirror of his eyes see the vague outline of myself, the ghost I am, the ghost I will become.

I am not dead, but I sometimes feel like I am. I say to him, I am already dead, mate, not really taking the piss, but he thinks I am. Having a go at him, diminishing him in some way—he can't tolerate this. I glance around at our surroundings. The jagged eucalypts, smoother ones on higher ground, the razor-wire clusters of parrot bush, birds chattering and processing the fibres in the air. Like dandelions—capeweed flowers transforming to seed—introduced, then dispersed. It's all fibres dispersing, spreading, working their way in. Taking root. I notice the beauty and the joy and the perverse balancing of the equation. I do people's taxes and know how to balance the books. This book cannot be balanced.

And so you ask, how has it got to this? Well, I'll tell you, just for the hell of it—no real reason, because it will have no effect. Nothing will change. Nothing will happen. Entropy. A stultified rebirth. A working-down to fibres … one day, atoms. My name is Ghost. I am fibres and atoms. I am cold. Asbestos keeps out the heat. Bushfire, soaring temperatures … and I remain chilled to the bone.

It came about when Seve started to knock down his old asbestos house with a front-end loader. He'd moved his girlfriend out, deposited her in the shed along with the contents of the house, and just started smashing the place down, lifting what he could with the loader into the back of his tip truck, which he then drove to a bush block a few k's down the road and dumped. I was witness to all this, and with a T-shirt wrapped around my mouth and nose, I went up to his place and told him what I thought. That was when he was about to dump his first load. He told me to get fucked, so I followed him in my car, suspecting that an illegal demolition would be followed by illegal disposal. Not hard to predict with Seve—it was the way he'd always done things, and anyone who opposed him got a thumping or a bullet in their water-tank. Even the cops and rangers were scared of him and his old biker mates, who every now and again took a run up from the city for a keg and sheep-on-a-spit rage. Seve even put on a live rock band sometimes, bikies and locals sitting together on hay bales arranged around the band, with electrics powered by a portable generator giving static and sibilance to the performance. At such times all wildlife bolted to my place, or further afield.

The remorseless *beep beep beep* as the loader reversed before charging straight into the mess of the fallen house. You could hear it across the valley. I waited for the asbestos removal people to arrive but they didn't—they weren't invited—this was a one-man show that followed its own anti-rules. The shire wouldn't take it on unless someone who had got under their skin in the past tried to do something outside guideless—these things were sorted in the sports bar. An eye for an eye. And every good turn deserves a favour. No room or time to listen to whingers and moaners. Just get on with it and people will forget. Bugger the fibres.

Another load of broken asbestos sheeting scrunched into the tip truck. No masks, just a loud stereo and *beep beep beep*. The grinding machinery, nerves on edge, through every muscle, rattling bones and making teeth chatter. Rrrr-r … Rrrr-r … crunch … *beep beep beep*. How can anyone sit there in a smudged glass box watching stuff crumple and snap and tear and shatter, and then back up and do it over again. As if there are no costs, as if there are no consequences. Dividends. But what sort of dividends? Compounding interest. *Beep beep* fucking *beep*. I have to repeat it just to remain stable, to block the sound out with the words that represent those sounds. Separate myself by degrees of illusion.

So I go into the sports bar and Seve and the shire president are having a beer in their crisp open-collar shirts, watching the Friday night footy on a television over the bar. They are both mauling peanuts out of an old ashtray—no smoking in pubs now. But both of them stink more of cigarettes than beer, and I know they'll break off at quarter time to nip out into the beer garden for a smoke. Seve has two rollies behind his ear ready to go—I suspect they might have a little hydro dope in there as well. Everyone knows Seve grows hydro in his shed but no-one rips him off because they know what will happen, that he will find them. The kookaburras are on his side—they're the only creatures that are. Now he and his girlfriend are sunning themselves under the grow lights while his redecoration project is going through its workout. I stand behind them and say, Seve, it's bloody criminal what you're doing. First wrecking that house without a care for your safety or anyone else around the area, and second for dumping your waste in the bush. Not just any waste, mate, but bloody broken and crushed and powdered asbestos. It's a jailing offence.

In hindsight, it'd taken me all the courage I had. I expected a fist in the guts—I was standing and Seve was sitting. But all Seve did, through a mush of peanuts and beer, was say to the president, They reckon this pub is haunted. Think I just heard the ghost of a loser who must have drowned in his own piss. The president laughed, lifted one bum cheek, and let out a cracker of a fart. The barman, who was leaning at an awkward angle back over the bar counter the better to watch the television, gave a brief burst of laughter, then stopped as abruptly. I walked out. I could hear that someone kicked a goal and the president cheered and Seve yelled, Fuck off—that grazed the fucking post!

Other than attending school, the kids have been inside for days. And even then I've driven them in rather than let them walk up the hill to where the bus stops. The air is full of fibres. We are under siege. I have rung authorities everywhere and they've said they'll get onto it. Seve has finished knocking down the old house and scooping the shit up and is now messing in a bed of particles, sorting the foundations. Where the old house was, he is excavating and installing sub-drains and yellow sand compacting and preparing to lay the new concrete pad. He is building a monument to himself. This is to be his legacy to the valley, the region. His girlfriend (I have no idea of her name), stands outside the shed with hands on hips watching him.

I worry about the shit dumped in the bush. I really worry. The animals … roos, echidnas … they could get asbestosis. I worry about children playing in the bush, walking to and from the bus, way out here, isolated, no-one noticing if they get a cloud of fibres, mess around in the rubble. I will broach the subject with him again. I am

not just being a picky dickhead. It's not because of my own health, honestly, it's not. I care about Seve's health as well. And his girlfriend's. And the president's. That doesn't make me noble or a hero, I can hear them now … it just eats at me, bothers me. You can't stay silent when something is so strong, so visceral, can you? The Australian Taxation Office says of capital gains tax: 'A capital gain or capital loss on an asset is the difference between what it cost you and what you receive when you dispose of it.' Seve picked up that place for a song, he's always bragging about it, and he will claim a bundle for the demolition. It's all topsy-turvy—he's profited from my misery, from putting fibres in the air. He enjoys the knowledge. He knows.

I'll offer him a bottle of Jacks. No, two bottles of Jacks. Even three. Meet him halfway. Bribe him. Pander to his better side—he has a girlfriend, she must care for him. I'll speak to her. Fuck off, ya poofter, she says when I see her in in town. I know you two haven't been together long, I say, but I go way back with Seve, known him for years—used to do his tax. But no, just a craning-back as if to spit, hair lassoing in the wind, and a Fuck off, ya poofter, didn't ya hear the first time? A carton of bottles of Jacks, Seve. Just clean it up. And then he sizes me up and laughs a sickly sort of death laugh: Fuck off, mate, not going near that—it's asbestos, don't ya know! Need to get a specialist in there to clean that shit up. Bastard who dumped it there should be shot. Then he cacked himself laughing and as suddenly—it's always abrupt— pulled a steel-straight face and said, If you don't fuck off my land, I'll shoot you, ya liddle retard.

Maybe I should have put up the white flag there and then. Cut my losses and put our place on the market and moved out, away from the fibres, from Seve, the president. But my wife would have had none of that. She's part of my ghosting as well.

When I was a kid I was surrounded by asbestos. My bedroom was asbestos, and I slept pressed against a rough, dimpled grey wall. A sheet of bitter cold and extreme heat—no matter which, I pressed my face against it. I didn't like the sensation, but was compelled. The fence between us and our neighbours on both sides was asbestos covered in a green growth. It had set root though it probably had no roots. It had connected with the fibres of the asbestos, which look as if they follow the same lines but when viewed through a magnifying glass are crazed and shooting off in all directions. Every now and again sheets of asbestos appeared in the deepest part of the back yard, stacked like football cards. On one occasion my brother and I drew one off the pack and smashed it to pieces with a hammer and then, covered in the disintegration, panicked and buried the bits in sand. We never got into trouble for that, dusting ourselves off before going in for tea. I have a relative who died of mesothelioma. A slow and terrible death. I grew up in a world of fibres and their consequences. I tell you this to ensure you understand my sanity, my caution, my caring. Even for Seve himself.

But Seve is of a 'breed' (prime bull) of Aussie men who will always call the likes of me Ghost or Poof or Jerk or Cunt, if they bother speaking at all. I know I will do the leaving, the moving, going elsewhere.

Searching for a Cigarette in the Blackout after a Flood
Brian Purcell

Bellingen 2013

I find it hard to remember
what it was like
drawing it in
filling my lungs
with its airy cream

to gild the solemn moment
with a wreath of desire
a sharp line ascending
in an art deco curl

as the river inches up the hill
I yearn for this definition
blurred, the heart's twinge
beside the candle flame

I see my wife
by her mother's side
the shattered lungs
the denial of that body's ache
for one last breath

I want it, some kind of air
to fill the lungs or heart, desire
for what we cannot have, and you
always at the corner of my eye
and turning

I am back in this small room
watching the candle flame
The power is gone
The river
inches up the hill

And I know it won't be selling and upping sticks, it'll just be me leaving the place to my wife—and I admit it's 50 per cent hers. She has as much right, and she'd be happier there without me. There, I've said it crystal clear. But it's all I've ever wanted, this place in the bush. I'd be leaving the songbirds to the knife-beaks of kookaburras, the kangaroos to the shooters. It's always that way. And between us, and again I am not bragging, some of us will always pay more tax than others on the same income, even when we know the tricks of paying less.

And Seve will stay for maybe a year or two after he finishes his new place in its silent, invisible—if you don't know how to hear and see—aura of fibres, then sell up and move on to the next opportunity or the next downfall. Whatever it is, he won't think any further of me unless I turn up as a witness against him in a court case. If I have the balls to see it all the way through. He's betting I haven't. And even with the photographs I've taken, authorities will cite a lack of evidence to prosecute or dish out a $2000 fine, which will have made it worth it. The rubble will stay in the bush for years and maybe for good. Sounds like I am vengeful, as if I want a draconian legal system, punishment. But it's not that. It's the air, the air we breathe and that all of us, ghostly or chunky and material, move through.

I mean, we're not that different. I like the footy, a beer, and will listen to Keith Urban if not quiet as loudly as Seve does in his truck. I don't mind looking at a pretty woman … Seve is renowned for going on and on about the town's pretty women. He fancies himself. He succeeds on occasion. He gets girlfriends. Always new girlfriends. And then they vanish. We're not *that* different, but now there's only room for one of us: him or me. *I will go now …*

Or I can choose to lay me down—be laid down and covered and not found until long after. A cold case. Be here for eternity—there'd be no getting rid of me and my permanence would be by Seve's own hand, with the acquiescence of the president and his folk. Like the kookaburra, I'd be here to the end. My children thinking I've deserted them, my wife … one of the town's pretty women, a woman who has—strayed from me.

I said to her, my wife, once: Seve shoots cats wild or domestic if they stray onto his property. Why would any cat want to hang around that revolting brick-clad place of his? It's an insult to the eye, to the atmosphere of the district.

Who do you think you are? she demanded. He's a working man and is proud of his house. She defended him tooth and nail. Whoo! I said. So-rr-eee!

A working man? So am I, running my small business from home. I work and work and don't leave my rubbish lying around.

What did she say to him about me? What rubbish did she go and fill his head with? The empty Seve head. Did *I* get under her skin, into her lungs to nestle among the residues of teenage smoking, second-hand smoke of her friends, the air of betrayal? After all, she was with me because I have … taste. I listen to my music at a reasonable volume, I know the difference between right and wrong, I don't want anyone to suffer from asbestosis. Did she say to him, alongside the three-bar radiator, drinking wine from the cask and listening to Slim Dusty, You're a glorious fuck, Seve, but you live in a slum? It's in her, you know. As the shire president and the bank manager and … pure class, indoors. My wife, thinking I've finally moved on—freed her from *me*. She could have left anytime. But then there are the kids. She'll look after them enough. Truth be told, we've probably both depreciated. Seve will always think of himself as top shelf, as being blue-chip stock. It's unbecoming of me to point out the ironies—I think you've already got it. No point gilding the lily. Like that mining entrepreneur who sprinkled asbestos on his Weeties to show how *harmless* it is. To prove to us. To let all the realities vanish into the shade of this one quotidian public gesture. I wonder what Keith Urban said to Nicole Kidman when she first broached her Scientologist past? Maybe she never brought it up. And us—me and my family—living out here, isolated. Red rag to a bull. Not a ghost of a chance.

My wife just won't believe … she wouldn't believe … that I am no more 'wimpy' than him. He just wimps around when no-one's looking. I can tell by the way his girlfriend stands out the front of the shed, glaring at him. He puts on his tough face. Even at those do-or-die moments, he needs to see a reflection of his power in someone else's eyes. He's a vampire. *His* wimpiness is hidden in his coffin, sleeping on his dirt and fibres when his lovers and mates have long gone, have been pushed aside. But this is no study of him. He's not worth it.

It was so petty—my wife telling him, I'm sure she did, I can sense the whispers still hanging around, impaled and transfixed by the fibres, Did you know he has a rellie who died of asbestos, the stuff your house is made of … he's fucking paranoid about the stuff!

Ha! Seve would have revelled. Ha! And then he would have ranted to her, probably making her go down on him while the new girlfriend was performing some other rite on his hairy, filthy body, It was your old man's bloody fault I got audited! He would have said this again and again, even early on when he was poking her by the light of the television, a cop show flickering across their eyes, teeth, nails … saliva.

I'd like to think she'd have replied, No, he's a good accountant, whatever else I think of him I've gotta give him that. Audit is just chance, as he says—as *Ghost* says (and they laugh a churning juicy guttural laugh from deep inside the septic tank), An audit is just fate …

Or I can choose to be laid down and covered by earth and night, fibres of my existence working their way to the surface, aestivating. There, in the gully, by the rubble of the house that wasn't quite up to scratch. If you scratch old asbestos walls and fences you should have them properly sealed. There are businesses dedicated to sealing and removing, spreading the love around. Relocating. James Hardie went offshore. There are laws, ways of enforcing them. But out here the threads are thin if fibrous. The kookaburras are laughing and my name is Ghost, and I am made of a tough, fibrous, dangerous and immutable material. •

John Kinsella's most recent collection of stories is *Crow's Breath* (Transit Lounge, 2015). He is a fellow of Churchill College, Cambridge University; a professorial research fellow at the University of Western Australia; and Professor of Literature and Sustainability at Curtin University.

THE BEST IN POLITICS, ART & STYLE

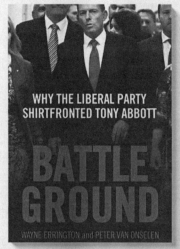

$29.99 RRP

$45.00 RRP

$19.99 RRP

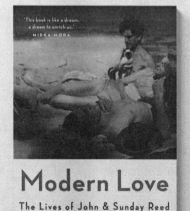

$45.00 RRP

$39.99 RRP

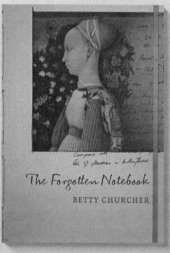

$44.99 RRP

AVAILABLE NOW IN ALL GOOD BOOKSTORES

or visit mup.com.au

MUP
BOOKS WITH SPINE

WRITTEN IN MY BODY

Na'ama Carlin

ON 26 JULY 2015 *New York* magazine rolled out its new issue with a cover that echoed across oceans. Seated in rows were 35 women. Thirty-five women out of more than 40 who had decided to go public with sexual assault and rape allegations against comedian Bill Cosby.

Seated alongside those 35 women was an empty chair, a symbol of the women who had not come forward, who did not want to expose themselves to public scrutiny. Social media loved it. Here were 35 women who refused to remain silent, go under a pseudonym or blur their image. And here was a large media outlet giving them a significant public platform.

The image of those 35 women on the *New York* magazine cover has not left me. I did not need a trigger warning I was elated. My heart beating rapidly, I drank in their stories. They were speaking out. They were seeking justice. They were doing everything I could not do. Everything I had always lacked the courage to do.

Almost immediately, comments started rolling in: 'If what they said happened to them actually did happen, why didn't they speak out sooner?' 'Why didn't they go to the police?' 'Why wait so long, unless this is part of a targeted campaign, not for their own

sense of achieving justice, but to destroy a man's life?' Predictable and frustrating.

People who have not experienced (even second-hand) domestic violence, rape, assault or abuse often underestimate the real difficulty of speaking out. Just recently in Australia the Royal Commission into Institutional Responses to Child Sexual Abuse has revealed to us how painfully draining speaking out on abuse can be, and the emotional toll it brings. I have thought at length about what prevents people from speaking out. What people often miss, when they ask 'why didn't you speak out sooner?' is the difficulty of admitting to yourself that you are in an abusive relationship; that what is happening to you isn't normal; that you don't deserve what you're getting; that you are a victim; and that you can—and deserve to—get out. I can appreciate how ridiculously obvious these statements may seem to people who haven't experienced abuse. But I also know how real they are. Nearly 20 years later, I am still coming to terms with them.

I had just turned 13 when I met him. I was at the central bus depot, waiting for the bus to my friend's house, where we were having a slumber party. He was nearly six years older than me, flirtatious, charming, intelligent. He wasn't handsome, or even pretty, but I was so flattered and charmed by his attention. I gave him our house number so that he could ask me out. Unknowingly, I had entered into what would become two years of emotional and physical abuse. I was young. I was so young, but I thought I was so much older and wiser.

One of the challenges of revisiting this relationship now is the visceral, physical reaction I get. Even when I bring to mind the moment of our first kiss—before 'it' all began—my stomach turns, and nausea rises up in my chest. But I bring this moment up regardless, to remind myself that there was a time when he *was* good, that based on that time I could not have known what was to happen. I do not doubt that he loved me. 'You make me crazy,' he would say. 'I am crazy around you.' That was just another way in which I was responsible for what happened, why it was my fault.

My parents, who did not know until much later, refused to let me see him. But I was steadfast in my ways and they couldn't stop me. I would skip school and walk two hours each way across the highway connecting our cities to meet him. At the start, because I wanted to. Then, because I was afraid of what would happen if I didn't go. I recall his rage. His face. But I went back. I tore my family apart, I broke my parents' hearts every day for two years, but still—I was breaking too, and they could not know. Not until my body had broken down and I had starved myself almost to death. I felt so full of secrets that I did not have the appetite to eat, so I told my mum and she told my dad and they too

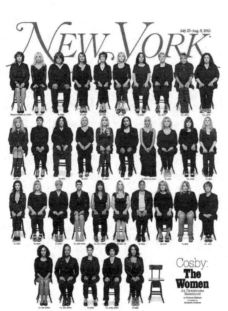

carry this pain now. I have broken them, in some way, but at least I am not the only one who is broken.

I could not speak when 'it' was happening because I did not know 'it' was happening. I thought that this is how men treat girlfriends. And in any event, it was all my fault. 'Look at what you're making me do', he said the first time. We had been together for less than three months. I had not even been naked around him. But I told him about a new friend—a boy in our neighbourhood—and how I went to his house and we chatted about books. My new friend tried to kiss me, and I said no, I have a boyfriend. But my boyfriend didn't believe me. He became overwhelmed with jealousy. I was cheating on him, he accused me, behind the closed doors of his room. Lifting his dog in his hands, he said she was worth more than me. I was *worth less* than a dog. I needed to make up for it, so he laid me on the bed. It was my punishment. This is how girlfriends are punished. A stabbing pain shot though my stomach. As it does now, nearly 20 years later.

I would be punished regularly. Always in his room. Always behind closed doors. Behind those doors was the bed, a single bed, and in that bed was a man, and this became my world. My whole world, for two years. All I knew was that this man who ruled my world loved me, and because he loved me he wanted me to behave like a proper girlfriend, and that I always did something wrong. I was late. I spoke to a boy. I didn't come the day before. I didn't come to the phone when he called. I went to a friend's place instead of his. Soon the need for excuses died out, and this would be my life, my routine. I would look out the window as day rolled into night, measuring the time that stretched out with silence, until I could go home.

Detaching myself emotionally from the situation, from the room, from the bed, became my method of dealing with what was happening. I was not present: just a body on a bed, underneath or beside a man, and this was normal. This was fine. This was how I managed, how I survived. Then and after.

> Then I doubted it was rape because it kept happening. Can rape be routine? Isn't it just a moment, an event?

It wasn't until I was in my twenties that I began using the word 'rape'. To this day I speak it under my breath; it's a word that doesn't roll off my tongue, but rather is pushed out with a wispy gasp of air. It exhausts me and my whole body to speak it. It is a physical word, and by this I mean I physically react to it. Whether it be reading, saying or hearing the word 'rape', my muscles will immediately tense up, my stomach tighten, and a deep sigh will begin inside. Today when I use it in a sentence like 'I was raped' I immediately think about the ensuing conversation. I anticipate the downcast expression on the other person's face. The sympathetic 'aww, I had no idea' (of course you didn't … how could you? I am not marked) and 'can I do anything to help?' If I confide in a friend, a lover, they will probably get angry, and express a desire to hurt the person who hurt me. But the truth is that I don't use the word 'rape' very often. Despite nearly 20 years since the first of many times, I still am coming to terms with what it means.

I recall reading as a child stories of rape in the daily newspapers. The victim—always a victim, as we did not adopt the language of 'survivors' back then—was anonymous. If she was identified at all, it was always only by the first letter of her name or a pseudonym. It seems important to pause briefly on language. In particular this one word: victim. In Hebrew, the language in which those articles and papers were printed (I grew up in Israel), the word for victim is *korban* (קָרְבָּן), a word with a biblical meaning. 'Korban' translates as 'sacrifice' (victim, sacrifice, offering, vow), and is the word used for the animals slaughtered as a sacrifice to God at the holy temples. Only the best beasts were brought to the altar. Thus the word victim invokes strong biblical connotations: helplessness, but also purity, sacrifice and holiness. And so we read the papers through the eyes of a child taking in stories of rape, and the anonymous woman, the victim, her body a sacrifice on the altar of power and sexual domination. There were, and are, many victims: anonymous, pixelated; sparse biography pieced together (she knew her attacker or did not, etc.). So we could place any victim in a given situation, as we could not distinguish horror story from horror story, pixelated face from pixelated face. We glossed over the words. 'The victim, anonymous, 17, attacked by a man while walking home from a friend's place' … and on it went.

Why are we so invested in anonymity for victims of assault? Seemingly, for their protection. But I think there is more at stake. There are a couple of elements at play: first, the hegemonic framing of 'victimhood' as something to be ashamed of, to the point where anonymity and disguise are necessary if one is to speak out. What are we telling victims here? Victims carrying so much burden and shame regardless. We insist on disguising victims of assault for our own protection, for our own social cohesion, rather than theirs. It is far more convenient to keep women silent, and with blissful ignorance we can put aside the fact that one in five women will experience sexual violence in their lifetime (and one in 20 men).[1] Think of five women in your life, and consider that at least one of them has experienced sexual violence.

Try to reconcile the fact that you may not know this because the woman concerned was too ashamed to come forward, and because we do not have systems in place to support victims. Indeed, we are reluctant even to hear victims when they speak out, questioning the legitimacy of their claims, doubting, distrusting, privileging the voices of non-assaulted men who speak for victims. This is systematic and ongoing silencing, whereby society tells victims that they should carry the shame and burden anonymously, and when they speak out, their claims usually fall on deaf ears, as we wait for a man to validate them.

But there is another more curious element under the surface and underpinning our reluctance to afford victims a voice. It is our fear of violence that drives us to avoid anything threatening, our desire to subdue any violent events. But what of a body that has known, and has come to know itself through, violence? In our attempt to hush victims, cross out their stories, blur their faces, we deny their experiences. We deny their right to justice, not only in a court but in other profoundly ontological ways too.

Our response to bodies that have known such violence is: be silent, hide your name, hide your face. This is a potential denial of lived experience and identity. We are too concerned with the need to 'protect' as an outcome of assault that we do not pause and consider whether we have taken the right approach to support victims. We need to stop seeing victims in terms of the 'momentary' or 'singular', whereby we only afford them a platform to speak out once as they give testimony in court. Through this they

satiate our egotistical social needs, as we cry in unison 'We have justice! We have been avenged!' We need to see it rather in terms of 'continuity of being' (to borrow from Donald Winnicott).

For the victim, the violence has already taken place. We cannot retroactively prevent it happening, and our attempts to protect victims with anonymity are concerned more with trying to protect us from *hearing* their stories. To invoke Winnicott again, our social obligation is not to eradicate the faces of those who come forward but rather provide a 'holding space'. Modelled on the nurturing emotional environment that a loving mother provides to her child (how she holds her baby, physically as well as emotionally, and how she is attuned and attentive to her child's needs), Winnicott's notion of a 'holding space' or 'holding environment' extends this nurturing environment to patients in psychiatric treatment. This is a measure that demands a *consistent responsiveness*, but it cultivates security and a sense of being. It is time for us to observe our role as that of the 'mother' and to this end be cognisant of the connection with and responsibility we have towards others. We must provide a holding space for victims to come to terms with and even share their experiences, ensuring they feel safe and secure doing so.

Thinking back to my teenage years, there were a few reasons I was certain it was not rape. One was because he was my boyfriend. Also, it was my fault. I made a mistake and I was being punished. Punishment isn't rape, right? Especially not if he's your boyfriend. Then I doubted it was rape because it kept happening. Can rape be routine? Isn't it just a moment, an event that happens once or maybe twice but not every day, surely? Is it rape if at some point I stop resisting because I am so exhausted from crying and lie mute

---

1   Centres Against Sexual Assault 2015, *Fact Sheet: Statistics about Sexual Assault*, <http://www.casa.org.au/casa_pdf.php?document=statistics>.

on the bed? Do tears qualify as resistance? Does silence? Also, the fact that I was 13.

Thirteen-year-old girls don't 'get raped' by their boyfriends. Rape is just something that happens to women who are dressed scantily and walk down dark streets unaccompanied. 'They are asking for it,' a friend told me one night. 'My dad told me so,' he said. We were taking a stroll and spoke about a recent rape case that featured in the news. I was 14, and still with that boyfriend. Incidentally, this friend's dad ranked high in the police force where we lived. My friend's dad had told him that girls who are raped are asking for it. Their short dresses whispering an unequivocal message. Surely me, in my long, ill-fitting jeans, my short hair, goth eyeliner, surely I was not asking for it … Rape only happens to women in short skirts, by strangers. But then, what if I was asking for it? Then I am still to blame.

A few years later I was hospitalised for an eating disorder. Keeping my abuse a secret from everyone made me feel constantly full. Additionally, I tried to gain control of my life, and food is the one thing I found easy to control. I didn't eat for months, and had been secretly starving myself for years,

Bach
David Wood

St Thomas's, Leipzig,
   all around
music, wings of counterpoint.

Bach climbs the stairwell to the organ loft,
to weave his tapestries of sound:
the congregation in stolid prayer
as fugal rhythms writhe, tower
to dominant, tonic;
   a lone church bell
tolls sweetly in the crystal air
to shuttle harmonies, cadential where
falling snow is lit by sun
bursting from cloud's immortelle.

I think of him alone, free,
of equal temperament in mind and key:
writing fugues, the *Forty-Eight*;
the *Brandenburg Concertos*, music
cerebratonic, quixotic,
at Cothen under Leopold
when *Aires* by Telemann were thought to be
more graceful; simpler harmony
spaced and balanced complement;

cantatas, the *St Matthew Passion*
staid, stentorian—the opening chorus
rolling all before it,
   arias
spun ingeniously from the whole
celestial sound—
   in craft the *Kapellmeister*
too complex for his time, insightful,
united in the ground of being.

St John's, Cambridge; I walk alone
down echoing precincts, three hundred years
beyond his birth, articulate
the freshness of the choral strains
undiminished, sweet refrains:
Jesu, Joy of Man's Desiring
within the ancient walls of stone;
the organ *dulcet* as it plays
beneath a melody of light
illuminating pathways, sanguine:
beyond the critics' spleen and rage
picayune and persiflage,
music for all time, the sunlit cosmos of the God who sings.

simultaneously implementing a punishment as well as a discipline. When my weight dropped to 36 kilos I knew I was dying, and I also knew that I didn't know how to stop. I had lost control.

I had no more food to bring up, so I vomited my secret to my mum, breaking down in her arms in a corridor of a hospital where my grandfather was undergoing heart surgery. I could not carry my burden alone any more. I have no memory of this conversation, I do not know how much I said, but clearly remember saying one thing: don't tell dad. I wanted to protect him. I was so ashamed. That evening, when I came downstairs from the shower and saw them both at the table, silent, their faces red and solemn, I knew she had told him. I heard his footsteps coming down to my room. I remember the blanket on my 15-year-old body, heavy, suffocating, drowning. Every part of me was shattered as he sat beside me, his face wet with tears, at a complete loss, not knowing what to do or how to help. I had been silent for so long, and I could not speak then, but at least I had room for food, and I knew I could live.

In the closed ward with other young girls like me who refused to eat or ate too much and then purged, I was made to see a therapist every day. Despite seeing a therapist for much of my life, even during the years the abuse took place, this was the first time I had ever told anyone. First my parents. Now a therapist. And with her, I remember, I defended him. I don't recall if I told my parents I had been raped, or just that he had hurt me very much, but I do remember not being able to say that word in front of the therapist. Was it shame? Probably. Disbelief? Likely. I couldn't believe this had happened to me. I was strong, powerful, in control, undefeated, and now I had to concede that I had been raped. Not just once (although I do remember that first time) but many times. This, in addition to the emotional abuse I

was subjected to, by a weak man who relied on me to build his ego and give him meaning. I remember him smashing his fist against the wall. I remember him telling me his dog was worth more than me. I remember him saying I deserved it, all of it, and more. I should be thankful—any other man would have killed me by now. That was my life for just over two years. This is my life sentence.

> I was hospitalised for an eating disorder. Keeping my abuse a secret from everyone made me feel constantly full.

The abuse does not define me. I am not a victim, sacrificial and holy on the foot of an altar. Nevertheless, I have grown up struggling to make sense of life as a young woman (even a girl) who was so hated and so loved (yes, loved), not knowing just how wrong and how damaging what I went through was.

We read about victims of abuse, rape. As ever they are anonymous, just a letter to their name, unidentified. They could be anyone, and everyone. But we do not read what happened to them. How they went on to negate everything that happened. Deny it, make excuses, lie. Carry the blame, feel ashamed.

Over the following 20 years I began to notice the paradigm shift, and observe as even the language around rape and assault evolved from 'victim' to 'survivor'. And then those pixelated images of anonymous women that were present in every rape story were replaced by 35 portraits on the cover of *New York* magazine. Bill Cosby's accusers, no longer invisible. Faces, names, details. One after the other their stories unfolded on the page, alongside powerful emotionless portraits, eyes penetrating the lens, as if to say defiantly: 'I am beyond your reach now. You can't hurt me here.' Sadly, in the case of the Cosby accusers, we cannot say that we did not know. Ten years ago, 14 women came forward and said Cosby drugged and assaulted them. We have a ten-year-old deposition that Cosby made, admitting he bought Quaaludes to drug women. All this, and still we needed comedian Hannibal Buress to repeat what those women were saying for us to *actually hear it*. It is easy to tell women, Go to the authorities, when we are so reluctant to listen and in any event, it is more likely someone will hear if a man speaks for us, in our place. You can recapitulate our stories but our bodies will always remember—this is not transferable.

One of the ramifications of living in a country with a statute of limitations on rape was that by the time I developed the emotional courage to begin to consider a legal process to seek justice for what happened to me, it was too late. Even then, courage isn't a thing that happens once and then remains with you. It may be fleeting, momentary. In fact, there is a continuous process of 'encouraging'. In similar vein, there is always a 'reawakening'. They come hand in hand. I like to think I was always strong. It takes a strong person to survive what I went through. It takes a strong person to shatter their family in the ways that I did. It takes a strong person to admit that they cannot be broken alone, and share their secret. It takes a strong person to turn 19 and tell her new boyfriend what happened to her. It takes a strong person not to break down when that new boyfriend tells her he can't be with her, because she is damaged goods, and because he is not strong enough to help her. It takes a strong person to say: I did not ask for your help. I am stronger than you could ever dream of being, and your weakness is weighing on me.

It takes a strong person to say the word 'rape'. Twenty years later, I am beginning to say this word.

When I was 15 my parents saved my life by moving halfway across the country. They had the courage I lacked. I couldn't walk away from him, and they dragged me screaming and shouting into the car, away. I did not tell him where we moved to, because I was so very relieved to be away. I was too tired. I wanted a new life—any life.

Despite moving hours' drive away, I would often see his car parked on our street. I would answer our new phone number and hear his voice breathing down the line. Every birthday he would call me, no matter how many numbers I changed. Every birthday I would cry. Years later I moved from the other side of the country to the other end of the world and now he doesn't call me any more for my birthday. Still, every birthday I cry. Every birthday I reject calls from unknown numbers with shaking hands. Twenty years later I am just as strong as I was back then and just as weak. A survivor, yes. A victim also.

I think about trying to explain how difficult it is to come to terms with being abused. To convince yourself it was not *your* fault. It wasn't *anyone's* fault but his. To refuse to let anyone other than him carry the blame. To say: I was raped and abused by my boyfriend for two years from the age of just 13.

Inevitably, people will want to save you. They will ask, what can I do to help? And you will say: how can you help me? Have you not heard what I said? Do you not see how strong I am to have carried this burden all this time? You cannot share this. You cannot help this. But you can listen. And you can allow survivors and victims of abuse to speak. And you can give us room. •

Na'ama Carlin is a PhD candidate at UNSW. She is interested in questions of violence and ethics, sociology of the body and deconstruction. She loves cats, Jacques Derrida, Danny Trejo and beer.

THAT'S NOBODY'S BUSINESS BUT THE TURKS'

Shane Maloney

BODIES ARE WASHING onto beaches along the coast. On the eastern border, an ugly war drags on. In the capital, President Recep Tayyip Erdogan has built a huge high-tech, mosque-centred palace from which to rule the country.

Istanbul is hot, beset by a late-summer heatwave. It is also cool. The central districts abound with little cafés and quirky shops, street fashion and juice bars. A fortune has been spent restoring historic sites to their Ottoman glory. The harem of the Topkapi now rivals the Alhambra. Tourists throng Sultanahmet and eat pastries on Istiklal Caddessi in Pera, women in niqabs and hipsters alike. For lovers of contemporary art, there's a biennial happening. Street vendors do a roaring trade in selfie sticks.

It is the first week in September and I am here for a family convergence. My daughter and her partner have come from Malaysia, where she works for an international humanitarian organisation. My son, a musician, flew from London with the Melbourne Ska Orchestra, which is part of the Australia–Turkey 2015 cultural exchange, a spin-off from the Gallipoli centenary. Their mother has dipped into her leave entitlements. We have booked an Airbnb in Galata with panoramic views of the Bosphorus. Deep

into a novel, I have brought my work with me. Whenever I get the chance I scribble away, keeping on the boil.

We sample *locum*, visit Orhan Pamuk's extraordinary Museum of Innocence, drink ayran in the Dervish Tea Gardens beside the Blue Mosque, get steamed in the Cemberlitas hamam and explore the markets and side streets. For all its cosmopolitan airs, Istanbul is a city holding its breath. Turkey is a country where religious piety, crony capitalism and assertive nationalism walk hand in hand, threatening to jostle aside anything that stands in its path.

Two years ago a peaceful protest against the removal of trees in Gezi Park in Taksim was smashed by the riot police. The cops were merciless, hosing the crowd with tear gas and breaking heads. Fleeing bystanders were hunted through the streets and baton-whipped. People opened their front doors to strangers and offered places to hide. For days on end, entire neighbourhoods were blanketed in tear gas.

'We were scaredy cats,' the waitress in a funky little café told me. 'We ran. The only ones who fought back were Kurds and football supporters.' Protests erupted across the country against Erdogan's corruption, authoritarianism and Islamist agenda. Millions took part, thousands were injured, several killed.

His opponents driven from the streets, Erdogan resumed his plans. Moving from prime minister to president, he sought to shift constitutional power from parliament, which was dominated by his AKP party, to an executive presidency. All that stood in his way was an election he expected his party to win.

A new party emerged, the HDP, pitching itself to the Kurds—who comprise 20 per cent of Turkey's population—Sunnis not in the AKP camp, women, religious minorities and politicised young people, the so-called Gezi Generation. In the July election, HDP candidates won 13 per cent of the vote, enough to deny Erdogan a majority. His response was to break the longstanding ceasefire with the Kurdish separatist PKK, stir up nationalist sentiment and tar the HDP with the terrorist brush. When the AKP was unable to find coalition partners, he called a fresh election for 1 November.

Before arriving, I'd contacted old friends from Melbourne, Saadet and Ozcan, now living in Istanbul. Saadet works with Yazidi refugee women. With money she helped raise, some from the Maritime Union of Australia, they have set up a bakery, bringing income, independence and dignity. I mentioned the possibility of writing an article and she offered to help.

We meet them at the Çiçek Pasajı, a beaux arts arcade filled with busy tables, rushing waiters bearing trays of mezze, wandering musicians and boisterous talk. Friends of Saadet arrive, the waiter puts dips and iced raki on the table and we talk Turkey. Saadet has lined up some interviews for me. When the bottle is empty, we head down a dog-leg back alley to Garajistanbul.

A stony-faced doorman pats me down for weapons. The MSO enters from the back, honking its way through the audience. Bandleader Nicky Bomba, straw porkpie, all arms and legs, is a man in ceaseless motion. Last week they played the Notting Hill Carnival, the holy grail of Caribbean rhythms. Immediately, everybody is dancing. Nicky works the crowd and it responds, captive to the infectious beat and zany antics. It's two in the morning before we unlock the heavy iron street door and climb the five flights to our apartment.

We hive off on separate excursions, then coalesce for dinner and the gigs. The call to prayer booms across the rooftops. My fiction progresses. The story involves a jihadi recruiter and some petty-crim dipsticks in Melbourne's northern suburbs. I pencil changes onto printouts and fine-tune dialogue.

On the second night, Joe Hockey ambles into the club just as the band is kicking into 'The Diplomat':

Who da pigeon who da cat?
Who da blamer who da rat,
Who you call to cool the pack,
Well you call the diplomat.

Some young Turkish Australians in the crowd mob the treasurer, grinning wildly and snapping pictures. Joe soaks it up. On his way home from a G20 finance ministers meeting in Ankara, he and his wife were dining with the consul when somebody suggested they catch the show. A big man who used to be even bigger, Hockey sways to the beat. In a salmon shirt on a warm night, he has the air of a man on a long slow cruise. In ten days, he'll be out of a job.

There is football on a screen in the place we eat on my second-last night, Turkey versus the Netherlands in a Euro Cup qualifier. Mid match the vision cuts away to military vehicles racing through an arid landscape. The PKK has killed 15 policemen in an ambush on a police convoy near the border with Iraq. The following afternoon, I speak to Levent Tuzel, a veteran of parliamentary politics and now an HDP deputy. The HDP condemns the PKK's actions, he says. Violence will not solve Turkey's problems.

I ask about the likely outcome of the election. Even if the HDP increases its vote, Tuzel tells me, Erdogan will still control the military, the judiciary, the universities and government agencies. What I don't realise is that attacks on HDP offices are in progress all over the county. Party headquarters in Ankara has been trashed and set on fire.

I join the rest of the crew in Kadikoy on the Asian shore. Supporters of the CHP, the Kemalist party, fill the roadway, waving the national flag. 'PKK murderers,' they chant. 'Erdogan murderer.'

It is more pleasant in the beer garden of the Nazim Hikmet centre. 'Living is no laughing matter,' the poet wrote, 'you must live with great seriousness—like a squirrel, for example.' I'd like to stay but I have an appointment with Filiz Kerestecioglu, HDP member for Istanbul's 2nd District.

We meet in the foyer café of a theatre. A songwriter, women's activist and human rights lawyer, Kerestecioglu sees being in parliament as just part of a wider struggle for social justice. As we talk, her phone rings with updates on the ongoing trashing of party offices. The government says it's not responsible, she says, but computers and files are removed before the mobs smash everything and light fires. 'They know exactly what they are looking for. The police do nothing.'

It is our last night here. We return to the apartment to find we have been burgled.

The Question
Nicolette Stasko

for Tony Abbott

Each day a homeless man picks
through the rubbish bin
I worry
what is he to me
or I to him?
memory pushes in

night of a birthday party
barbecue and circle of torches
in the park
we were packing up
when a figure appeared
from the cold silent dark
he asked for something to eat
we gave him all
that was left
bread sausages and tomato sauce
perhaps too much
later we went back
to give him a coat
but he was gone
the next day or maybe two
a homeless man was found
in the bleachers
of the disused club
his throat was cut

the question remains
what was he to me
and I to him?

There is no sign of forced entry but our passports are gone along with credit cards, iPads and my laptop and case. My notes, my drafts, five years of work are gone. Sick at heart, I ring the Airbnb owner. A young guy is sent from the office. Let's call him Semih. He is followed by two policemen. The cops peer through the open door, decline our urging to look inside and tell us to go to the station.

The streets are deserted and the doors of Karakoy police station stand open. An officer is sitting on a bench out front, his legs spread wide and a walkie-talkie crackling on the low table in front of him. He is quite the pasha. We approach with due deference. Semih's English is limited but sufficient. All we need is a police report for the insurance.

Officer Caparli ponders our request. He makes a short speech. He stands and goes into the station. Semih shrugs. Ten minutes later, the officer returns. What is the population of Australia, he demands? We are given a lecture. Everything must be fully investigated, top to bottom, beginning to end. We are part of the investigation. Again, we are left to cool our heels.

After a while, we are taken inside and put in an empty office. Our questions are met with obstruction and obfuscation. It is unclear if we are free to leave. Semih looks increasingly uncomfortable. I ring the insurance company in Australia and explain that a police report is proving impossible to obtain. No report, no payment, no exceptions, I am told.

Hours pass. My daughter's husband is escorted back to the Airbnb by constables who spray black powder around and snip a square from an empty plastic slip-cover. On return, he is fingerprinted. Even as a pretence at forensics, it is ludicrous.

I call a consular assistance number and a Turkish woman about my daughter's age arrives. The obstruction continues. The pasha is enjoying himself, lording it over two young women. They are sequestered in a separate office. Who do you work for? What is your monthly salary? What is your job title? Why do your parents have different surnames? Policemen crowd into the office to watch. A constable laboriously types the answers. Proceedings halt while the boss disappears for a 'cigarette break'. It is past 3 am. We have been here for four hours. I urge Semih to go home. This country, he groans ruefully. Things might improve, I offer, not really meaning it. The election, the HDP. Astonishment lights his face, immediately damped down. 'You know of this?' I nod. He glances around furtively. 'I am a member.'

Finally we obtain a report. We are free to go.

Five days later, back in Melbourne on an emergency passport, filled with despair at my irreplaceable loss, I ask a friend to translate the document. He thinks there is something odd about it. It is definitely not standard issue. He asks what I did that day, then draws a conclusion that had not occurred to me.

As a matter of course, Erdogan's security service would be monitoring Levent Tuzel and Filiz Kerestecioglu. Contact with a foreign journalist would raise a flag. Who was this Australian who consorted with undesirable elements? A sham burglary was arranged and the police instructed to keep us tied up while my laptop and notes were examined.

It's just supposition, of course, but an intriguing one. The thought of the Turkish secret police poring over my account of a band of wannabe terrorists called the Sons of Islam, the pages replete with references to ASIO and the AFP, is nothing if not consoling.

Perhaps they can tell me how it ends. •

Shane Maloney is the author of the Murray Whelan series of novels. His writing has appeared in *Best Australian Essays* and *Best Australian Short Stories*. He is a recipient of the Australian Crime Writers' Association Lifetime Achievement Award.

in their apartment
Daniel John Pilkington

she's caught the greys, apostrophic above the ears
he says of himself he's distracted, paler, light

    the TV switches off like a hypnic jerk
    the city floating in the colours of its industry

she breathes, she waits, she wears a new acid-wash, and the day is peeled
he fusses how his feet will tuck into the sheets

    the night is cold, meticulous
    the light in the corridor assuring them they're as young as they fear

her parents only visit when she dreams
his when his father's certain, urging on his eschatology

    the morning is always on time
    the alarm: final, ending unconscious appeal

she therefore needs a shower, a shower to begin *anything*
he has his one glass of water

    the succulents crossing the sill strike preferences for a northern view
    the city is but arranged orthographies of chance

he burns his toast
she watches the morning sun play knife, butter, plate

    the kitchen separates them with its polished gravity
    the space: polite

he chews and chews away his sleep (chewing with volume)
she turns the TV on, sits for its time in the corner

    the icecaps melting
    the fridge is empty so it's sushi for lunch

she says we should despair because … because she cannot feel it
he says of her hair dyes: ashen, ashen, rather than auburn

SYDNEY TAKES SHAPE

Re-reading Christina Stead's *For Love Alone*

Madeleine Watts

THE SHAPE OF the city is hazy. From above, Sydney looks like somebody spilled ink on a map, let the rivulets run and shrugged when the mess began to dry, saying 'fine, that can be Sydney'. The way it actually happened wasn't so different. The city was first a prison, not a place. Roads were built with no logic or forethought. The city sprang up hastily, and it was too hot and too hard ever to go back and try to make sense of it. The roads are thin and winding. They adhere to no grid. The tree roots splinter the bitumen. Sensible-seeming routes peter out into dead ends and one-way streets.

The inner suburbs are clogged with pollution and clinging heat because Sydney is a city ruled by the car, with traffic its defining feature, snaking out along Parramatta Road, across the bridges, down the Princes Highway, unmoving and seemingly infinite. But then there's the water. Driving over a hill at Coogee or Rushcutters Bay and seeing the ocean laid out before you never fails to feel like a minor miracle. Sultry, shallow, cocksure, contradictory—this is Sydney spread wide. Slinking its way through the red tape and traffic into absolute raw, ravishing beauty.

If there is a single book that captures Sydney in all its sweltering loveliness and brash parochialism, it might be Christina Stead's 1944 novel *For Love Alone*, the novel that Stead wrote immediately after her best-known book, *The Man who Loved Children*. When Stead published *The Man who Loved Children* she was persuaded by her publishers to rewrite the story so that it occurred not in Sydney but in Washington because, her publishers argued, Americans don't care about Australians. The dissonance is clear in the prose. The cadences are off, somehow. It's an Australian novel putting on a third-rate American accent, the vowels all wrong, filled with awkward idioms, 'by jiminy's and 'ain't much for tuh see's. When Stead came to write her next book she was adamant that her instincts would win out. The book would be set in Sydney.

Christina Stead was one of Australia's great twentieth-century writers, and a modernist to the core. As the world became more urbanised, more complex, Stead along with a legion of Western writers did away with the idea that old realist techniques were enough to describe and diagnose the condition of the times. The 'city novel' was a defining feature

Study for The Bridge in-curve, by Grace Cossington Smith, 1930
National Gallery of Australia, Canberra

of modernism, driven by a need to thematise the fragmentation, complication and subjectivity of the world as it looked in the first half of the twentieth century. These are books in which the city is key to their emotional foundations. What was overlooked when *For Love Alone* was published was that with this book Stead did for Sydney what Woolf did for London, Joyce for Dublin, Dos Passos for New York, Döblin for Berlin. These books contend that a city affects the rhythms of consciousness itself.

Christina Stead was born in a still-unassuming suburb of Sydney in 1902 and her childhood was a notoriously unhappy one. Her mother died when she was two years old, her father remarried, and her stepmother did not love her. She lived miserably with her father, half-siblings and stepmother first in Bexley and then in Watsons Bay.

Incredibly intelligent, Stead couldn't go to the university, but instead went to Teachers College. She hated teaching. She wanted to write. To do this successfully she set upon leaving Sydney. And so she worked and saved and schemed and in 1928, at the age of 26, she left. With her partner William J. Blake she lived variously in London, Paris, Antwerp, New York and Spain, and wrote novels that focused not on the subjects expected of lady novelists—the home, love, the small dramas of private life—but on class warfare, unionism and one, *House of All Nations*, an 800-page doorstop on international banking. Stead was a cosmopolitan writer. But she never ceased to be an essentially Australian writer. The island continent was in her marrow.

These days *The Man who Loved Children* still has the reputation of being Stead's masterpiece, possibly because by the 1970s it was the only book of hers that remained in print. While a revival of interest in Stead's work was largely due to the feminist movement of the 1970s, her own feelings about women's liberation were decidedly equivocal. When, in her spiky and contrary old age, Stead was asked about her attitudes to the feminist movement, her response was terse. 'It's nonsense. It's eccentric. It's not a genuine movement. It's totally, purely middle class.' It wasn't that Stead disagreed with their conclusions; it was that she thought they were going about it all wrong. 'I know what women have to put up with; I've written about it, I know,' she declared. In short, Stead alienated those who would best defend her. But in 2010 Jonathan Franzen reappraised Stead. He lionised *The Man who Loved Children* in the *New York Times*, placing it among the best works of twentieth-century modernism and throwing Stead's name into the same literary pool as Gertrude Stein, Virginia Woolf and William Faulkner

If *The Man who Loved Children* was about Stead's childhood, *For Love Alone* is about her early adulthood. Which is to say that it is a novel shot through with longing, 'spun', Stead explained, 'out of anguished reminiscences'. It operates at a pitch of ferocity that is overwhelming, like the riptide, sometimes hard to bear.

For Love Alone is Stead's fifth novel, written for the most part in New York. She had been away from Australia, by then, for 14 years. Set largely during the years of the Depression, the book opens with Teresa Hawkins, the 19-year-old protagonist, attending her cousin's wedding on one of the hottest days of the year. Teresa lives with her family in Watsons Bay in a situation recognisable as Stead's at the same age, at a time when the South Head community was still wild and relatively inaccessible from the city except by boat. Working as a primary school teacher, she takes night classes and dreams about the University of Sydney, of Oxford or the Sorbonne. She falls in love with her tutor, Jonathan Crow, and makes up her mind to follow him to London, to a life of ardour and the intellect that feels impossible at home. Teresa is lonely, desperate, roaming, verging on manic. She works herself to the edge of exhaustion, becomes utterly consumed in her effort to leave Sydney. Divided into two sections, the London part of the book is significantly shorter than the Sydney part, and operates as a way for Stead to attempt to give an ending—marriage to a nicer man—to an experience that defies the regular constraints of plot. All the blood of the book is in Sydney and Teresa's agonising peregrinations across its sandy hills.

When *For Love Alone* first appeared reviews were tepid, and warned readers away from the 'five hundred pages of lust and abnormality'. The novel was printed on flimsy rations-era paper with a cover that only bolstered the impression that the book was a cheap novelette written by an unserious lady novelist. It served only to lose Stead the readers who might have appreciated her work, and attracted only those who were drawn to the image of the half-naked girl on the front cover, who all in all found Teresa to be exceptionally dreary.

· · ·

I first read *For Love Alone* when I was eighteen. My stepmother had an old Angus & Robertson copy on her bookshelf in Melbourne, and I had just finished high school. I had never heard of Stead, but the title appealed to me. I took the novel back to Sydney with me, where the days, without structure or plan, yawned open ahead of me. It was November. The weather was threatening to get very pretty again, and I was wandering around Alice-like, afraid of advancing adulthood. For five days I sat in the garden under the gum tree where the lorikeets screeched at sunset and I read *For Love Alone*.

Stead's prose captures Sydney in all its livid, dissolute loveliness. The velvet air. The sea breeze after the westerlies. The worn impermanence of the landscape. In the opening pages, Teresa and her sister make their way across the harbour on the ferry, the air about them full of the stench of sea-weed and fishing nets, while in the distance bushfires cast a red and smoky glow across the horizon. This is Sydney at its Sydney-est, a place that can be simultaneously wet and burning. For Stead, Sydney is textural. Her prose gathers up the life of her protagonist and imbues it with all the qualities she attributes to the city.

Teresa longs for the 'sensual life' she knows she is best suited to, and believes that 'she smelled, heard, saw, guessed faster, longed more than others'. She imagines a kind of intellectual and emotional utopia in London, but even the most cursory reader will note that it's Sydney that makes Teresa who she is. In *For Love Alone*, the heat of Sydney, its disarray and humidity and the threat of the night are metonymic of Teresa's internal condition; the city is part and parcel of her longing for a life of the mind and a meaningful future as well as a longing for the 'love' alluded to in the novel's title.

For Love Alone is a novel that resonates particularly with young, bookish, female readers. Drusilla Modjeska, in her introduction to the 2011 reissue of the novel, notes that she was drawn to Stead 'for her insistence that the intellectual settings of the mind are woven into the drama of the person': what's appealing about the book is Teresa. The love story is supplementary, and subverts nearly every idea of what we imagine a love story to be. The loved one, Jonathan Crow, is truly awful. He is full of coldness and hypocrisy. What Teresa is in love with is what she makes him represent—and this is what a lot of arrested love affairs in your early twenties are for. The relationship is as much about the experience, the feeling of wildness, than the person himself. The thing that's at stake in *For Love Alone* is Teresa and the untamed state of her emotional and intellectual topography.

Teresa Hawkins leaves her mark all over Sydney. She goes trudging through Sydney with broken shoes, without a winter coat, contemplates sleeping in the Domain, in Surry Hills alleyways, in the factory where she works, just to save energy. Her self-sacrifice is both pious and excessive. The dark beaches where Teresa walks at night are full of groaning and strange cries. We are led to believe they are sounds of sex, but anyone with a working knowledge of Sydney will also entertain the thought that they might be the sounds of death. Watsons Bay is the site of The Gap, Sydney's most infamous suicide spot.

Hazel Rowley, Stead's biographer, describes how as a teenager Stead would wander the coastline, fascinated by the cliffs, and worry that the jumpers wouldn't fall lightly into the water below but that their bodies would instead be slammed against the rocks. On one of these walks along the shore at night, Teresa passes by the body of a woman lying beneath a tarpaulin recovered from The Gap that afternoon. 'It did not cause much comment. They lived there, among the gardens of the sea, and knew their fruits; fish, storms, corpses, moontides, miracles.' The term 'on the beach', famous as the title of Nevil Shute's post-apocalyptic novel from the 1950s, comes from a naval expression. 'On the beach' originally meant 'retired from service'. Any place defined by its beaches, as Sydney is, also aligns itself with these latter-day meanings of a place by the sea. Liminal zones where things wash up, are left abandoned, can be created and re-created continually. Because surely Stead herself was formed by the walking, by the international vessels sailing in and out of the heads, by the grid-less city streets and the dark places where the noises you hear could be sounds of sex or sounds of death.

A city isn't its roads and beaches and bridges. Alone, they don't tell you anything. It's the stories, the imaginative work, the memories that flow in as you pass through the streets. The imaginary city rises and expands sponge-like over the topography, and we live in both. These stories of the city sustain the intellectual and emotional life of a place. English-language literature abounds with stories that evoke New York and London and Chicago and Dublin, but Sydney is an under-written place, and to that extent it has yet to be fully imagined. It's possible to grow up in one of Australia's major cities and never read a book set in the place in which you live.

If *For Love Alone* resonated with me because I was young and female, it was made all the more potent by being set in the city I had grown up in. In the days of that November reading *For Love Alone* in the garden I would look towards the skyline from the verandah and see in the weird, distancing hieroglyphs of skyscrapers, for the first time, a sense of meaning, an intention to communicate. I needed to read about Sydney to fully experience it as a place that had anything to do with me.

When it was suggested to Stead in her advancing years that she might try her hand at a memoir, she responded with rage and contempt. Stead insisted that 'the truth' could be located in her books. The daughter of a scientist and the first student in the

Jealousy?
Trevor Bailey

Were the moon a laughing face—
a mouth enwidened by delight—
I'd be all for changing place
with it; knowing too that flight

of fun at gibbous wane
is no farewell at all,
that in the wax it comes again.
And so my heart would fall

and rise in revolution but not
revolt: a clockwork doll sans
consternation whose lot
it ever was to glance

away from mortal fear
of happenstance and pain;
of the dissolution near
each man's horizon.

For life, unlike a moon of phases,
must wane without return:
it steadily erases
that small and glib concern

of self without remorse.
(The unfeeling moon the while
will wax and wane, but worse
perhaps, beam a hollow smile.)

history of Sydney Girls High School to write 'No Church' on the registry form, she fiercely prized an adherence to objectivity and fact. But artists are tiny dictators who derive pleasure from controlling the kingdoms of their various creations. Stead could bend the past in her novels, control the outcome in a way she could not in real life. The Jonathan Crow of the novel bears traces of Keith Duncan, a one-time university medallist who, when Stead met him, was whiling away his time on an MA before he took off to do academia properly in London. Stead believed her portrait of Duncan accurate, yet some of the descriptions of the man are grotesquely Dickensian—she has him slinking down the street like a black-coated villain as the book ends. This is writing as punishment, literature as revenge. Rowley writes that 'Writing had become a means of attaining power over others, and resisting their power over her. By writing—and showing her writing to others—Christina could reduce people by ridicule or raise them to great heights.'

For Love Alone is Christina Stead claiming her early twenties for herself, making Sydney *hers*. And the proverbial pink elephant in this essay in praise of *For Love Alone* as the quintessential Sydney novel is that it's also a novel about wanting desperately to get out of the place. As Stead did, and as I have. In Australia in the 1920s, Stead was one of the women writers who experienced themselves as 'exiles at home', to borrow a term from Drusilla Modjeska. While no Australian who voluntarily moves to London or New York is really an 'exile' in the truest sense of the word, for many Australians in the twentieth century, the place they felt exiled from was Australia itself. To leave was to release oneself from internal exile. This was especially so for artists, writers, intellectuals. There simply wasn't enough in Australia to sustain them.

In *For Love Alone*, Teresa articulates the conviction Stead and many Australians felt,

and still feel: 'If I stay here I'll be nobody.' She longs to 'sail the seas, leave her invisible trace on countries, learn in great universities, know what was said by foreign tongues'. Stead's writing was profoundly different to that of the writers who stayed behind in Australia during the 1920s and 1930s. Instead of learning to write in the model of the 'dun-coloured' realism that Patrick White inveighed against upon his return, Stead was in Paris reading Joyce. As a result her work was some of the first Australian literature to break free into more challenging, poetic territory. Big cities of the world are still filled with Australians attempting to break through into more challenging territory. As I sit writing this on a park table in Brooklyn, just across the East River from Gramercy Park where Stead wrote *For Love Alone*, it makes perfect sense to me that the most resonant of Sydney novels would be written on the other side of the world. That's the paradox. You love your birthplace most when you're furthest away, as far away as you could possibly be without treading water hopelessly in the mid Atlantic.

Christina Stead returned to Australia in 1974. She was old by then, at a loose end. She was hailed as a genius upon her return, her books were being reissued, but she was living in Hurstville with her brother, uncomfortably close to where she had started. She was drinking too much, she dithered, she never really wrote again. At her last lunch with Patrick White she arrived in a taxi and thrust at him a number of empty bottles wrapped in a brown paper bag. She told him to throw the bag into his rubbish, so that nobody else would discover it, and by implication, her alcoholism, in the bin at home. She spent the last years of her life stuck in creative inertia, desperately lonely, shuttling between the houses of the friends and relatives who would take her in.

Writing is not, by its nature, cathartic. To write about things that have happened to you doesn't make you feel better. The only real reason to do it is for the brief moment when it feels as though you've made something that's brought you closer to other people. The catch is that the writer can never be sure that communication is happening. A relationship between a writer and a reader is fragmentary. It exists in a vacuum.

Part of the impact of *For Love Alone* was that it helped me think about something that I had always been too afraid to confront—how to work and live in Australia, as a woman and a writer, and how to feel that those three details might not be fundamentally incompatible. Even the most overworked, most hopeless passages soothed me. Sentences etched themselves into the sealed metal box of my self, and I have carried them with me, will do, always. Stead had no knowledge of me as a reader, no guarantee that I would pick up her book and read it on the other side of her death, nor you, who may read the novel now if you haven't already. All she did was write into the vacuum, filling the space. All a writer can do once they've finished is hope that some other receives what they've sent out, blends it with their own stories, understands, expands, takes the story in and makes it mean something. •

Madeleine Watts has written fiction and essays for the *Believer*, *Griffith Review*, *Los Angeles Review of Books* and the *Lifted Brow*. Born in Sydney, she now lives in New York.

Things on an Iron Tray on the Floor
Trevor Bailey

After the painting by Grace Cossington Smith, 1928

You have to hand it to the artist—
cobble together some kitchen commonplaces
on a shiny tray of iron: not the *smartest*
assembly you'd think; not the faces

of beauty most people seek
out Narcissus-like, hanging mute
but loudly and tongue-in-cheek
on gallery walls waiting to suit

some hungry, questing Id
(that centre of self-delusion).
Here instead a saucepan lid
and jug find communion

with some other homely stuff
in similar circles. Still life,
though inanimate enough,
can bring to bear a knife

to cut the blinding veil
that hides our being from death:
underlying order will prevail
beyond our final breath.

THE POISONED CHALICE

How an unsung architect filled Utzon's shells

Anne Watson

I N JANUARY 2015 the new Philharmonie de Paris concert hall was opened by President François Hollande. The event was controversially boycotted by the building's architect, Jean Nouvel, in protest at the French government's decision to open the 2400-seat auditorium well before it was finished. The architect has since lost a court battle that hinged on what he called the 'sabotage' of his design. Way over budget and schedule and with many construction hurdles, the problematic project and the repercussions for its architect strike a familiar chord.

Half a century ago a similar scenario, but with even more drastic consequences, played out in Sydney when Jørn Utzon spectacularly resigned as architect of the unfinished Sydney Opera House. In April 1966 he flew out of Sydney, never to return. He left behind a set of magnificent but empty concrete shells: not only was the building unfinished, the plans for completion of its interiors and cladding were far from resolved.

It was into this perilous void that the 34-year-old Sydney architect Peter Hall bravely, or perhaps naively, stepped in April 1966 as part of the government-appointed consortium Hall, Todd & Littlemore. Charged with finishing the building, Hall,

as design architect, was confronted with a perplexing logjam of problems, not the least of which was the pressing need to resolve the impasse over the conflicting seating and acoustic requirements of the dual-purpose main hall. The rights and wrongs of Utzon's abrupt departure have been widely discussed over the years, but it is the narrative of the misunderstood 'creative genius', thwarted by an unsympathetic client and uncooperative consultants, that has stuck and has fed the compelling Utzon myth. So entrenched has this myth become that even 50 years on it continues to eclipse the achievements of those who completed the building. Join one of the very popular Opera House guided tours and you will hear little if anything of those responsible for the interiors—principally the Concert Hall and Opera Theatre—you visit. The 40th anniversary celebrations in 2013 made almost no mention of the post-Utzon work from 1966 to 1973—more than half of the building's total construction time

But worse than the enduring disregard and ignorance is the continuing vilification of Hall. To this day the mere mention of his name in connection with the Opera House is enough to send many architects into paroxysms of indignation. In Hall's

Photo courtesy of Tim Ritchie (@timritchie)

own time he was snubbed by many in the profession and his career post–Opera House never fulfilled the promise of his considerable early achievements, including the Royal Australian Institute of Architects' Sulman Medal in 1965. His family was threatened and his colleagues sidelined in their subsequent careers. The controversy over his appointment in 1966 effectively ended his first marriage and Hall's premature death at the age of 64 in 1995 was, I believe, partly precipitated by the rekindling of old prejudices in the highly partisan, and uninformed, response by the media to the 'Unseen Utzon' exhibition at the Opera House in 1994–95.

I recall the exhibition well: the beguiling drawings of Utzon's final schemes for the halls, the captivating models, the underlying thesis that Utzon's designs were 'ready to go', as one journalist put it. Ten years on, as a curator at the Powerhouse Museum, I was still blissfully ignorant of the possibility that the powerful Utzon narrative was only part of the story. In 2006 I was editor and a contributing author of a book of essays on the Opera House. Like almost every Opera House historian before me, I adhered to the belief that what was designed after Utzon left was heavily compromised and thus not worth bothering about. Ken Woolley's book analysing Utzon's last designs and Peter Webber's biography of Hall were still some years off. Unlike, for example, the gripping yarn of Utzon's supposed Eureka-moment discovery of the spherical solution for the shells when contemplating an orange, what happened on Hall's watch seemed decidedly less, well, fruity. The epic struggle to solve myriad technical and functional hurdles of the interiors *after* the shells had been constructed, not the reverse as should have been the case, was simply too challenging to consider. That perspective was to change, however: soon after my book, *Building a Masterpiece: The Sydney Opera House*

was published I was introduced to Hall's son Willy.

When Peter Hall died it was Willy who salvaged his father's papers. Willy and his young family live on a rambling, picturesque farm in the NSW Southern Highlands and it was there, one freezing July day in 2007, that I sat in a cavernous corrugated-iron shed with an ineffective one-bar heater unexpectedly absorbed by the diaries, letters, reports and photos that documented Hall's career, and most particularly his seven years on the Opera House. Paradoxically, I was supposed to be there not as a researcher but with my curatorial hat on to provide advice about a suitable institution in which to deposit the archive. Call it an epiphany, but several hours later I was seriously re-examining my prejudices about the value of Hall's contribution.

The archive told a very different story to the one I was familiar with. Here was a highly talented and committed architect, steeped in modernism, but also in the pragmatics of function. Here was an architect who not only greatly respected Utzon, but who was willing to challenge the bureaucrats, as Utzon had done, to ensure the best for the Opera House. And here was a human being who, perhaps unaware of the magnitude of the problems he was taking on at the outset of the project, was professionally and to some extent personally undone by the controversies and misunderstandings that have persisted to this day.

Peter Hall was a typical high-achiever. Born in Newcastle in 1931, he won a scholarship as a boarder to the Sydney private school Cranbrook, another scholarship to Sydney University, where he achieved a double degree in Architecture and Arts, majoring in the classics, and a trainee bursary in the NSW Government Architects Office. Newly graduated in 1957, he was awarded a prestigious travelling scholarship that took him and his soon-to-be wife Libby

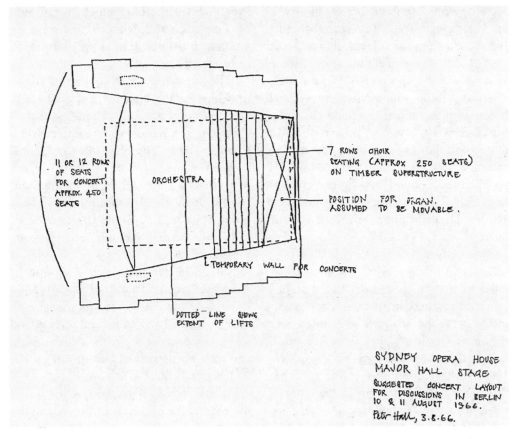

Drawing by Hall of a 'Suggested Concert Layout' for the Major Hall stage prepared for discussion with the acoustic consultants Cremer & Gabler in Berlin, August 1966. (Peter Hall papers, private collection)

Bryant on an extended tour of Europe, a trip that was to be pivotal for the affirmation of his interest in modernism and his introduction to the architecture of the Mediterranean countries. Perhaps not pivotal, but certainly portentous, was Hall's travel to Denmark to meet Utzon, just a year or so into the Opera House design after Utzon had won the competition in January 1957. Hoping to secure some short-term work on the project, Hall was, ironically, unsuccessful because Utzon at this early stage needed a more long-term commitment. It was in the Government Architects Office that Hall designed the Sulman Medal–winning Goldstein Hall at the University of New South Wales in 1964. It is tempting to speculate that had Hall not

garnered the accolades that accompanied the award, the trajectory of his life after 1965 might have been very different. As it was, Hall's obvious talents and growing reputation were what motivated the government architect, Ted Farmer, to approach him in April 1966 and offer the role of design architect in the consortium set up to complete the Opera House. 'He was a ... very fine designer, and a man of many parts,' wrote Farmer many years later. 'I had enormous respect for him.'

Why Hall took on the job when other more experienced architects such as Ken Woolley and Col Madigan had rejected Farmer's overtures is conjectural. In March 1966 when Hall had just left the Government

Architects Office to forge a career in private practice, he signed a petition acknowledging Utzon as 'the only architect technically and ethically able to complete the Opera House as it should be completed'. Nonetheless Hall was ambitious, no doubt flattered, and liked nothing so much as a good challenge. Satisfied that Utzon had no intention of returning following a phone conversation with the architect, and after a month of 'independent enquiry' and much deliberation, Hall agreed to take on 'that immense and complicated thing', as he described the building in a 1973 interview.

Hall's papers are revealing for both the new narrative they uncover and the significance that he must surely have attached to what he kept. One of the earliest documents is the list of drawings handed over to the new team—Hall, Lionel Todd and David Littlemore—by Utzon's office in May 1966. Perhaps conscious of the fact that this was a critical moment in the complicated history of the building, Hall retained copies of the various drawing lists and their annotations. Of the 131 drawings on Utzon's list he identified 14 that were missing in the transfer, including, crucially, two drawings showing the most recent seating layouts for the Major Hall. Not on the list at all were the final Major Hall ceiling drawings on which the Utzon office had been working in late 1965/early 1966. Hall's notes record that 'critical items, seating and ceiling, are either not shown or not in the set'. The transferred drawings also included design work for paving and cladding, the glass walls and the Minor Hall ceiling. Peter Hall's comments on his handwritten list ranged from 'useful' to 'design idea' to 'practically useless'. There was unanimous agreement among all three architects that 'there were no working drawings available, nor any complete detail drawings'. David Littlemore later remarked that examination of the drawings 'took place in an atmosphere of suspense and fear'.

Presumably expecting a much greater level of completion, the architects' first confrontation with Utzon's Stage 3 legacy was clearly somewhat disturbing.

The lack of resolution in the Utzon drawings for the interiors and glass walls, after six years of work, reflect more than anything the tangled web of complex issues that had stymied progress in early 1966. It is the misguided oversimplification of these issues that has obscured clear thinking about the rationale for the solutions that were eventually adopted. To the Utzon diehards all that was needed was for Utzon to be given more time, more money and more support to solve the building's many significant design and technical hurdles. But as the post-Utzon team soon discovered, solutions could only be found by radical compromise; and it was compromise that Utzon, both before and after his departure, had shown he was unable or unwilling to accept.

Apart from budget and schedule, at the core of the problems in the mid sixties were three key design issues: Utzon's wish to use the technically innovative, but largely untested, long sheets of plywood for the theatre ceilings and the blade-like mullions of the northern glass walls; the compromised acoustics likely to result from a dual-purpose concert and opera theatre; and the impossibility of squeezing the required 2800 seats into it. Solving the first was dependent on the concurrence of Arup's, structural engineers on the project since day one. Solving the second and third issues was dependent on the ABC, then manager of the Sydney Symphony Orchestra and the principal user of the main hall, relaxing its insistence on the seating quota and ideal concert acoustics for the hall. But Utzon's relationship with the Arup office in Sydney had soured considerably—to the point where communication was highly strained and at best formal and sporadic—and the ABC remained bullishly intransigent over its requirements.

Two important sets of documents in Hall's papers reflect the inception of a strategy to come to grips with these issues. The first records the discussions at the joint consultants summit held on site on 4–10 May, to which Ove Arup himself flew from London, and which was apparently the first comprehensive conference since the project started. The second set—diaries, letters and photos—details Hall's first overseas study trip. In June 1966 Hall flew to San Francisco, the first stop in a three-month trip to North America, Britain, Europe and Japan to meet with acoustic and engineering consultants, theatre-design experts and architects, to visit concert halls, opera houses and a range of landmark buildings, and generally to equip himself to supply the brief to complete the remaining design of the Sydney Opera House. As he wrote:

Ideally this brief should have been for-mulated before planning was begun … Otherwise the brief could have evolved during planning, with the users and a project manager contributing to the work of the architect and consultants. On any kind of official basis, neither had ever been done, with the result that after nine years we were confronted with the statement of the principal prospective user [ABC] that the pro-posed accommodation was in no way acceptable. The job was being built, in effect, without definition of what was expected of it … One of the accusations made against the Minister and our-selves in 1966 was that we would reduce the quality of the job. We had no such intention. The big question, though, was what were we supposed to build?

Hall alludes here to the ineffectiveness of the Sydney Opera House Trust in formulat-ing a management brief for the building over the years. Had the trust not lost sight of the original competition requirements, the stale-mate of 1966 might have been avoided. For the competition clearly articulated that the first priority of the Major Hall was to be for concerts and the second priority to be opera, but that 'Compromises which will prejudice the entirely satisfactory performance of a function with a higher priority … should not be made.' At the core of Hall's study trip then was the need to garner best-practice opinion to enable an informed decision about the advisability of building a multi-function main hall.

Hall's recommendation to the govern-ment, with the support of international theatre and acoustic experts, was that a single-purpose main auditorium was the ideal around which the new brief should be structured. Released, perhaps strategically, just a few days before Christmas 1966, the 'Review of Programme', with its central proposal for a 2800-seat concert hall and the relocation of opera to the Minor Hall, pro-voked a furore unprecedented even by Opera House standards. In a project long troubled by controversy, the meetings, reports, media coverage, resignations and recriminations generated by the review over the next three months—much of it documented in Hall's papers—would severely test his dedication to the project.

Not surprisingly the ABC, whose require-ments were comprehensively met by the review, gave its 'unreserved support' for the changes to the brief. Less supportive, indeed positively disgruntled, was the Elizabethan Theatre Trust (ETT)—the national manag-ing body for ballet, drama and the country's fledgling opera company under the helm of the redoubtable H.C. 'Nugget' Coombs—which understandably took exception to what was considered the 'relegation' of opera to a much smaller hall designed for drama productions. For the government, and Hall, it was an unwinnable situation. But what was the alternative? The idea of a convertible main hall had been studied but abandoned because its extensive technical requirements were considered unworkable under the restrictive curve of the shell perimeter. And while the Sydney Symphony's subscriptions audience had already outgrown the capacity of the orchestra's then home at the Sydney Town Hall, the ETT's Opera Company had had a somewhat problematic recent past, with variable production standards, patchy attendances and an inexperienced administration contributing to a decade of what colourful music writer and broadcaster John Cargher described as 'unending traumas'. Inevitably, after several conferences and numerous reports by various consultants, including Ernest Bean, imported for the occasion from London's Festival Hall, the minister for works, Davis Hughes, announced in March 1967 his decision in favour of the review's recommendations.

Peter Hall in New York on his first study trip, mid 1966. (Peter Hall papers, private collection)

With some modifications they effectively provided the blueprint for the as-built Opera House interiors.

The review acted as a necessary circuit breaker to the impasse of 1966, but there were, of course, consequences. The dual-purpose, proscenium-stage Major Hall that Utzon had laboured over for six years now had to be redesigned as an auditorium with an orchestra platform and choir seating behind, negating the logic of Utzon's last design for a curved plywood-ribbed ceiling converging at the proscenium arch. The inadequacies of the stage and orchestra facilities for the newly designated Opera Theatre were recognised from the outset and Hall, theatre consultants and the engineers explored possibilities for their improvement for more than a year.

Short of extending the stage wings into the foyer space, there was little that could be done. The proposal now under consideration for a redesigned Opera Theatre—the result of Utzon's re-engagement in 1999—requires the technically difficult severing of the beam that ties the shell arches together, an extremely radical, and expensive, intervention that was unthinkable in Peter Hall's time. With the decision, after much agonised deliberation, to abandon Utzon's ambitious scheme for the northern glass wall plywood mullions as both too experimental and an impractical intrusion into the foyer's harbour views, the glazing had to be redesigned by the new team—perhaps the most challenging of all the remaining work.

In retrospect the changes to the building brief introduced by the 'Review of Programme' were, arguably, unavoidable. Yes, the now necessary redesign of both auditoria impacted on Utzon's integrated vision for the building. But it was the very magnificence of this vision, unachievable within the constraints of the unorthodox shell structure on the narrow Bennelong Point site, inflexible user/client requirements and the limitations of 1960s construction and acoustic technology that, paradoxically, set the project on an inevitable trajectory to its perplexing denouement in early 1966. What was the architect's great imaginative masterstroke in 1956 was also a classic example of creative overreach. Utzon was mostly correct when he said, 'it is not I but Sydney Opera House that creates all the enormous difficulties'. 'Mostly', because the wild cards of human nature, political intervention, interpersonal conflict and client mismanagement also contributed significantly to the frustration of progress in the first half of the 1960s. They were all issues with which Hall also grappled in his determination to make the building fulfil the functions for which it was conceived.

But while Utzon and Hall were both victims of the great speculative venture that was the Sydney Opera House, Utzon's reputational rehabilitation has been absolute, while Hall's reputation has languished in an enduring mire of controversy. It is as though the monumental presence of the building precludes the possibility of alternative readings that are less than heroic, that challenge the simplistic myth and that suggest the project was beset by all-too-human failings and contradictions. As the 50th anniversary of Utzon's withdrawal approaches, it is perhaps timely to reconcile the two halves of the Opera House story—before and after 1966—to embrace Utzon's great achievement and Hall's hard-fought endeavours to complete the building. They are not mutually exclusive. For what they reflect, separately and together, is history. Not the stuff of legend but the muddy reality of the collision between the pursuit of creative perfection and the limits of imperfect human knowledge and behaviour.

Despite its epic and conflicted gestation, the Opera House has been a spectacular success—with audiences, performers and visitors and as an inspirational masterpiece of twentieth-century architecture. The extraordinary global marketing power of brand 'Sydney Opera House' is probably unequalled by any other modern building. Utzon benefited inestimably in his later career from the building's star status but for Hall, acknowledgment has been negligible. Yet despite the opprobrium he suffered during his lifetime, Hall never publicly complained about his treatment or the lack of recognition for him or his team. Indeed, in his 1990 report outlining a conservation strategy for the building, Hall was generous in his praise of Utzon and credited the teamwork among architects, engineers and consultants for making the building the triumph it is. Five years later, after Hall's death in May 1995, former government architect Ted Farmer wrote a moving eulogy that is as poignantly apt now as it was then:

> I had to choose a design architect who would replace Utzon. I then asked Peter if he would do this but warned him that the project would always be mixed up with politics. That it could lead to fame for him or the reverse … After a great deal of thought he accepted. He succeeded beyond doubt but there is no doubt he sacrificed his career in loyalty to his profession and to me personally. •

Anne Watson is an independent design curator and writer. Her 2014 PhD thesis examined the work of Peter Hall at the Sydney Opera House following Jørn Utzon's departure in 1966.

Meanjin:
It's Australian for fine writing.

Subscribe and save 20%.
Essays, fiction, poetry and
memoir delivered to your
door four times a year.

Subscribe online at
meanjin.com.au
Or call us on 03 9342 0317

WITHIN AUSTRALIA
1 year (4 issues)
for $80

Find more information about
subscriptions at the back of
this issue

OVERSEAS
1 year (4 issues)
for $140

Missing

Omar Musa

MARIA SLID THE toilet window across and pressed her aquiline nose to the flyscreen, searching the car park below uneasily. Nothing but the gleam-wobbling macadam and a few cars. 'Bickie!' she called in a sing-song voice. 'Bikkiiiie!' Usually, as soon as she called, she would see the cat's stripy form appear from behind a bin or emerge from a bush and come loping over the asphalt from afar. Then, after half a minute, he would burst into the flat, both needy and haughty, waving his tail with patrician entitlement. Like a dog, the way she could call and he would come. But not this time.

The Cat that Walked by Himself by Rudyard Kipling.

Gato travieso, she muttered as she bustled into the kitchen—'naughty cat'. Her walk was lopsided, rump hefty, floral blouse bunched up at the hip, and she grunted in pain with each step. From a drawer she pulled out a trendy knife her children Eva and Pedro had bought her for Christmas and used it to cut potatoes into thick chips, careful to keep her fingers shy of the keen blade, which sliced through the spuds almost too easily. She flicked the grubby potato skins into the sink. Once she had cooked the chips she piled them into a pyramid, soaking their oil into absorbent paper. Then with a fork she carefully laid a rich, red steak, an inch and a half thick, in the remaining oil. It hissed like an alley cat. Lately, Eva had forced Maria into a 'paleo diet' and regularly came around to the flat to check that she was keeping up with it. But Eva was at the theatre tonight, so Maria was going to treat herself.

Paleo diet. Didn't cavemen die at about 25? Let an old woman live in peace and eat what she wants. The fat on the steak popped. Maria grinned and the lines on her dark face deepened and wrinkled.

Yes, she was going to cook it perfectly until it charred and blistered, the way they used to do on the grills back home, until it was *just right*. Chips, steak, beans, tortillas and rice—a huge meal for one. Maria often caught Eva looking at her sideways, then smoothing down her dress over her legs in a repeated motion as if it might cast a spell of everlasting skinniness. A family of strong, squat Mayan women, *mija*—the genes are there, no matter how hard you try to battle against it.

She eyed the front door. Where could that cat be?

The TV was on softly, a newsreader's rectangular head saying something serious. Maria knew what he would be talking about. On everyone's lips and minds, the killer on the loose. The killings had been going on for three months now, and still he hadn't been caught. At first the main suspect had been a Pakistani student who hadn't been seen for a month, and the prime minister had even gone so far as to say it was a potential terrorist threat. However, in a bizarre turn of events, the student had been found dead at the end of a drain on the outskirts of town, seemingly also a victim of the murderer. Each murder was horrifying and perverse. The killer would wait for hours on end in cupboards, so the story went, and watch people before he butchered them, and in this small, convivial town people had taken to locking their houses for the first time. Men accompanied women down the street after dark. Maria crossed herself quickly.

Bickie's brother Coffee appeared suddenly and rubbed his head against Maria's ankle. He, unlike Bickie, never strayed too far from home. He was the runt of the litter and much more timid, awkward, a light brown tabby with a front paw constantly lifted, as if injured. She wrestled his rangy limbs up into her arms and greedily fussed over him, tickling

behind his soft ears and sniffing his paws. Coffee closed his eyes with pleasure and bobbed his wet nose in the air. Maria loved the way they smelled, especially when they'd just woken up. She set him down after a minute, puffing. She rubbed the small of her back with her thumb, then pressed directly into the most painful spot, what she imagined as an infra-red tangle of nerves between the vertebrae, but it did no good. The pain was constant.

Coffee miaowed. He was missing his brother. She bent over slowly and tipped some dried biscuits into a bowl to distract him, but he ignored them and continued miaowing. Maria cursed herself for not getting Pedro to install a cat flap. It wasn't safe to leave the door open. But what choice did she have? The summer had been brutally hot, and without a cross-wind coming through, it was unbearable in the flat. Not only that, but the cats had been getting restless, unused to being locked inside for days on end, pacing tirelessly along the windowsill and making a hell of a racket, so much so that her neighbour Freddy had complained. She had taken to leaving the door open during the day, and counting on the cats to go out for a maximum of three hours only, well before it got dark. Coffee always came home before Bickie. Where was it they went every day? She was glad that she coddled them so much as kittens because it meant they couldn't bear to be away from her for very long and regulated their absences. Until today. Bickie had been out for five hours already.

It was still light outside, still safe. The sky was murky, sepia like an old photograph, burned out at the edges. She went onto the steps of the flats and called out, louder this time. She leaned out and yelled at the Korean kids from the flat below kicking a soccer ball in the front yard, 'You seen Bickie, kids?'

'No, Mrs Flores!' they yelled back.

She stretched out over the railing and could see the next landing. Freddy, the bachelor from directly beneath her, had set up a mini grill on the landing, turning over sausages and sipping a beer. He was quite big, with a foppish haircut and sharp eyes. Even before the killings he had been a paranoid bastard, a stickybeak, up at all hours checking on his new Mazda and for suspicious activity around the flats, which was mild solace to Maria. If any dodgy activity was going on, Freddy would be onto it in a flash.

She had a neighbour once in Guatemala, Julio, strong and brave, whose courage did him no good in the end. She thought of his face, with its proud Mayan nose and intelligent eyes, that it was almost unrecognisable when she saw him dead in the street the day she and her husband fled their homeland for good. Eva and Pedro didn't understand war or true sacrifice, and it was good they didn't. Eva didn't want to, preferring to tell people she had royal Spanish blood somewhere back up the family tree. Pedro was different. He wanted to know a bit too much. When he asked her about the war, the killings, the death squads, she noticed a greedy look in his normally placid eyes that she didn't like, as if his parents' suffering would lend him pity or prestige among his university friends.

She knew there was no way he could understand, no way she could word a phrase to take on the shape of absolute horror. Every now and again, rarely, she would try to explain about *los desaparecidos*, the so-called 'disappeared'. She would say that she had known people who had gone missing, that even when mass graves appeared many years later, there was no closure for their families. It seemed to both intrigue and terrify Pedro, but still, he didn't get it. Maria's grandchildren understood even less. Once, at a family Christmas,

she had asked Eva's daughter, Barbara, what magic power she wished she had. Barbara had replied instantly, 'Invisibility!' Maria had smiled and in a voice she didn't recognise, said 'that is not a super power, my darling. There are millions of people in the world who are invisible and wish to God they weren't.'

Suddenly she smelled something burning and swore to herself. The steak. Hustling as fast as she could into the kitchen, she cursed herself, but was glad that Eva wasn't there to witness it. She would take it as yet more evidence of Maria's growing infirmity. As if she needed any—she seemed to find evidence in every stumble, every forgotten appointment. So critical, that girl. Maria took the steak off the heat and eyed it. It wasn't unsalvageable, she realised, cutting into it with the trendy knife; it was burned only on the outside, leaving the meat inside rich and juicy. She smiled to herself proudly. *Just right.*

She sliced it into thin strips, for easy consumption.

Lately Eva had been hinting that Maria should move into a retirement home, but Maria had refused outright, saying she wanted to stand on her own two feet, in the flat that she *owned*, and would make a great show of throwing pamphlets from the nursing homes into the bin. But Eva was getting more and more persistent. She had a steely determination that terrified Maria. Her father's daughter. The type of cunning tenacity a person had to have to survive danger, to flee a homeland and to start a new life, had transmuted into something else in a new generation. Pedro, though—he was Maria's hope. As placid as he was, he was a mama's boy and if there was one thing he would fight for, it was her dignity.

She set the table with a glass of red wine and sat down heavily, grunting again. She shifted to get comfortable, then shifted again. It did no good. She savoured the first bite of the steak, and the second and the third, chewing slowly, imagining that it was filling her limbs with strength. She needed it. As well as getting her pension, she still worked stubbornly a day a week as a cleaning lady at a local primary school. Everyone loved her there, but she would have to give it up soon, because she was getting too slow at even the smallest tasks. She got a quarter of the way through the steak and set it aside. She wasn't as hungry as she had thought and plus, it was too gristly and it hurt her teeth. A little pile of chewed gristle sat on the side of the plate. She transferred the steak, rice, beans, tortillas and chips onto another plate, put it in the fridge, then carried the plate of gristle to the front door. But what for? Was she forgetting something? Maybe Eva was a little bit right. Sometimes Maria's memory floated from her like a balloon and she had to use all her concentration to catch it and bring it back.

She stood there, looking down the darkening stairs with a plate of gristle in her hand. Coffee rubbed against her ankles again. The cat! Of course. She tossed a piece of gristle to Coffee, who sniffed it, chewed it once, then let it drop to the floor. She stooped over and set the plate of gristle on the floor in the doorway. Cats have a good

On the Death of the Past
Christopher Palmer

there will be momentary mourning.
Even as people come out of their houses
to question themselves, and each other
the streets will be lit with expressions of the minute
reflecting instead the day's empty shine.
Entering forever the Modern Era
a time that no longer knows when it is,
where history has never been.
Ancestors can't inform their descendants;
the elderly will be looked upon with puzzlement.
Stonehenge will become contemporary art
and ammonites pretty ornaments.
People will be born with the conviction
that one moment is like every other,
and move between them
with all the speed of electricity;
without glimpsing the horizons of their language:
the tongue will no longer taste words
such as tradition, veteran, or antiquity
and all that was ever written by Plato,
or Shakespeare, will be written today;
because experience is extinct, and insight is instinct
the days will see the world merely as it is
within the palling echoes of their lineage.

sense of smell, didn't they? Bickie would smell it a mile off and come bounding in. He would be starving by now, surely.

It was dusk now and the sky was strange, brown darkening into black. She sat by the window and watched it through a mess of cobwebs. Coffee jumped on her lap and miaowed loudly, trembling. As she patted and calmed him, she looked at the framed pictures of her cats and children next to a crucifix on a bookshelf, at the brightly coloured painting of her namesake Maria and the photograph of her dead husband. There were more photos of the cats than the humans. She hadn't always loved cats. Her husband had thought them a pestilence, but when he had died she had been so lonely, mourning for hours in the dusty flat, weeping and refusing to eat, to take visitors. One day, Eva and Pedro had bought her the kittens and said they would be good for her. She laughed at them then, saying she was not the crazy cat lady from those cartoons Barbara liked. But then Bickie began to tug at her sock with his little teeth while Coffee tried to clean him and their loveliness stirred something within her and brought her back to life. She had been devoted to them ever since and thought of little else, not her husband, not God.

She no longer believed in God. How could she? Whenever she crossed herself, it was only out of habit. Her crucifixes were mere artefacts. If God does exist, she thought, he is a torturer. If not, then what remains? War remains. As much a war today in Guatemala as back then. The same M16s as *el ejército* used. That poor young generation, knowing no better life than the black blood that trickles between tiles and pavements, then turns mercury bright when police lights appear, a generation living in the spaces between bodies that would never be found, that went missing and were forever missed. A people who were somehow still brimming with humour despite the carnage, or maybe because of it. War remains. What Australians found so terrifying about the killer's violence was its grotesque novelty. They were not used to it. It was not banal. It was not the everyday.

She suddenly realised the phone was ringing. Eva. No-one else would call at this hour, not even those telemarketers, whom Maria was not sure whether to pity or despise. Maria hovered over the phone, her left arm crossed over her body, propping her right arm straight, resting her chin on her right palm, tapping her nose with the index finger on the same hand. It rang out. There was a moment of silence before it started ringing again. She picked it up.

'Mija?'

'Mum,' came Eva's serious voice, the one she had modelled on ABC newsreaders. Maria imagined her on the news, talking sombrely about the killer. 'Mum, we need to talk.' Wasn't that something people only said in American movies?

'We're talking now, *mija*.'

Her daughter's voice cracked. 'How's Bickie? How's Coffee?'

Get to it, girl.

'They're good. Right here in my lap. They just ate.'

'Mama … we need to … we've found the perfect retirement home for you. It's near us. They have a spa there, they even have a chef.'

'I can cook for myself. Just did. We've talked about this already.'

'I know, I know. But, but, they have a nice big lawn and a waterfall. Perfect for your afternoon walks. They have an art studio with painting classes every Thursday.'

'What am I going to do in a studio? I haven't got an artistic bone in my body.'

Eva's voice was getting desperate now. 'We're doing it for you, *mama*. It's the best thing for you. You can barely get up and down the stairs of the flats any more.'

'It's only *you* who are saying it.' Maria decided she would talk to Pedro, her sweet

Pedrito. He would go in to bat for her with this stubborn Eva. She tried to change the conversation. 'Let me talk to Barbara. I miss my granddaughter.'

'She's asleep.'

'That's a lie. I can hear a cartoon on in the background.'

Eva was nearly at her wit's end. Maria could hear the aggression bubbling in the crucible. Smoke was rising. Yes, that's it. Get angry, *mija*. Eva started again. 'Mama, please listen to me. We're doing it for your own—'

'You let that child stay up much too late.'

It was then that Eva's temper broke, as did the urbane accent she had tried so hard to cultivate. She suddenly became a girl from the flats again and spat the words out. 'Mum, fucken hell. Are you being a pain in the arse on purpose? I don't have time for your bullshit. I don't wanna be the one to have to clean up your shit and wipe your arse every day when you can't do it yourself. It's not our fucken problem.'

Maria smiled, enjoying the sport of it. Her voice rose too. 'Ah, now the truth comes out. I'm a burden to you, is that it?'

There was a suck of breath and it sounded like Eva was going to retort when suddenly Pedro's wispy voice appeared on the line. He had been listening the whole time. 'Mama. Mama? I think Eva's right. It's not safe for you to be by yourself in that flat. What if you fall and hurt yourself? Mama, at least come and look at the place.'

Maria said nothing. Eva spoke again and this time she was calm and triumphant. Her 'reasonable' voice. 'It's for the best, mama. We've made an appointment. Take a look at least.'

Maria didn't want her voice to betray her, so she remained silent for a moment. 'You are a hard child, Eva,' she wanted to say, and 'Pedro, how could you betray me? *Pedrito, mi corazón*,' but instead she spoke softly, 'Okay, okay. I'll come with you. See you tomorrow.'

She bowed her head and put the phone gently in its cradle, her face shining with tears. She looked around the flat and went to the kitchen, running her hand over the faux marble kitchen bench again and again. It was *hers*. Years of exile, years of toil. Had it made her happy? Her hand tightened around the trendy kitchen knife.

What was happiness? If happiness existed, it was a skein whose knotted lengths were lost and tangled among those of pain and loss, inextricably, loose leads threaded through the remains of bodies and bullet shells. Eva spoke endlessly about happiness, and did all manner of things—diets, yoga, cosmetic surgery—but she didn't seem happier. Maria thought of how from even a young age, she would pick up an apple with one bruise and look at it as if it were wholly unclean. She would refuse to cut the bruise off and eat the good bits.

Maria placed the knife in her pocket. She nodded to herself and made a decision, wiping the tears from her face and jutting her chin out. She would go outside into the darkness to find her cat Bickie. But she would have to leave the door open, just in case he came home when she was gone.

What to do with the other one? She had an idea. She laboriously took the catbox down from a shelf in the laundry and opened it up. Coffee was shaking, but he went inside without her having to push him. She shut the grill and his wet nose and eyes shone from behind the bars. The louder you miaow, the more chance your brother will come home, she said to him. She carried him to the top of the stairs, in front of the open door. Bait!

Each step down the stairs sent excruciating pain down her back and into her legs, then down into her feet, where she felt a dangerous tingling. She looked back up the stairs and all was dark, just a dull rectangle of light from her doorway. She compelled herself down the stairs and was breathing heavily by the time she got to the bottom. 'Bickie,' she called out in a thin voice. 'Bickiiiie!'

A light went on above her and there was a shadow behind a curtain. She walked forwards step by step into the yard of the flats and kept calling to Bickie. There was a toy ball on the ground and she would have stooped to pick it up if it wasn't such a waste of energy. She went out the front gate. She faced a row of houses and flats, all locked shut and silent, turned strange colours by blinking streetlamps and the particulate air. All else was shadow and there was no movement whatsoever.

She climbed the hill next to the flats slowly, each step more plodding than the last. Excruciating. She suffered forwards and the air was malevolent, almost choking her. She had once enjoyed the town's dry heat but now its grit seared her throat. She kept looking around. Every tree, every fence, every garbage alcove could be a hiding place. She touched the knife in her pocket. I wouldn't even know what to do with it, she thought. Suddenly something appeared at her periphery, a spark of white-hot movement and a pair of flashing eyes. 'Bickie?' her voice quivered, almost gone. Yes, it was a cat, but it was pure white. Actually there were several of them, fleeing across the road and somehow they looked like birds flocking against a very black sky. Her heart leapt for a moment, thinking that maybe this was where Bickie went during the day, to join a gang of white street cats to go on adventures. But he wasn't with them.

She stumbled to the crest of the hill and could feel something trickling down her leg. Maybe it was blood, maybe it was sweat, or maybe something else. She couldn't control her bladder so well these days. Up on the corner, against a streetlight, she saw the shapes of two humans, but couldn't make them out. People said they dealt heroin on this corner. Drug dealers wouldn't be afraid of a murderer, would they? Not if they were armed. By the time she made it to the corner there was no-one there.

When she got to the bottom of the hill, her throat was burning. Her breath came out in heavy rasps. It was the furthest she had walked in a year and she wasn't sure how she would get back home. Maybe in her absence Bickie had come running up the stairs and was sniffing around Coffee in the catbox, trying to lick him, warm and safe again. She stood facing a square vacant lot with an open stormwater drain next to it, often filled with plastic bags and deformed crab apples that fell from a tree that arched over it. It was once home to a melon patch, an orange cat and its kitten. Maria had often thought she could take the scabby creatures up and look after them, but she knew how her coddled cats would be terrified. 'Wouldn't be worth it,' she said aloud. The lot was empty now, but the drain caught her eye. It was at the other end of this drain, on the edge of town, where the water empties out into the river, that the Pakistani student had been found. An early-morning jogger had come across the lipless body.

She moved towards the drain, feet somehow sure of themselves again, and now stared into the darkness, an abyss or black mirror, and it seemed to shift somehow, like waves on the surface of the deep, blackness on blackness, and at its epicentre she thought she could see something, two eyes maybe, and she peered back at them, and in that moment she cared little about pain or death, about the labyrinth of streets and the countless dreams and nightmares being made and unmade around her. She stared and stared, drawn forwards until, at last, she recognised what it was that she saw. •

Omar Musa is a Malaysian-Australian author, rapper and poet who lives in Queanbeyan. His debut novel *Here Come the Dogs* was long-listed for the Miles Franklin Award.

BOMB SIGHTS IN JAPAN

Photographing Australian-occupied Hiroshima

Robin Gerster

ATOMIC-BOMBED HIROSHIMA, Maria Tumarkin observes in *Traumascapes*, has become 'the lens through which other sites of destruction and death can be witnessed and remembered'.[1] Tumarkin is suggesting Hiroshima's reverberating significance as a set of images against which other tragedies are measured in the public imagination; she is also cannily implying the importance of the camera as the primary contemporary tool to represent and communicate massive devastation. In 2015, the 70th anniversary of the atomic bombings of Hiroshima and Nagasaki that heralded the nuclear age, it is worth reconsidering the role of photography in documenting an unprecedented level of destruction for which existing language seemed inadequate, and a sight that reduced early visitors to stunned silence.[2] One visual record of Hiroshima that illustrates the power of photography (and its limitations) is that produced by the Australian men and women of 'BCOF', the British Commonwealth Occupation Force in postwar Japan—relentless sightseers and habitual photographers who rarely ventured anywhere without their cameras.[3]

Japan was in ruins when the first Australians arrived in early 1946 to participate in the American-led military occupation. Sixty of its cities had been pulverised and incinerated by a saturation bombing campaign that included the prodigious use of napalm. The postwar homeless numbered up to 9 million; people were dying of malnutrition; orphans scrounged in gutted buildings and blackened streets. Prostitution was the only thing to thrive in the wreckage, catering to an influx of foreign troops intent on enjoying the spoils of war. The traditional Japan of temples and teahouses that had attracted generations of Western photographers was horribly scarred. But of all the devastated sites of a devastated country, it was Hiroshima that exercised a special fascination for the Australians.

Partly this was due to proximity, for the Australian contingent was largely based in Hiroshima Prefecture, in the port of Kure just down the Inland Sea coast from the devastated city, and in nearby camps and residential enclaves where many servicemen lived with their wives and children from 1947. The remote and ravaged BCOF sphere of influence in western Honshu was the dubious gift of the Occupation's commander, General Douglas MacArthur, comfortably ensconced in central Tokyo across from the palace of the ruler he had effectively usurped, Emperor Hirohito. But there was also the pull of a place that was both morally troubling and seductive as a portent of a dangerous new epoch.

Shirley Hazzard, who visited Japan as a child a year after the bombing, writes in her novel *The Great Fire* (2003) that Australian members of the Occupation exhibited 'the unease of conquerors: the unseemliness of finding themselves a few miles from Hiroshima'.[4] Nonetheless the nuclear notoriety of the place immediately dubbed 'The Atomic City' made it a must-see on the tour of duty, and the Australians visited in numbers, either individually and informally or on group tours organised by the military, which advertised the opportunities for taking pictures of the destruction.[5] They travelled to the place heedless of the risk, for the official guidebook *Know Japan* provided to the troops never once mentioned the word 'radiation'.

By May 1947, when the English-born Australian illusionist Maurice Rooklyn travelled to Japan to entertain BCOF servicemen, a tourism industry was already in evidence in Hiroshima. Bomb debris was being peddled to tourists, mostly household items remoulded in the tremendous heat caused by the explosion. Australians were enthusiastic clients, buying (or looting) a piece of Ground Zero to take back home. Back in Australia, Rooklyn had billed himself the 'Human Target' for his most famous theatrical feat, in which he conjured to 'catch' a bullet fired directly at him. In Hiroshima he tried something rather less ambitious, having himself photographed in a field of rubble, surveying local devastation (see Figure 1).

It is not known whether the 'Human Target' realised the irony of situating himself at a site where tens of thousands were summarily killed one bright summer morning. The bomb that destroyed Hiroshima was surely no illusion. What the photograph does evoke is the element of spectatorship of the Australians in Japan, and the uneasy combination of voyeurism and self-consciousness with which they first apprehended the

Figure 1 Maurice Rooklyn views the Hiroshima devastation, c. 1947, W.G. Alma conjuring collection (photographs), State Library of Victoria, a10007 13

tremendous damage inflicted on a country for which some still harboured a deep dislike, verging on hatred.

But the Australian photographs reveal something else, not just about the death of a city but also its rebirth. Equally importantly, they provide a self-reflexive view of the way Australians perceived postwar Japan, and the evolution of attitudes towards the wartime enemy. Photographing Hiroshima, more than any other place in the country, was the means through which they mediated the ethical and perceptual confusions of a military occupation that was part punitive and part exercise in reconstruction.

. . .

The very first foreign reportage from atomic Hiroshima, that of the Australian journalist Wilfred Burchett in early September 1945, inadvertently indicates the problem that was to beset representation of the bombing—its indescribability. Striving to convey the colossal material damage, Burchett wrote of a city that looked 'as though a monster steamroller had passed over it and squashed it out of existence'.[6] This is a revealingly anachronistic metaphor for the technological obliteration caused by one small bomb, aptly codenamed 'Little Boy', containing the body weight in enriched uranium of a jockey-sized man. In the Australian spring of 1945 the first peace-time issue of *Meanjin* (then called the *Meanjin Papers*) also selected an old-fashioned image to indicate the sense of historical severance occasioned by the use of nuclear weapons. The bomb, it editorialised, had 'severed the old world from the new with guillotine-like decisiveness'.[7] In the early days the bombing literally *was* indescribable. The Hiroshima daily newspaper the *Chugoku Shinbun* did not possess the movable type for 'atomic bomb' or 'radioactivity', and hence could not properly report on what had taken place in its own back yard.[8]

In distant Australia, relief at the end of the war was tempered by inarticulate trepidation at the tremendous new source of power science had unleashed. A couple of days after the destruction of Hiroshima, and the day before an even more powerful weapon wrecked Nagasaki, the Brisbane *Courier Mail* contemplated the atomic bomb. 'Even scientists', an editorial remarked, were 'lost for words' as they considered its magnitude. If scientists couldn't describe it, who could? Australian members of the BCOF advance party were struck dumb by Hiroshima upon their arrival in the country in February 1946. The men 'had no word to describe it, which is unusual for Australian soldiers', said a brief report of this first landfall in postwar Japan, published in the Melbourne daily broadsheet the *Argus*.[9]

Photography filled this representational vacuum. The *Argus* report is dwarfed by photographs taken by the newspaper's staff photographer. These include a panorama of the extensive damage in the centre of the city, highlighting the skeletal structure of what was to become the iconic symbol of both Hiroshima and the nuclear age, the so-called 'A-bomb Dome', another wide-angle shot of the heavily bombed harbour at Kure, and a scene of a genial Australian soldier interacting with Japanese women and children. In the publicly circulated photography of the early days of the Occupation, the military might of the conquering force was balanced by an imagery of benignity. The Allies had won the war with technological efficiency, and were now rebuilding Japan and helping it mend its militaristic ways.

In pictures often supplied by the army's Directorate of Public Relations or taken by newspapermen still enlisted in the services, early Australian press photography contrived to make the Australian 'Diggers' look good, and so convince a doubting public that MacArthur's project to remake Japan was both worthy and appropriate. In Figure 2,

Figure 2 Australian soldiers in Hiroshima, c. 1947, *Argus* Newspaper Collection of Photographs, State Library of Victoria, H98.100/282

from the extensive *Argus* online collection held by the State Library of Victoria, a group of crisply uniformed Diggers stroll past the A-bomb Dome with a conqueror's self-assurance. The symbol of the city's nuclear destruction serves as a decorative back-drop; the Australians' eyes are fixed firmly ahead. Images like this, along with those of inquisitive soldier-tourists rummaging through the rubble for atomic souvenirs or traipsing through the wreckage of ruined shrines, suggest a force free of self-doubt or moral qualms.[10]

The atomic bombs that ended the war were greeted with relief: a Gallup Poll of Australians taken in September 1945 revealed that 83 per cent thought their use justified.[11] While there was widespread alarm at the development of nuclear weapons and concern that no Australian city in future would ever be safe, there was little pity for the Japanese. As further revelations came to light about the manifest iniquities of Japan's military during the war, the country was still widely excoriated. In September 1949, four years after the war's end, MacArthur issued an order relaxing the (largely ignored) policy of 'non-fraternisation' between the occupier and the occupied, and encouraging instead 'friendly interest and guidance toward the Japanese'. This edict challenged the priorities and predilections of the Australian mili-tary command, which continued to regard the Japanese as a conquered enemy. Being 'kind to Japs', as one press report put it, was still unconscionable.[12]

The landscape of devastation surveyed in these early published photographs is pleasantly free of signs of human suffering. This was both calculated and shameless. Anxious not to disturb what it called 'public tranquillity', MacArthur's GHQ imposed a strict code of press censorship in September 1945, as one of its first disingenuous acts to democratise totalitarian Japan. This systematically silenced the *hibakusha*, the survivors of Hiroshima and Nagasaki who had lived to tell the tale. Years later, the Hiroshima poet Sadako Kurihara expressed her frustration: 'We were not allowed to write about the atomic bomb during the Occupation. We were not even allowed to say that we were not allowed to write about the atomic bomb.'[13]

During the first year of the Occupation, the portrayal of the misery inflicted by the bombings was strictly the privilege of the foreigner, and could only be communicated to foreign audiences. In October 1946, a month after MacArthur slapped the home ban on Japanese testimony, the *Australasian Post* published in full John Hersey's *Hiroshima*, a 30,000-word reconstruction of the A-bombing written from the viewpoint of survivors, which had first appeared in the *New Yorker* that August, in an entire issue devoted to it. The *Australasian Post* supplemented Hersey's powerful narrative with graphic photographs. Unfortunately, an aerial shot of bomb-blasted Hiroshima is counterpointed with a full page advertisement for Australia's leading winemaker, Penfold's, with a nurse offering a seated gentleman a glass of red beneath the legend, 'Nature's blood transfusion'.[14]

In Japan, MacArthur's ban applied to the publication of photographs as well as the written word. Ostensibly it was latent Japanese resentment that the Occupation wanted to contain. But there was another, deeper reason—the prestige of the United States as a beacon of enlightened humanity was at stake. The home public had been bombarded with horrifying pictures of the Nazi death camps in the months after the end of the war in Europe. Documentary images from Japan of burned corpses or massed remains would not do. The US Secretary of War Henry Stimson had sounded the alarm

before August 1945, in response to the relentless firebombing of Japanese cities, confiding in his diary that June that he did not want to have 'the United States get the reputation for outdoing Hitler in atrocities'.[15]

Accordingly, the publication of intimate ground-level photographs capturing the horror of the immediate atomic aftermath was prohibited, including the handful of harrowing images of Hiroshima taken on the day of the bombing by the *Chugoku Shimbun* photographer Yoshito Matsushige, and those of Nagasaki taken the day after by Yosuke Yamahata. These images were not published in the United States until *Life* magazine presented them in a photo-spread in September 1952, after the implementation of the Peace Treaty formally ended the Occupation. A month earlier, on the seventh anniversary of the levelling of Hiroshima, the venerable Japanese weekly *Asahi Graph* had published an issue dedicated to explicit photographs of the bombings and their victims.[16] In their absence, images of the destruction circulated on the black market in the form of postcards (with titles such as 'Terrible Sight'), many of which were acquired as souvenirs by BCOF servicemen. Thus during and well after the Occupation, photographic imagery of the atomic bomb was monopolised by the uncensored sight of the mushroom cloud spiralling high into the sky, camouflaging the horrors down below. This 'abstract image', argues Adam Harrison Levy, was essentially exculpatory, freeing the bombing from 'human agency'.[17]

The official Australian visual record of the Occupation is revealing. Photographers attached to the Military History Section (MHS) were handed a brief to construct a faithful, 'impartial' view of the Occupation. Yet they were selective in what they chose to photograph.[18] The first photographer appointed to 'MHS BCOF', Alan Cuthbert, produced several panoramic photographs of Hiroshima and its neighbourhood,

Figure 3 Allan Cuthbert, view south from central Hiroshima, 28 February 1946,
Australian War Memorial 131583

including Kure. Soon after arriving in Japan in February 1946, he photographed from the roof of the *Chugoku Shimbun* building, in which more than 100 employees had perished on 6 August (see Figure 3). The elevated vantage point provides a perspective of a devastated landscape that is virtually devoid of people, save a few anonymous figures walking along the crossroads, as well as two small clusters of uniformed personnel in the foreground, by the shell of the Jesuit church that served Hiroshima's small Christian community.

Objective and methodical, Cuthbert's vista of absence and annihilation is highly reminiscent of the photographs taken by the Physical Damage Division of the Strategic Bombing Survey (1946) commissioned by the US government after the war to assess the effectiveness of the aerial campaigns in

Germany and Japan, with a view to informing the future civil defence architecture of the United States.[19] But while it provides an impressive image of the astonishing spread of the nuclear devastation, Cuthbert's panorama conveys an aloof and sanitised picture of the atomic-bombed city. By 1946 much of the debris had been cleaned up and the streets are neat and tidy; only picturesque ruins remain of what was Hiroshima. What this impersonal image does not show is the pervasive misery and persistent sickness of a traumatised population. Like the imagery of the mushroom cloud, this structured absence of human suffering is troubling.[20]

Not that Cuthbert confined himself to working from a comfortable remove. He also scoured the streets of Hiroshima, photographing crowded tramcars as the shattered population began to regroup, and visiting

Figure 4 Allan Cuthbert, Japanese labourer at work in the Kure shipyards, 1948, Australian War Memorial 145572

the docks at nearby Kure to photograph Japanese labourers under BCOF supervision dismantling naval infrastructure to provide the scrap metal needed for the immense task of rebuilding.[21] One of Cuthbert's ground-level images displays an acute and possibly ironic eye for detail. In Figure 4, a Japanese labourer works with an oxyacetylene torch in the shipbreaking yards. His clothes are virtually rags except for the straw boater: suitably nautical, perhaps, but incongruously jaunty and indeed ridiculous in the gritty context. Military defeat and occupation had effected a transformation in fearsome Japanese male stereotypes. The fanatical Japanese warrior had become something other altogether—dutiful and hard-working, but faintly vaudevillian.

Hiroshima's rebuilding was symbolic as well as pragmatic, and the city was well on the way to becoming the 'place of pilgrimage for pacifists' anticipated by the globe-trotting Australian writer Frank Clune in

his travel book *Ashes of Hiroshima* (1950), the product of a trip to the BCOF areas in 1948.[22] The making of Hiroshima as a self-styled 'Mecca for World Peace' began almost immediately, with the formation in January 1946 of the Hiroshima Reconstruction Bureau. The creation of what we now know as 'Peace Park', with its host of commemorative structures (including the prolific use of plaques bearing 'before and after' photographic images of the city), was just a few years away. In 1948 the slogan 'No more Hiroshimas', taken from an article in the US service newspaper *Pacific Stars and Stripes*, was applied to a local campaign to make the city a focus for the advocacy of world peace. It has stuck as an anti-nuclear catchcry ever since, paradoxically linking the city forever with the historical fact of its destruction.

'No More Hiroshima's' [*sic*] made its first appearance on a large banner at the second of the official annual Peace Festivals, on the third anniversary of the bombing,

6 August 1948. Cuthbert's MHS colleague Alan Queale was there to record an event that was to become notorious (see Figure 5). In what would later be a ritual at this solemn event, doves had been sent fluttering into the summer sky; bells had tolled; poets had recited commemorative odes. And then BCOF's Australian commander-in-chief, Lieutenant-General Horace Robertson, Gallipoli veteran and hero of the North African campaign in the Second World War, strode to the podium.

In 1946 Robertson had demonstrated his goodwill by offering the services of Australian engineers and town planners to rehabilitate Hiroshima as 'a city dedicated to the idea of Peace', a gesture vetoed by MacArthur. But on this special day he chose to tell the assembled citizens, many of them young children who would have lost beloved family members in the blast, that it was their own fault. The bomb was a 'punishment' handed to the city as 'retribution' for Japanese militarism. To emphasise his point, he had detailed a squadron of Mustang fighters to fly low over the ceremony—an ear-shattering reminder of the bolt from the blue three years earlier. Perhaps that is what prompted the Japanese man standing on the jeep in Queale's picture to point skywards.[23]

So much for 'peace'. Civilian Australians such as Frank Clune may have been impressed by Robertson's harangue. In *Ashes of Hiroshima* Clune is both callous and flippant in his view of Japan's atomic 'punishment', blaming the wholesale devastation

Figure 5 Alan Queale, scene of the Peace Festival, Hiroshima, 6 August 1948, Australian War Memorial 145724

wrought by the bomb on the Japanese for being 'too stupid and ignorant to build solidly'. Yet even Clune had his enmity qualified by the sight of Japanese children, in particular. 'No man could see the ashes of Hiroshima and fail to feel qualms,' he wrote. Driving along the perilously narrow coastal road back to Kure, he sees Japanese kids playing in the water. 'They at any rate had no war-guilt,' he remarks. 'We couldn't honestly say it served them right.'[24] Certainly many among the common soldiery of BCOF responded with sensitivity to the plight of the people of Hiroshima Prefecture, and regarded helping them rebuild their lives and their city as the force's main achievement in Japan.

Away from his professional duties recording BCOF activities, Queale—the brother of the novelist Jessica Anderson—sought out the common folk of Japan for a series of portraits collected in his private albums, held in the photographic archives of the Australian War Memorial in Canberra. He photographed another local festival, the *O-bon*, which has evolved over time into a Buddhist summer holiday honouring the departed spirits of ancestors who return to Earth in midsummer to visit their relatives (see Figure 6). In Hiroshima it often coincides with the remembrance of the atomic bombings. It is not the spectacle of the festival that is the object of Queale's camera, but a young, traditionally dressed girl, posing for him away from the crowd of spectators. Here we see a gently beguiling image of essentially feminine Japan rather than the country demonised by wartime propaganda, one that no technology of destruction could erase.

The penchant for photographing Japanese children extended to common servicemen such as Neville Govett. A sergeant in a Transport Company, Govett was an active member of the BCOF Tourist Club, which enjoyed group tours to various locations throughout the length and breadth of

Figure 6 Alan Queale personal collection, girl dressed for the Odori, c. 1946–1949, Australian War Memorial P1197.017.001

the Japanese archipelago; out of it emerged a camera club. Complied by Govett, *The Story of the B.C.O.F. Tourist Club* (1950) records the full itinerary of some 200 outings, well over 20 of which were to Hiroshima and environs. The book is copiously illustrated with photographs of the club's activities, but only one of Hiroshima, a humdrum view of the A-bomb Dome. Perhaps the club thought it in questionable taste to highlight a voyeuristic interest in a site of mass death. Several of the photographs are the work of the MHS photographer Claude Holzheimer, clichéd pictures of castles, mountain views and tea ceremonies. Govett's own unpublished photographs are much more compelling. Taking to the streets of Hiroshima, he made effective use of the winter sunshine in a photograph of a boy selling black market cigarettes (see Figure 7). The boy confidently faces Govett's

Figure 7 Neville Govett, boy selling black market cigarettes, Hiroshima, c. 1947–1949, Mitchell Library, State Library of New South Wales, PXE 1498 Box 1

Box Brownie, to the evident amusement of his friends. Hiroshima was full of uprooted youngsters, living rough, supporting themselves as best they could. Many had lost their fathers to the late war, or one or both parents in the bombing. The survival instinct was strong, if not always especially edifying.

Stephen Kelen, who served with BCOF Intelligence before joining the military newspaper *BCON*, was less reticent than Govett about publishing his graphic scenes of Hiroshima. Several of the personal photographs that illustrate his memoir *I Remember Hiroshima* (1983) are now lodged in the Hiroshima Municipal Archives, and are among the most significant taken by a foreign soldier in Occupied Japan. Indeed, Stephen Kelen himself personifies the tentative process of Australian rapprochement with the old enemy that took place in postwar Japan.

Born in Hungary in 1912, Kelen arrived in Australia in 1937 as an international table tennis champion, playing a series of exhibition matches. Refusing to return to Hungary for military service, he settled in Sydney and joined the Australian Army instead, enlisting in May 1945 and serving briefly in New Guinea and North Borneo before joining BCOF. In the early, edgy days of the Pacific War, Kelen's knowledge of Japan acquired during his global table tennis odyssey gave him credibility as a commentator on the country. In a series of articles published in late 1941 and 1942 in the *Sydney Morning Herald* and the Melbourne *Argus*, Kelen critiqued Japanese customs and culture as a means of understanding a people he called 'strange, unscrupulous and … reckless'. The wartime climate hardly encouraged a sympathetic view of the Japanese. He wrote that he had originally gone to Japan naively believing that 'the differences between the Nipponese and the Occidentals' were 'purely ideological', and that essentially 'they are just the same human beings as we are'. But firsthand knowledge taught him otherwise. The Japanese, he proclaimed, are 'as strange to us as the inhabitants of the moon'.[25]

A different tone pervades Kelen's writing on the Occupation. By the time of the first anniversary of the bombing, he had already visited Hiroshima several times, walking its streets, speaking to the survivors and taking photographs. Attending the commemorative services on 6 August 1946, he expected to encounter sorrow and possibly anger. Instead he found acceptance, and the experience becomes an epiphany of cultural reconciliation. The first anniversary of the dropping of 'Little Boy' coincided with the *O-bon* festivities taking place in the vicinity of Ground Zero.

In the flickering light of kerosene lamps and to the sound of drums and the clapping of hands, the people of Hiroshima danced the festival dance, the *Bon Odori*, 'forming a circle, moving round and round, greeting the dead whose souls had been liberated from their sufferings in the Buddhist hell and elevated to a state of celestial bliss'. The only foreign observer, Kelen felt uncomfortable. 'How would we have reacted if the enemy had destroyed Sydney a year ago?' he asks himself. Then the music suddenly stopped and someone called to the Australian: 'Come and dance with us, honourable soldier.' Two grimy Hiroshima urchins took him by the hands and led him into the circle. There on the riverbank, Kelen writes, 'In front of a grotesque skeleton of a building, with the people of Hiroshima I too danced the *Bon Odori*.'[26] Commander Robertson would not have approved.

But it is in the many photographs illustrating his text that Kelen's conciliatory attitude to emerges most vividly. Kelen appears to have been especially keen to capture uplifting images of a tenacious Japan emerging from the ashes. Along with his photograph of groups of Hiroshima orphans, his photograph of an open-air schoolroom, set up in the rubble, is one of the best-known images of atomic Hiroshima, and features in online educational material published by the Hiroshima Peace Memorial Museum, to spread the anti-nuclear gospel.[27] Kelen also took several images of a citizenry busily getting on with the life, far from demoralised by the enormity of what had befallen their city and neither cowed nor kowtowing to their occupier. His intent is revealed in one of his lesser known photographs, not included in *I Remember Hiroshima*. Here the Digger is a shadowy, indistinct shape in the background; the focus is directed at the perky, business-like market woman, cursorily posing for the Australian photographer (see Figure 8).

Australian and American photography of the Occupation characteristically highlights women and children in order to reframe Japan as a potential peacetime ally—the men were still too closely identified with the horrors of the war.[28] Kelen was more inclusive. In a carefully conceived photograph, two

Figure 8 Stephen Kelen, Hiroshima market woman, c. 1946–1948, courtesy S.K. Kelen and Hiroshima Municipal Archives

middle-aged Japanese men walk purposefully toward Kelen's camera, in a typical tableau of Hiroshima devastation. As two Diggers slouch back into the bombsite and towards the vanishing point beneath the cluster of stripped trees, the two conspicuously civilian, Western-attired Japanese walk out of it, away from the militarist past that led to such destruction, defeat and military occupation, and into a future that would be independently determined by men such as them (see Figure 9). It is a photograph that is rich in allegorical significance.

By contrast with the responsive but also artful work of amateur photographers such as Kelen and Govett, the work of the celebrated artist Albert Tucker in postwar Japan is remarkably tame. Tucker spent three months attached to BCOF in early 1947, photographing, sketching and painting the bombsites of Hiroshima and Kure, and also visiting Osaka and Tokyo. He took some engaging pictures of children, but his obligatory photograph of the A-bomb Dome is duller than many made by amateurs, and his paintings and sketches are undistinguished.[29] Years later, Tucker confided that he was 'too young and inexperienced' to grasp the immensity of Hiroshima and that his 'empathic abilities weren't developed as fully' as he would have wished. Given that he was well into his thirties when he travelled to Japan, and had already produced some of his best work, including the *Images of Modern Evil* series depicting sordid urban life in wartime Australia, this is a strange comment. Nonetheless it is a revealing nod to the challenges posed by Hiroshima, and the difficulty of getting beyond what Tucker calls its 'superficial aura'.[30]

Tucker's photograph of a piece of twisted metal at the Kure shipyards is the work of an artist unable to register a response to destruction other than one that is purely aesthetic (see Figure 10). The industrial detritus of the bombing that killed and maimed so many is

Figure 9 Stephen Kelen, Hiroshima scene c. 1946–1948, published in *I Remember Hiroshima* (Hale & Iremonger, Sydney, 1983), p. 27. Courtesy S.K. Kelen and Hiroshima Municipal Archives

turned into a modernist sculptured object of aesthetic contemplation, and pleasure. 'There is beauty in ruins,' Susan Sontag has suggested, citing photographs of the 'Ground Zero' site in downtown New York City in the aftermath of 9/11. But photographing human tragedy is ethically fraught. Photography 'that bears witness to the calamitous and the reprehensible', she writes, 'is much criticized if it seems "aesthetic"; that is, too much like art'. In Tucker's defence it might be argued he is merely responding like the artist he is, bearing witness to destruction by framing it as an image, according to the conventions of his craft.[31] Nonetheless Tucker's photograph seems too detached, just as Cuthbert's sweeping views of Hiroshima's destruction seem a little too clinical, or 'overconstructed' in the sense meant by Roland Barthes in his discussion of 'shock photos'.[32]

The arresting photographs of amateurs such as Kelen and Govett support Sontag's contention that the work of an untrained and inexperienced photographer is not necessarily inferior to that of a professional, and enjoys 'the bias toward the spontaneous, the rough, the imperfect' that can make for good pictures.[33] Moreover, they reveal the ability of ordinary Australians, freed of professional compulsions or the official obligation to provide an unproblematic perspective of a sometimes controversial occupation, to respond with sensitivity to the travails of a people who were still distrusted, especially back home in Australia, where many considered the Occupation indulgently benevolent and disarmingly constructive.

• • •

The documentary value of the photography of violence has become a topic of debate in recent years, especially after Susan Sontag's dismissal of the genre in *Regarding the Pain*

Figure 10 Albert Tucker, Shipyards at Kure, 1947, Albert Tucker Archive, Heide Museum of Modern Art, Melbourne

of Others (2003), where she contentiously remarked that, while narratives 'make us understand', photographs merely 'haunt us'.[34] It is true that the potency of Hiroshima imagery has tended to overwhelm subsequent disasters, such as the meltdown at the Fukushima nuclear complex in eastern Honshu following the earthquake and catastrophic tsunami in March 2011.[35] On occasion it has also proved an impediment to accurate historical accounting. In 2008 the august French daily *Le Monde* published grisly pictures of human cadavers that were purportedly 'lost' photographs of the bombing, taken from rolls of undeveloped film discovered in a cave outside Hiroshima—photographs released by the Hoover Institution Archives at the prestigious Stanford University. To Stanford's great embarrassment, it was soon proved that they are images of the carnage produced by the Kanto earthquake in 1923.[36]

Yet the pictures of Australian-occupied Hiroshima are more than 'haunting'. They pose searching moral as well as aesthetic questions about the act of taking photographs of a human tragedy in which Australia was complicit. They also reveal in postwar Australians a capacity for empathy and an eagerness for historical reconciliation that was to prove productive in the coming years, as the two former bitter antagonists forged a bilateral relationship based on mutual respect (and not a little economic self-interest). •

Robin Gerster is a professor in the School of Languages, Literatures, Cultures and Linguistics at Monash University. With Melissa Miles, he is working on 'Pacific Exposures', a cultural history of Australia–Japan photographic exchange.

Notes

1 Maria Tumarkin, *Traumascapes: The Power and Fate of Places Transformed by Tragedy*, Melbourne University Press, Melbourne, 2005, p. 186.

2 See for example the mute response of Lorraine Stumm, Australia's first accredited female correspondent in the Second World War, to her first sight of Hiroshima. In Lorraine Stumm, *I saw too much*, Write-On Group, Coopernook, NSW, 2000, p. 140.

3 Robin Gerster, 'Capturing Japan: Australian Photography of the Postwar Military Occupation', *History of Photography*, vol. 39, no. 3 (2015), p. 281.

4 Shirley Hazzard, *The Great Fire*, Virago, London, 2003, p. 8.

5 See the pamphlet *Tour of Hiroshima Japan: 'The Atomic City'*, conducted by the British Commonwealth Occupation Forces and the Eighth United States Army military government, Hiroshima Printing Co., Hiroshima, c. 1946. The author thanks Dr Ran Zwigenberg of Pennsylvania State University for supplying this document.

6 Wilfred Burchett, 'The Atomic Plague', *Daily Express*, 5 September 1945, p. 1, quoted in Burchett, *Shadows of Hiroshima*, Verso, London, 1983, pp. 34–6.

7 *Meanjin Papers*, vol. 4, no. 3 (Spring 1945), p. 149.

8 See Kenzaburo Oë, *Hiroshima Notes*, Grove Press, New York, 1981, p. 67.

9 'New Era', *Courier Mail* editorial, 8 August 1945, p. 2; 'Atom bomb ruin staggers Australians in Japan', *Argus*, 18 February 1946, p. 20.

10 See the *Argus* Newspaper Collections of Photographs, State Library of Victoria, H98.104/563, H98.100/172.

11 Prue Torney-Parlicki, '"Whatever the Thing may Be Called": The Australian News Media and the Atomic Bombing of Hiroshima and Nagasaki', *Australian Historical Studies*, vol. 31, no. 114 (2000), p. 61.

12 'MacArthur's "kind to Japs" order poses dilemma', Melbourne *Herald*, 29 September 1949, p. 1.

13 Monica Braw, *The Atomic Bomb Suppressed: American Censorship in Japan 1945–1948*, Liber Forlag, Tokyo, 1986, p. 14. The author interviewed Kurihara in 1978.

14 *Australasian Post*, 10 October 1946, esp. pp. 12–13. Hersey's *Hiroshima* was extracted in Japan in the service newspaper the *British Commonwealth Occupation News* (*BCON*), the readership of which was almost entirely non-Japanese. See 'Death came swiftly with the atomic bomb—and lingers', *BCON*, 12 October 1946, p. 5.

15 Stimson quoted in Braw, p. 141.

16 'When the Atom Bomb Struck—Uncensored', *Life*, 29 September 1952, pp. 19–25; *Asahi Graph* special issue, 6 August 1952: see Hirofumi Utsumi, 'Nuclear Images and National Self-Portraits: Japanese Illustrated Magazine *Asahi Graph*, 1945–1965', *Bulletin of the Kwansei Gakuin Institute for Advanced Social Research*, vol. 5 (2011), pp. 8–9. Utsumi notes that a few images of the bomb damage had been published in Japan just before the press ban was introduced in September 1945, and again, in the *Chugoku Shimbun*, in July 1946.

17 Adam Harrison Levy, 'Hiroshima: The Lost Photographs', *Design Observer*, 23 October 2008, <http://designobserver.com/article.php?id=7517>, accessed 13 July 2015.

18 Photography of the Military History Section both during the war and in the Occupation is discussed at length in Shaune Lakin, *Contact: Photographs from the Australian War Memorial Collection*, Australian War Memorial, Canberra, 2006, pp. 113, 137, 173–4.

19 See 'Hiroshima: Ground Zero 1945', International Center of Photography (New York City) website, <http://www.icp.org/browse/archive/collections/hiroshima-ground-zero-1945-may-20-august-28-2011>, accessed 14 July 2015.

20 On this representational issue, see Robert Hariman and John Louis Lucaites, 'The Iconic Image of the Mushroom Cloud and the Cold War Optic', in Geoffrey Batchen et al. (eds), *Picturing Atrocity: Photographs in Crisis*, Reaktion, London, 2012, pp. 135–45.

21 Allan Cuthbert photographs in the Australian War Memorial collection, for example AWM 131784 and 131785; 145575 and 145576.

22 Frank Clune, *Ashes of Hiroshima: A Postwar Trip to Japan and China*, Angus & Robertson, Sydney, 1950, p. 103.

23 See Clune's interview with Robertson in *Ashes of Hiroshima*, pp. 148–9, in which the BCOF

commander discusses the rationale behind the speech. A short film of the occasion, made by the Military History Section, is held by the Australian War Memorial, F07474.

24 Clune, *Ashes of Hiroshima*, pp. 89–90, 93.

25 Stephen Kelen, 'Japan's Cult of Death', *Sydney Morning Herald*, 3 January 1942, p. 9; 'Japs differ from us in many little things', *Argus Weekend Magazine*, 6 June 1942, p. 3; 'What sort of person is the Japanese soldier?', *Argus Weekend Magazine*, 24 January 1942, p. 3.

26 Stephen Kelen, *I Remember Hiroshima*, Hale & Iremonger, Sydney, 1983, pp. 30–2. Kelen also wrote sympathetically about the Japanese wives of BCOF servicemen who started entering Australia—to open hostility from some quarters—from 1952. See his article '"New Australians"—from Japan', *Sydney Morning Herald*, 12 April 1952, p. 6.

27 'Children in Postwar Hiroshima', Hiroshima Peace Memorial Museum website: <http://www.pcf.city.hiroshima.jp/kids/KPSH_E/hiroshima_e/sadako_e/subcontents_e/12kidssengo_1_e.html>, accessed 14 July 2015; also on the same website, Kelen's photograph of a group of children living in makeshift shacks: 'Hiroshima Returning to Life', <http:///www.pcf.city.hiroshima.jp/kids/KPSH_E/hiroshima_e/sadako_e/subcontents_e/12yomigaeru_1_e.html>, accessed 17 August 2015.

28 See Morris Low, 'American Photography during the Allied Occupation of Japan: The Work of John W. Bennett', *History of Photography*, vol. 39, no. 3 (2015), pp. 263, 275.

29 Tucker's photograph of the A-bomb Dome: State Library of Victoria, H2010.72/16.

30 Albert Tucker, interview with Robin Hughes, ABC Radio National program *Verbatim*, 14 February 1994, <http://www.australianbiography.gov.au/subjects/tucker/intertext3.html>, accessed 14 July 2015.

31 Susan Sontag, *Regarding the Pain of Others*, Picador, New York, 2003, p. 76. On the dynamics of witnessing and representation, see Jane Blocker, *Seeing Witness: Visuality and the Ethics of Testimony*, University of Minnesota Press, Minneapolis, 2009.

32 Roland Barthes, 'Shock-photos', in *The Eiffel Tower and Other Mythologies*, Hill and Wang, New York, 1979, p. 71.

33 Susan Sontag, *Regarding the Pain of Others*, p. 28.

34 Sontag, *Regarding the Pain of Others*, p. 89. Sontag's view has been trenchantly tackled by Susie Linfield, who argues for the genre's ability to promote empathy and, indeed, to mobilise social and political action. See Linfield, *The Cruel Radiance: Photography and Political Violence*, University of Chicago Press, Chicago, 2010.

35 Reportage of the Fukushima disaster customarily defined it by comparative reference to Hiroshima, including photo-spreads juxtaposing images from the two events. See for example 'The nightmare returns: Chilling echoes of Hiroshima's destruction in images from the aftermath of tsunami', *Daily Mail Australia*, 15 March 2011, <http://www.dailymail.co.uk/news/article-1366126/Japan-earthquake/html>, accessed 4 July 2015.

36 'Le Monde says disaster pictures weren't of Hiroshima', *New York Times*, 13 May 2008.

Elegy Written in a Dead Metropolitan Library
Corey Wakeling

Preferring the ceilings of turnpikes and mountains, stay put
for change, a coming gravitational reversal.

It's laughable season of family unity, and tempest
in the yuletide spondee: past dark.

Cheap lamentations but for pointing out the sun
by the above-ground poolside glitter Jung preserves.

What are Maida Vale dispensations, the approach like this:
\\\
the departure like that: //

the jewels, though shaken, elude the international
syndicate that had our bounty on their list? So for now

the shade, four seasons delicately rocked, the panda
breeding itself off the endangered list,

the fox, now stifled at the turnstile and chemically castrated,
beloved.

You are now all our friends, climate servile,
laughable or tempest.

My shadows come to your apartment and move your furniture for you.
It's easier tossing your furniture from the slate,

it pulverises better. I like that your telephone stand is obsolete,
it will keep my microwave company.

Maida Vale is so rude when it hears of your tranquillity,
the calm come after tragedy. How many Christmases have you

missed? Yes, all the pseudonyms we can use for you that won't sound
like euphemisms, because the apartment has relieved you

and the redundancy package is indefinite.
For service to the implacable sunshine, even the international

crime syndicate takes you off their list, my shadows steal your bike,
and Christmas has come again.

Your entombed library of undead things is screeching now.
International law shrugs. Sure, the electric wire won't mute

the screams, but Tesla would be proud of the field of shock
even Edison would feel if he tried to take a piece of this partition.

Don't they know how happy the tranquillity of the relief of catharsis
of tragedy of future of calm is, the company kept

of shadows innumerable where London delights, the tailored spines
and the tempered promise and the tapered bounty

of your super?

And so a demiurgic suspicion for the ice-land of your peace
looks sillier still when departure is prolix

and you contemplate a seaside life, if only to be the cargo
of your fugitive, the demon of chance stuttering his free advice

which is plagiarised from a lost poet's grave,
which it is my obligation to share with you here, verbatim:

burying your library confirms its tenure,
vermiform it does not ensure a future.

MAD MONKS AND THE ORDER OF THE TIN EAR

The Medievalism of Abbott's Australia

Louise D'Arcens and Clare Monagle

THE MIDDLE AGES have had a lot of bad publicity lately.

Take, for instance, *Wolf Hall*, the BBC miniseries adaptation of Hilary Mantel's Tudor novels, which appeared on Australian screens in 2015. Here the spirit of the Middle Ages is embodied in Thomas More, played with fastidious spite by Anton Lesser. In Mantel's take on Henry VIII's break with the Roman Church, More the urbane humanist is replaced by More the obdurate Catholic, whose protection of the Church's authority 'stretching back for a thousand years' is shown to be pious, sadistic and political—a triangulation that has become received shorthand for medieval. Even More's most defining quality, his conscience, is shown to be shot through with intransigence and a perverse pleasure in martyrdom. Far from being the Man for All Seasons, he has become the Man of the Past, superseded by his nemesis Thomas Cromwell, played with roguish appeal by Mark Rylance. The Machiavelli-reading Cromwell is Mantel's figure of modernity. Self-made, cosmopolitan, pragmatic and sceptical (indeed almost secular), he is less 'hammer of the monasteries' than jackhammer to the entire creaking edifice of the pre-modern.

Cromwell finds, though, that it's not so simple to erase the medieval from modern politics. Around him bristle mighty families whose power rests on ancient claims to land and title; street prophets who see the coming of the Antichrist in the regime he is brokering; and unctuous diplomats of Church and Holy Roman Empire, who circle menacingly, waiting to reverse their masters' waning fortunes. And those of us anticipating the final instalment know that that over Cromwell hangs an axe, and that his tale of incipient modernity will end with the most gruesome beheading of them all.

It's little wonder that this story has been met with acclaim in Australia, just as it has across the English-speaking world. Apart from the sheer quality of both novel and miniseries, their use of the Tudor era to depict an epochal struggle between the modern and the medieval offers an uncanny refraction of Australia's current political moment, in which commentators everywhere keep coming across the unwelcome re-emergence in the modern of 'medieval' views, institutions and practices. From the time that Tony Abbott's political star began to rise, and especially once his government took power, there's been a corresponding exponential rise in politicians and commentators condemning government policies on

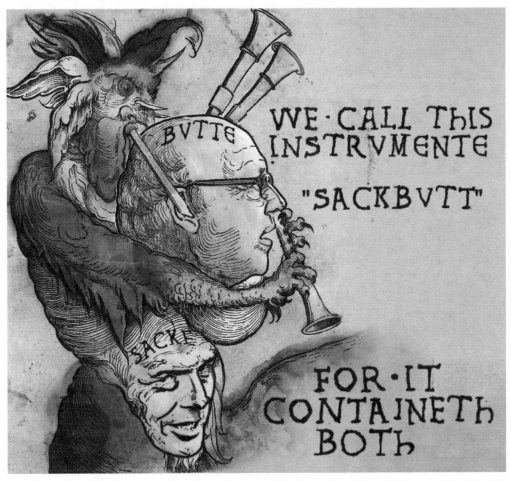

WE·CALL·THIS
INSTRVMENTE

"SACKBVTT"

FOR·IT
CONTAINETh
BOTh

Artwork courtesy of the George Brandis Live Art Experience (@artofbrandis)

climate change, marriage equality, border protection and religious education as 'feudal', 'anachronistic', 'medieval', 'dark ages', 'pre-Copernican' and 'closing the draw-bridge'. It's yet to be seen whether this will continue under the prime ministership of Malcolm Turnbull, but if Liberal MP Steve Ciobo's description of Turnbull on *Lateline* as 'a Renaissance man' is anything to go by, the epochal struggle within government ranks could well become a new theme ... or else Australia could be entering a new stage in which aggressive, Cromwellian modernity becomes a new leitmotif.

The recently deposed prime minister Abbott, whose religious past had long branded him 'the mad monk', began to be singled out for intensive medievalising in March 2014, when his revival of the 30-years-defunct honours system—an act reminiscent of Margaret Thatcher's conferral in 1983 of the first hereditary peerage in almost two decades—led to him being dubbed Australia's 'Rege Mediaevalibus'.[1] This year his seemingly unfathomable awarding of a knighthood to Prince Phillip caused an avalanche of satire depicting him as a knight, including, most amusingly, as First Knight

---

1   Rocco Fazzaro, 'Tony Abbott, rege mediaevalibus', *Age*, 27 March 2014.

of the 'Order of the Tin Ear'.[2] None of this, however, has stopped Abbott from joining the chorus characterising the actions of Islamist groups as 'medieval barbarism'.[3]

This domestic phenomenon needs to be seen in an international context, especially in the Anglophone world, since al-Qaeda's attack on the World Trade Centre on 9/11. The notable jump in allusions to the 'medieval' in Australian parliamentary records dating from that time has been matched and raised in British Hansard, while George W. Bush's call for a 'crusade' against Islamists in the immediate aftermath of 9/11 instituted a widespread public language of religious war. From that time the re-emergence of religion as a shaping force in global politics has led many to diagnose a global return to the Middle Ages. Some quarters of international relations theory, meanwhile, have predicted that a post-national 'neomedieval' world order will emerge in response to the pressures placed on the model of national sovereignty by international economic and legal organisations.[4] Economic critics, too, have seen in global capitalism a return to feudalism dominated by banker overlords who preside over a modern precariat lacking even the nominal security afforded the medieval serf by feudalism's bonds of mutual service and protection. Others, echoing the forecasts of the IR theorists, predict an eventual fragmentation and return to regional 'fiefdoms'.

In a world caught up in crazed fandom over HBO's medievalist-fantasy TV series *Game of Thrones*, for many the medieval has come to be seen as *the* political era par excellence. And Australians have not been backward in likening the revolving door of prime ministerial power to the show's treacherous dynastic politics. On the night Tony Abbott was deposed, memes circulated with his face photoshopped onto images the assassinated king Joffrey Baratheon, with Turnbull 's face superimposed onto the accused assassin Tyrion Lannister (who is, incidentally, the show's ironist and sceptic—in short its modern character). This view of *Games of Thrones* isn't just held by the pundits, but also by leaders: US President Barack Obama, British Prime Minister David Cameron and former Australian prime minister Julia Gillard have all said that the HBO series reminds them of their working lives, though only Gillard has felt the urge to tweet in Dothraki, the adopted language of the show's exiled female leader, Daenerys Targaryen.[5]

Despite being part of a global trend, the current Australian discourses of political medievalism also have a domestic pedigree, reaching back to the colonial and early federal eras, when newspapers of all stripes reached for the idiom of chivalry to evaluate the values of local politicians and statesmen. Indeed, the tradition of condemning 'medieval' prime ministers has been going for as long as we've had prime ministers: a February 1902 cartoon criticising Australia's involvement in the Boer War has the inaugural prime minister Edmund Barton dressed as a monk baptising the baby 'Commonwealth, born January 1, 1901', with 'the blud [sic] of the State Contingents'.[6] The negative depiction of the Middle Ages has

---

2   See Louise D'Arcens, 'Satire returns to the dark ages to make sense of modern machinations', *Sydney Morning Herald*, 1 February 2015.
3   See <http://www.openaustralia.org.au/debates/?id=2014-08-26.41.1>.
4   Clare Monagle, 'Sovereignty and "Neo-Mediaevalism": Hedley Bull's The Anarchical Society and International Relations Theory', in Louise D'Arcens and Andrew Lynch (eds), *International Medievalism and Popular Culture*, Cambria Press, Amherst, NY, 2014.
5   Lenore Taylor, 'Julia Gillard's Dothraki tweets translated', *Guardian Australia*, 29 May 2013.
6   *Bulletin*, 11 February 1902.

traditionally been the province of the Left; in the *Bulletin*, as the mouthpiece for federalist and Labor movements, 'medieval' was a byword for caste and barbaric despotism.[7] But this was at least partly balanced out by the Left's 'positive' medievalism, with labour unions mythologising themselves through the chivalric ideals of fraternity and service.[8] The idea that Australia's governance structures and political culture were new and yet rooted in medieval practice, as well as in 'medieval democratic' traditions such as the Anglo-Saxon folkmoot or Magna Carta, was expressed in political rituals and objects, as well as in public discourses. At the same time, prominent figures such as Melbourne's Sir Redmond Barry urged Gothic Revival as the perfect architectural idiom to express the city's political and economic ascendancy, seeing no contradiction between the Gothic's deeply religious origins and the modernist élan he wished it to express.[9]

While the colonial and early federal periods witnessed far more ambivalence and debate about the legacy bequeathed to Australia by the medieval past, this seems no longer to be the case in Australian political discourse, where the positive connotations of the medieval have all but vanished. Now it stands unilaterally for backwardness, cruelty and superstition—that is, for the opposite of the modern, for all that has apparently been superseded. The historical narrative of this supercession varies in popular consciousness: sometimes it's attributed to the Reformation, elsewhere to the emergence of the Enlightenment and scientific Reason, occasionally capitalist individualism is said to have ousted static feudalism and medieval group-think, while sometimes, less specifically, 'the Renaissance' is deemed the birthplace of the modern. Our point here is not to arbitrate between these accounts, but rather to point out that despite their discrepancies, large or small, the one truly stable element across them is the conceptual and rhetorical position of the medieval as the obverse term.

The fact that this term's usage is chiefly conceptual and rhetorical rather than properly historical becomes clear when we consider that in the vast majority of political debates where 'medieval' or its synonyms crop up, they refer to generalised and negative notions of the medieval rather than to the factual Middle Ages. To offer just one example, when Attorney-General George Brandis last year characterised the Left as 'medieval' in their rejection of climate-change scepticism, he clearly wasn't primarily concerned with whether he was accurately representing, say, the active ethos of debate within medieval Scholasticism or the robust, even adversarial, traditions of commentary fostered in medieval textual culture. Rather, by invoking the medieval as a byword for enforced unanimity he was positioning his political opponents as enemies of the post-Enlightenment values of free thought and free speech, which according to Brandis are more highly valued under the liberalism of the political Right.[10] Examples such as this proliferate in all kinds of debates across the political spectrum, with two things in common: 'medieval' could readily be replaced by any number of non-historical adjectives (in this case 'conformist',

---

7   Louise D'Arcens, *Old Songs in the Timeless Land: Medievalism in Australian Literature 1840–1910*, UWAP, Nedlands, WA, 2012, pp. 142–4.

8   Helen Hickey and Stephanie Trigg, 'Medievalism on the Streets: Tinsmiths, Knights, and the International Labour Movement', in D'Arcens and Lynch, pp. 83–105.

9   'The halls of Europe', *Age*, 10 September 1866.

10 Brendan O'Neill, 'The state should never be the arbiter of what people think': interview with George Brandis, *Spiked*, 17 April 2014.

THE ORDER OF THE TIN EAR

Illustration courtesy Jon Kudelka (@jonkudelka)

'absolutist', or Brandis's other word 'ortho-dox'); and it is virtually always intended as an insult.

But another question arises: if the medieval is everything we believe we've left behind, why is there so much talk of its return? In a world convulsed by war, inequality, oppression, religious extremism and continued intolerance towards ethnic and sexual minorities, we find ourselves contemplating the fragility of our modern myths of progress. Yet according to the logic of this reckoning, modernity and its maladies aren't seen to be the problem. Rather, for today's commentariat, as for Mantel's Thomas Cromwell (and his modern avatar, Malcolm Turnbull), the cause of the problem is the persistence of the medieval, which comes to stand for what should have been killed off but remains frustratingly, even frighteningly, revenant, the zombie that keeps coming at us despite the axe lodged in its rotting neck.

As noted earlier, the Australian figure in whom medievalism has been most insistently identified is former prime minister Abbott. This characterisation has not been limited to the Left. In his 2008 memoir, Peter Costello wrote about Abbott that he 'always saw himself as something of a romantic figure, a Don Quixote ready to take on lost causes and fight for great principles'.[11] It was perhaps inevitable when Abbott declared his aesthetic (and implicitly ideological) objection to wind farms that Costello's Quixotic Abbott would be ripe for a return; and so in June this year Rocco Fazzari, who had previously satirised Abbott as 'Rege Mediaevalibus', depicted the prime minister astride a steed, in Speedoes and bike helmet, smashing wind turbines with a lance while coal generators billow black smoke over the landscape.[12] This vision of Abbott tilting at windmills is a comedic one, and portrays him as something of a delusional knight errant living in

11   Peter Costello, *The Costello Memoirs*, Melbourne University Press, Melbourne, 2008, p. 55
12   Elizabeth Farrelly, 'Windmills can't blow away a love of the land', *Sydney Morning Herald*, 17 June 2015.

a lost Middle Ages. Looked at more closely, though, the case of Abbott shows us that medievalism as a modern phenomenon does not consist solely of the practice of arbitrarily deeming policies and practices 'medieval'. There has been a genuine strain of medievalism in contemporary Australian politics, and Abbott has been its main champion. Given what we know now about Abbott's intellectual and spiritual commitments as prime minister, it is worth pondering the extent and breadth of his medievalism. It goes much deeper than simply awarding a knighthood to Prince Philip.

As the cartoonists have rightly intuited, the concept of the knight itself does help us understand Abbott, as it corresponds directly with his Catholic and Cold War political foundations. In the same section of Costello's book, the former federal treasurer also declared that Abbott 'used to tell me proudly that he had learned all of his economics at the feet of [Catholic anti-communist activist] Bob Santamaria. I was horrified.'[13] Don Quixote and Santa, then: two crusaders who deployed a medieval imaginary of a glorious, chivalric Christendom to drive their quests. Don Quixote, of course, was seeking to protect his fantasised pure lady, his Dulcinea, and in the process ennoble himself and his vision of a glorious past. Santamaria was seeking to protect Catholicism and Australia from the ravages of both liberalism and communism, seeing the Holy Roman Church as the only international organisation capable of conquering these dark forces. Costello's marriage of Quixote and Santamaria in his description of Abbot, however comical and derisive he intended it to be, actually offers an acute insight into Abbott's desire for the Middle Ages.

Some commentators, most particularly David Marr, weighing the 'values Abbott' against the 'politics Abbott', have read the former PM ultimately as a political animal, driven by the pleasures of the fight; indeed, as libidinally pugilistic. In his rightly lauded essay Marr writes: 'The Abbott that matters is Politics Abbott … His values have never stood in his way.'[14] This Abbott is a scrappy fighter, who will do whatever it takes to gain and keep power. What this account misses, however, along with Waleed Aly's statement that '[Abbott's] political conservatism means he understands the folly of trying to recreate the past',[15] is the deep sense of the long past that underscores politics as Abbott sees it, and which has been the glue between his politics and his values. This became more apparent once he came to power, and remained conspicuous right up to his resignation speech, which concluded by invoking a historical tradition of Christian service, citing 'the first Christian service ever preached here in Australia' by Richard Johnson, which parsed the theme 'What shall I render unto the Lord for all his blessings to me?' In *Battlelines* Abbott recounted the lessons of his childhood reading about heroic figures 'in which duty and honour held the day'.[16] Abbott may well have presented to us as a devious and savvy political operator, but there is a notion of chivalric honour that has always lain beneath his political performance, one that has its eyes on a cosmic prize.

Battlelines was no glib title. It was the title of a warrior, a knight, for whom the sacred and the secular are intermingled. Crusaders were fighters, yet they understood their violence to be sanctified by the holiness of the mission. Santamaria, Abbott's earliest

---

13 Costello, *The Costello Memoirs*, p. 55.
14 David Marr, 'Political Animal: The Making of Tony Abbott', *Quarterly Essay* 47 (2012), p. 92.
15 Waleed Aly, 'Inside Tony Abbott's Mind: This Is Serious', *Monthly*, July 2013.
16 Tony Abbott, *Battlelines*, Melbourne University Press, Melbourne, 2009, p. 7.

political Godfather, was known for deploying underhand, potentially undemocratic, tactics to achieve his political ends. This could be justified, however, due to the necessity and the urgency of the cause. Abbott called Santamaria a 'political crusader', and in a Catholic context this means much more than a campaigner or an activist. Rather, the use of the term 'crusader' implies a necessary relationship between the doing of dirty deeds in the world and the achievement of sacred outcomes. What was at stake for Santamaria, and has remained so for Abbott, is nothing less than the success of Christian civilisation. Yes Abbott has ever been a political animal, but one who considers himself to have a Catholic soul engaged in a fight for human history.

In *Battlelines* Abbott declares his three key foundations to be honour, duty and Christianity. When these three concepts are imbricated they are medieval. This is not the orientalised 'medieval' in which Abbott places Islamists—a time-space some commentators have referred to as the 'mid-evil'[17]—but a distinctly European Middle Ages. Our European medieval imaginaries have two interrelated sides. On the one hand, we imagine Medieval Europe as a time of the Church, of Gothic cathedrals and great theologians. On the other, it looms as a place of romance and chivalry, of the sacred quest. In the chivalric economy, the knight is bonded to his lord through an oath of devotion. Abbott has been wedded to both forms of the Middle Ages as a source of political nourishment. When he declared Prince Philip 'a great servant of Australia' he was implicitly, and typically, venerating these medieval concepts of devotion and duty. Abbott's devotion to Cardinal George Pell, the most princely of Australian Catholics,

has also revealed a love of the monarchical and the feudal. Pell has done more than any other post–Vatican II leader in Australia to claw back the liberalising and pastoral reforms of that epochal council.

In his medievalism Abbott has been part of a larger international conservative Catholic movement that has no hesitation in playing hard politics if it means that souls will be saved and liberal pluralism overturned. John Paul II is the heroic figure here, the pope who saved the Soviet Union from its godlessness, was embraced warmly by US Republican president Ronald Reagan, and who made pro-life campaigns a clarion call for conservative Catholics. The 1980s was a crucial moment for conservative Catholics in the developed world. In places such as Australia, Canada and the United States the old sectarianism that had made Catholicism a minority with marginalised status fell away. Rather than seeing Protestants as the enemy in a sectarian turf war, conservative Catholics began to realise that they had more in common with evangelical Christians than they did with left-wing 'social justice' Catholics. And what they had in common was a passionate belief that liberty ultimately meant the freedom to worship God as one saw fit.

This is why Abbott's medievalism, his erstwhile traditional conservatism, is real and has seemed radical. His love of chivalry and of faith, that is, his medievalism, resulted in some very modern alliances. The combination of the happy-clappy evangelicalism of Scott Morrison with the 'traditional' Catholicism of Kevin Andrews would have been unthinkable 20 years ago. They could not have existed in the same party, and there is a good chance that neither of them would have found much comfort in the Liberal

---

17 See Nickolas Haydock, 'Introduction: "The Unseen Cross upon the Breast": Medievalism, Orientalism, and Discontent', in Nickolas Haydock and E.L. Risden, *Hollywood in the Holy Land: Essays on Film Depictions of the Crusades and Christian–Muslim Clashes*, McFarland, Jefferson, NC, 2009, p. 13.

Party. But in the medievalist fantasies of Abbott, in which he has been fighting ultimately for the Christian soul of Australia, he has more in common with passionate evangelical Christians than with left-leaning or progressive liberal Catholics (including his successor, Turnbull) who are comfortable with homosexuality and the legality of abortion, are not quite sure whether or not the Virgin Mary was a virgin, and do not really mind if the Eucharist is merely bread.

His vision even—or perhaps especially—departs from that of today's most prominent medievalist Catholic, Pope Francis I. In his recent encyclical *Laudato Si': On Care for Our Common Home*, Francis (whose name is in any case something of a giveaway) calls for social justice and environmental stewardship by invoking the starkly different medieval legacy of St Francis of Assisi, hero of the Italian Left. Although hagiographies of St Francis emphasise his love of the ideals of chivalry, his legendary love of nature and of the poor was matched by his unease with institutional authority and his rejection of feudal inequality. Whatever the Pontiff's limitations, his Franciscan Middle Ages remind us that medievalism need not be synonymous with conservatism. This throws into stark relief the ideological commitments underpinning Abbott's brand of medievalism.

Medievalism, as we've shown, almost always expresses more about modernity than it does about the historical Middle Ages. When we describe things as medieval, for better or for worse, we are usually casting the period and its practices as being in opposition to the present. Hence we have become used to seeing forms of fundamentalism and terrorist violence described as medieval, in as much as they seem other to ourselves, and we must place them outside time. For Abbott the Middle Ages have offered an antidote to modernity, a happily illiberal time of Church, monarchy and chivalry. This is the logic in which Prince Philip's knighthood—an anathema to Catholics on the Left—makes some sense. It is a way of speaking to a past of hierarchy, loyalty and institutionality, as Abbott sees it. While for Thomas More such a collusion would have been impossible, the Protestant–Catholic divide, as corrosive as it once was, obtains no more in the medievalist framework of Abbott's cabinet. What has mattered more for Abbott, and for much of his cabinet, is a commitment to the shared Western Christian values that makes politics a servant of God. Whether this will continue, or how it will be managed, in Malcolm Turnbull's cabinet is a story still unfolding. But between the flurry of allusions to him as 'Machiavellian', the fulminations of the pro-Abbott shock-jocks, and reports of resentful plotting among the conservatives in his government, Turnbull has never seemed more like Mantel's Cromwell who, readers will remember, is haunted always by More's downfall. If Turnbull himself is aware of the parallel, he can only hope that he is able to bind his enemies close ... and that if there are any changes of leadership ahead, the instrument is the ballot box and not the executioner's blade. •

Louise D'Arcens is Professor and ARC Future Fellow in English Literatures, University of Wollongong. She has written and edited five books on medievalism, including the forthcoming *The Cambridge Companion to Medievalism* (2016).

Clare Monagle is an intellectual historian who works on medieval thought and medievalism in contemporary political thought. Her current project is titled 'Sexing Scholasticism', and will offer a feminist reading of medieval theology.

A WORD IN YOUR EAR

The speech is the poetry of politics

Joel Deane

MOST DAYS MY DOG Berkeley, a black labrador–cocker spaniel cross, takes me for a walk. If there's time to kill, we weave through the 1960s-era suburban streets of Doncaster and follow an underarm of greenery that runs beneath the shoulder of the Eastern Freeway. If Berkeley and I are full of beans, we run to the freeway and back—a circuit just shy of five kilometres—although we've never mastered the heartbreak hill that is High Street. If time is tight, or I'm lazy, we amble to the oval at the end of my street, where Berkeley sniffs the backsides of my neighbours' dogs for 20 minutes then announces she's ready to return home by crapping in the grass beside the concrete cricket pitch.

The day Keith Sinclair popped into my head was a lazy day. Berkeley was working her way towards the concrete cricket pitch while I walked laps, listening to the *New Yorker Poetry* podcast (I know he's not Scottish, but Paul Muldoon sounds like the poetry world's answer to Sean Connery) and gazing at the craggy outline of Melbourne's CBD to the west.

I wasn't thinking about anything at all, and then I was thinking about Keith Sinclair in particular. This surprised me. After all, Sinclair had been dead for 20 years and I'd never met him nor read a word he'd written. All I knew, from a Claude Forell obituary, was that, as an editor, Sinclair 'seemed an aloof, forbidding figure to many young reporters, but he was courteous and kind to those who worked closely with him'. Why, then, did Sinclair's name keep floating out of my subconscious?

The answer was easy to divine. Sinclair, like me, had served time as a political speechwriter. Of course, the old boy had done more than crank out speeches for the duration of his four score years and one. He served in Bomber Command over the skies of Europe during the Second World War, rose to the pinnacle of his profession as the editor of the *Age*, and was a husband and a father. But what I'd stumbled upon during a researching sortie for some long-forgotten speech was that Sinclair had also become—at the age of 53—the first speechwriter to work for an Australian prime minister.

Graham Freudenberg—speechwriter for a litter of Labor leaders beginning with Arthur Calwell—may well have found Canberra first, but Sinclair beat him to the PM's office, qualifying the former *Age* editor as the first man of prime ministerial letters. Sinclair's PM was Harold Holt—a leader remembered more for dying in office than linguistic calisthenics—although, to be fair, two Holt one-liners have stood the test of time: his genuflection to US president Lyndon B. Johnson over the Vietnam Way ('All the way with LBJ'), and what were supposedly his last words before disappearing into the surf at Cheviot Beach ('I know this beach like the back of my hand').

Walking laps of the oval, I toyed with the notion of establishing a luncheon party of superannuated political speechwriters. We could eat yum cha in Little Bourke Street once a month and call ourselves the Keith Sinclair Society. Membership would be by invitation only, like the Melbourne Club, only without the chauvinism or financial security or social status, because sophistry, much like prostitution, is an ancient profession without gold or glory.

Still, I keep bumping into people who think otherwise. I've been out of politics since 2009 and have cranked out books of poetry, fiction and nonfiction, but what most people are both repulsed and fascinated by is the main game: politics. As a consequence, if people want to talk to me about anything it's usually speechwriting or politics.

One of the first questions I'm usually asked is: How did you become a speech-writer? The honest answer to that question is: Fucked if I know. That's because speechwriting is a strange, nebulous way to make a living. There's no university course, no training, no secret handshake. You're asked to write something for someone else to say to a roomful of strangers about, say, the economy. Or a town. Or a suburb. Or a new factory or building or bridge.

You might have a week to come up with something. Or a day. Or a few hours. So the speechwriter will sit in his or her office and google random dates, names and places. And bivouac in the Parliamentary Library, sniffing at old books the way my dog sniffs at stale turds. And they'll sit in a café and drink a coffee and doodle with their favourite pen.

They'll procrastinate and read the paper or text their boyfriend or girlfriend. And, maybe, with a deadline looming, they'll panic and cocoon themselves in their office and, surrounded by a crater of papers and books, bang out a piece of oratory wallpaper, then print out the mess and rush down to the leader's office and leave it in the in-tray of his or her executive assistant. Then they'll wait. And, perhaps, fingers crossed, the somebody they're writing about something for will like what they've written well enough that they won't have to go back to square one and write something else. The next day they'll be asked to go through the same process again. That, in a nutshell, is the life of a speechwriter.

Living such a solitary and subterranean life does strange things to the human spirit. If you don't believe me, consider the career trajectories former political speechwriters. Some drink too much (we all know his name). Some become radio shock jocks (Alan Jones). Some become prime minister (Tony Abbott). Others become fixated on names such as 'Keith Sinclair' and words like 'conflagration'.

I was the kind of speechwriter who became fixated. My conflagration fetish occurred during my second year as the chief speechwriter for Steve Bracks, the former premier of Victoria. 'Conflagration' came into my head—like Keith Sinclair's name—and refused to leave, demanding that I find it a home. So I did.

I engineered a line into a draft of a Bracks speech, scheduled to be delivered to a roomful of Melbourne businessmen, left the offending item in the in-tray of the premier's executive assistant, and started working on another speech that would be free of the con-flagration fixation. My conflagration speech didn't bounce back to my desk demanding amendment. It was accepted as written. And then the day came for the delivery of the conflagration speech.

To understand what happened next it's important to understand the ways different people speak. Some people breathe deeply and are therefore able to deliver long, convoluted sentences. John Thwaites, the then deputy premier of Victoria, was like that. As a consequence, when I wrote a speech for Thwaites I usually installed a few verbal chicanes—a long, convoluted sentence with a hydra of ideas and images he would have to slow down and savour to properly deliver, followed by a short, sharp statement where he could put his foot to the floor. Steve Bracks was a shallow breather. That meant complicated sentence structures were a no-no. Instead, I usually built momentum through a succession of short sentences connected by the repetition of words or phrases (anaphora is the fancy word for this technique) that either ascended or descended to a unifying thought or image or aphorism. I enjoyed writing in this way for Bracks. It came naturally to me and felt, at times, close to poetry in manner if not matter. And it suited his preference for big-picture storytelling.

Bracks had a reputation as a poor public speaker, but I thought differently. Most politicians sound like someone else. If you listen hard you can usually hear the cadence of the person who influenced them most, the former politician whom, consciously or unconsciously, they're mimicking. Bracks, though, only ever sounded like himself. He may have swallowed the odd word or mangled the occasional sentence or strangled the name of golfer Ernie Els so that his surname sounded like *Eels*, but none of that mattered. What mattered was he sounded like a real person instead of a robot.

A robot would have made a better fist of conflagration. I must have known this. Must have known in my heart of hearts that I'd booby-trapped the premier's speech by embedding 'conflagration' in its body, but I was so fixated on the word I couldn't admit my error. So I did nothing. Instead of attending the luncheon and witnessing the carnage I stayed at my desk, writing yet another speech.

The premier's chief of staff, Tim Pallas, did make it to the lunch. Pallas—a rolly polly former unionist who went on to become a politician himself—didn't usually visit my office. On this day he made an exception after witnessing the premier deliver the conflagration speech. Rather than walk into the premier's private office and take a right up a driveway of racing green carpet to his palatial office, the COS took a left and motored down to my paper cave. Pallas stood in front of my desk and said, 'I just want you to know that the premier gave "conflagration" a red-hot go.' And then he walked back out again. Not another word was spoken.

Needless to say, the offending word never found its way into another Steve Bracks speech, although when, a few years later, Pallas asked me to help him write his maiden speech as a parliamentarian I did insert 'conflagration' into my first draft.

I mostly loved working as a political speechwriter. Loved it because the job combined two of my passions: politics and poetry. The career path that led me to speechwriting—if you can call the goat track I took such a thing—was tangled and reaches back into my childhood. I grew up in an Irish Catholic family. We were ex-Labor, part of the tribe of right-wing Catholics that split from the Australian Labor Party in the 1950s, supported the Democratic Labor Party then, gradually, migrated to the Liberal Party.

What stopped me from becoming a conservative was poetry. You see, I attended a few Young Liberal meetings as a teenager, but decided it wasn't for me. Poetry was for me. Having decided I was going to be a poet, I took the next illogical step and quit studying. This was during my final year of high school. Instead of writing essays, I filled up an exercise book with doggerel. Needless to say, by the time my October exams rolled around I was failing half of my subjects. At one stage I was dragged into an office by a teacher I liked, Mrs Hollingsworth, who demanded to know what drugs I was taking. I told her my drug of choice was the poetry of Emily Dickinson.

I stopped writing poetry long enough to weasel through high school and land a job at the *Sun News-Pictorial* in Melbourne as a copy boy. After that I began following the goat track towards politics. By the time I was 18 I was working as a crime reporter at the *Sun*. Three years later I was covering the 1990 federal election in Canberra and shortly after that I was departmental speechwriting for the health minister in the run up to the 1992 state election. By the time I was 26, I was press secretary to the then leader of the state opposition, John Brumby. A year later I was living in San Francisco and working as a TV and internet producer—and covering the 2000 US presidential election. By the time I was 31, I was back in Melbourne working as press secretary to the attorney-general, Rob Hulls.

All the while I kept writing poetry, some good, some bad. It wasn't until 2004 that all those poems would start to come in handy, politically speaking. By the middle of that year Bracks had been premier for almost five years. He'd also burned through four speechwriters and was looking for a fifth. I didn't volunteer for the job—I was too busy writing poetry in my spare time—but, when possible candidates were being bandied about, my name was put forward by a fellow press secretary, Ben Hart. The reason Hart suggested me was that I had published poetry, which suggested I might have a facility with words.

I was called up to the premier's office for a meeting. Bracks asked me a few questions and asked me to write a speech. And, just like that, I became his chief speechwriter. In other words, poetry made me a political speechwriter.

That's not to say speechwriting was all about the words. What drew me to politics to begin with was a belief in participatory democracy: the conviction that, unless I was involved, I was in no position to complain; and the realisation that, as Cicero once wrote, you can't choose your time and place to get involved. To quote the great Roman orator: 'The opportunity of rescuing the country, whatever the dangers that threaten it, does not come suddenly or when you wish it, but only when you are in a position which allows you to do so.'

> I was the kind of speechwriter who became fixated. My conflagration fetish occurred during my second year as the chief speechwriter for Steve Bracks.

It's as Camus said: time does not belong to us, we belong to it. That means circumstances not only define us, they choose us. Political speechwriting chose and defined me and I, in return, chose political speechwriting because I believed I should make a contribution and thought the language of ideas was the best way in which I could make a meaningful one.

As for the work itself, my life as a poet was perfect training for politics. That's because, at its best, speechwriting is writing for performance. It is the spoken, not the written, word. You are writing to be heard, not read. You must therefore use language that has punch and verve. You must therefore use rhythm. You must be awake to the sounds different words make when you bang them together. And you must tell a story—something that encompasses past, present, future; where we come from, where we are, where we're headed—because stories are what people remember.

I'm not saying speeches are poetry. I don't buy what Shelley once wrote in his essay 'A Defence of Poetry' that 'poets are the unacknowledged legislators of the world'. Shelley obviously never read the Crimes Act, because it's more like Leviticus than Philip Larkin. As for me, I think the late Peter Porter was closer to the mark when he called poets 'politicians of the printed page'. However, the best speeches can approach poetry. To achieve that, speeches must do more than parrot junk phrases or bureaucratic babble or the latest sound bites: speeches that fall into those traps come off sounding like bad rap songs. They must, to paraphrase the poet William Carlos Williams, become machines made of words that are able to transport the language and the listener.

Language is the root of our democracy—and demagoguery—because words define public affairs and words can be recalibrated to say just about anything. You see, language is not concrete. Is not black and white. Language is an identikit of words stuck together to try to represent a position that is—at its primal cognitive level—organic rather than linguistic. That is why language is, as writer Eva Hoffman has said, the 'hob-goblin of abstraction'; or, as the poet George Szirtes has said, 'the thin skin of ice over a fathomless pond with its black bed. With dark above and dark below.'

Language is not solid. It is not the raw material from which the three little pigs would choose to build a house. At best it is an avatar that offers the barest inkling of the dark, speechless matter that shimmies around inside us all. Language may well be a thin skin of ice over darkness, as Szirtes said.

And a poem or speech should 'like a piece of ice on a hot stove … ride on its own melting', as the poet Robert Frost said, but without that ice there is only darkness.

Language is flawed, but remains the means by which we can approach consensus, if not truth; and that is why speeches matter—at their best, they can illuminate the darkness. All of which goes to the heart of what makes speechwriting a nebulous endeavour.

Finding the right words is difficult enough when you are writing in your own voice. Try writing in the voice of someone else. That requires imaginative projection. The speechwriter has to place him or herself in the shoes of the person delivering the speech—picture the audience they will be speaking to—and speak to that audience in the words of the speechmaker. Not the speechwriter's words; the politician's words.

That's why, ideally, the person writing and the person talking are breathing the same air, thinking the same thoughts and speaking the same language. Simpatico of that kind is hard to attain and harder to hold onto. I can't tell you how to attain simpatico, but I can tell you what it feels like. It feels like when you're trying to solve a 3-D wooden puzzle in the dark, and there's only one right way, and you have to fumble and feel your way around until the pieces click into place. And when they do, it feels a lot like poetry. •

Joel Deane is a poet, novelist, journalist and speechwriter. His most recent book is *Catch and Kill: The Politics of Power* (UQP, 2015).

Shit-Lips, Cat-Knackers and The-Dog-Fondler

Warwick Newnham

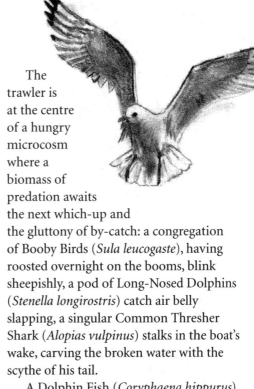

> *Bliss* was it in that dawn to be *alive*,
> But to be young was very heaven!
> —Wordsworth

Flying fish

Beaufort wind scale: 0. Mean wind speed: 0. Limits of wind speed >1. Wind descriptive terms: Calm. Probable maximum wave height in metres: –. Sea state: 0. Sea descriptive terms: glass

Scott Reef in the morning and as the sun begins his haul upwards fixt upon the zenith the sea is glass coruscations of red reflected iron ore deposits in the Kimberly. Dawn is magnificent. The ocean is stilled like opal opulence save for the wake astern a lone trawler as she ploughs her way along the contours of the Nor-West Shelf. Mackerel skies are reflected, ruddy refractions of the dawn's early light.

Frigatebirds (*Fregata ariel*) slowly circulate the heaven. They ride the thermals circling the trawler and scream to each other. They fall down to the ocean and re-ascend on the thermal until almost the very Eye of God before falling again from the sky. They swoop the boat's wake screaming and then ride the thermal rising higher and higher until mere specks in the sky.

The trawler is at the centre of a hungry microcosm where a biomass of predation awaits the next which-up and the gluttony of by-catch: a congregation of Booby Birds (*Sula leucogaste*), having roosted overnight on the booms, blink sheepishly, a pod of Long-Nosed Dolphins (*Stenella longirostris*) catch air belly slapping, a singular Common Thresher Shark (*Alopias vulpinus*) stalks in the boat's wake, carving the broken water with the scythe of his tail.

A Dolphin Fish (*Coryphaena hippurus*) male and bull-headed like a bullet herds an air armada of Flying Fish (*Cheilopogon olgae*) from aquaria to aqueous. Fish take flight in salvos, prolonging flight in ricocheting skips along the oceans glass. The Dolphin Fish traces their trajectories, aiming for the next and final splash and prey. One Flying Fish, more avian perhaps than others, more agile in flight when frightened, launches himself like Icarus towards the sun: it takes flight and …

Shit-Lips, Cat-Knackers and The-Dog-Fondler

Three youths sheltered in the inboard lee of the poop deck, behind the sorting trays where they could not be seen, and smoked illicit cigarettes. The Skipper (*Arse-Hole*) had decided to give up smoking and there-for all smoking had been banned.

They are callow with youth and Play-Station; unused to work. They range in age from 16 to 20. They have spots and facial hair ranging from fluff to tufts of bristles. They are pasty, ill exercised and unsuited to the rigours of a life at sea and yet they come of their own will, drawn to whatever lure the sea held for them.

They pass around a desultory cigarette; a hidden rebellion, an act of defiance in face of what they perceived as tyranny on the high seas: a cruel and unusual punishment. On boarding the vessel they had been awarded nicknames for the trip, as The Skipper said they needed their sea names or else they would never gain their sea legs and be able to stand up in the storm: Shit-Lips, Cat-Knackers and The-Dog-Fondler.

'Shit-Lips: shy one, eh? Don't say shit, eh? Shit-Lips!'

'Cat-Knackers: a fookin' cat's got more hair on its ball-bag than you got on your chin, son!'

'The-Dog-Fondler: his parents bred greyhounds. The name was awarded after a conversation regarding stud breeding techniques.'

As they pass around a desultory cigarette, a Flying Fish (*Cheilopogon olgae*), more avian, more agile when frightened, launches itself towards the sun, taking flight and easily clearing the gunnels. The fish crash-lands amid the three youths. They are startled by the sudden explosion of rainbow scales and dragon-fly wings beating upon the steel deck. They ditch their cigarettes and lighters over-board for deniability,

fearful like school-boys caught smoking behind the shelter shed by the head-master. When nobody appears the youths are taken with the notion that The Skipper (*Arse-Hole*) had somehow thrown the fish at them.

The-Dog-Fondler: 'The cunt is throwing fucking fish at us now: arse-hole!'

The Flying Fish beats itself insensate in a welter of pea-cock scale and mucus as the heat transferred through the steel deck from the engine-room desiccates. It flops slower and less and then stops completely, mouthing silent fish prayers for release.

The Skipper

Beaufort wind scale: 5. Mean wind speed: 10. Limits of wind speed >13. Wind descriptive terms: Fresh breeze. Probable maximum wave height in metres: 2.5. Sea state: moderate. Sea descriptive terms: whitecaps, spray

The Skipper (*Arse-Hole*) takes the afternoon watch as per usual; the wind blows up in the afternoons and he likes to be on the helm through the afternoon and evening when the sun is less in his eyes. He has had little sleep in the past six days since leaving port. He has been catching steadily, profitably and with an almost full green crew save his engineer many hours have been spent on deck breaking them in. He half dozes in the chair with the afternoon sun slowly setting abaft and abeam his left shoulder as he trawls the afternoon shot to the nor-east, away from the sun and quarter to the rising swell. A lit cigarette smoulders, trapped between two fingers in a closed fist held in place by crossed arms. It is an ad-hoc yet well-practised guard against sleep proper with burnt fingers a wake-up.

He can hear the three youths whispering urgently to each other in the galley. He has seen the 'look' in their eyes and he knows what to expect; he's done this a hundred times or more: pasty youths, ill exercised and unsuited to the rigours of a life at sea. The youth he has named 'The-Dog-Fondler' has drawn the short straw.

The Skipper (*Arse-Hole*) says, 'Come on then … out with it!'

The youth blushes and stammers.

The Skipper (*Arse-Hole*) says: 'Le' me just check I got this right. You want to get off? You speak for the other two? And the reason you want to get off is that, and I am quoting you here: we're just not enjoying it as much as we thought?'

The youth blushes and, stammering assent, nods.

The Skipper (*Arse-Hole*) says: 'Je'S'us' fucking Christ. The fucken' things I gotta do …'

The contract

The Skipper (*Arse-Hole*) orders the youths out of his fucking wheel-house to wait for him in the galley. The youths comply quickly and not without some anxiety; The Skipper (*Arse-Hole*) is Old-School, 'Nam. Imposing, a fright. They assemble stood-to.

The Skipper (*Arse-Hole*) appears with share fishing agreements in hand; he says: 'Je'S'us' fucking Christ … Sit down for fuck's sake! Here you are: Contracts. One signed by each of you. One for Shit-Lips. Ahh. Cat-Knackers, and for you, Dog-Fondler. One for you too. Do you all see your own signatures?'

The youths all nod, eyes down they won't look up, they can't: he is the very devil to them at this moment; The Skipper (*Arse-Hole*) waits to see if they would make this easy for him, if they would dare to lift their eyes in defiance and peek at the apparition of their night terrors: The Skipper (*Arse-Hole*) enraged.

The Skipper (*Arse-Hole*) says: Je'S'us' fucking Christ … the fucken' things I gotta do. Turn to page … page 11; clause 11.3 paragraph B. Let me read it to you, just in case there are any literacy issues here:

'Cessation of duties as a partner. Any partner who wishes to end their participation in the enterprise shall, Except in that of the cases outlined in paragraph C, give two weeks notice at the minimum. Paragraph C states exceptional circumstances as: death; injury; illness; family emergency. Hmm. Just not enjoying it as much as we thought? No. With me so far?'

The youths all nod, eyes down.

Syaw
Erin Shiel

After Regina Wilson, 'Syaw (Fish Net)', 2005

It takes more than one day to weave a syaw
to catch a prawn's swimmerets, or the fin of a fish.
Time finds the gaps we've tried to ignore.

Over and under, over and under, the net forms.
Our mesh must be fine to trap a floating wish.
It takes more than one day to weave a syaw.

Some years it's easy to weave more and more,
yet some years we struggle with one loose stitch.
Time finds the gaps we've tried to ignore.

Some nets have patches and don't hide their flaws.
Other nets' seams have been sutured to vanish.
It takes more than one day to weave a syaw.

A net woven carelessly leaves an open door.
It's not just for fun, no net means no fish.
Time finds the gaps we've tried to ignore.

We strip the pinbin vine to weave the core
of days that form the years we cherish.
It takes more than one day to weave a syaw.
Time finds the gaps we've tried to ignore.

Note: A syaw is a fishing net in the language of the Ngangikurrungurr people.

The Skipper (*Arse-Hole*) continues: 'Paragraph D, immediate cessation of part-nership other than described in paragraph C: 'Any partner who insists on an immediate dissolution of partnership, other than as described in paragraph C is liable for all costs associated with the facilitation of the immediate dissolution of the partnership including though not limited to fuel, berthage costs, replacement crew transporta-tion costs. Etcetera. Etcetera. With me?'

The youths all nod.

'So let us count the costs for getting off immediately. I assume that's what you meant isn't it? You've all had enough and you want to go home now?'

The youths nod.

'Mmm. 'Fuel. Three days from Dampier … 2.5 tonne of fuel per 24-hour operation is seven and a half tonnes of fuel by 0.87 specific gravity to get literage is—mmm—rough, rough, 10,000 litres at—well Dampier is one of the most expensive ports for fuel too, so let's call it dollar 80 for the fuel—is, what's that, 18 grand? So 18 plus your airfare and the airfare of your replacement from Dampier to Perth, 800 or so, for two is 1600. Plus stores, berthage … Do you know what it costs per day to tie up alongside the wharf? It is $2000 a day. Expensive parking bill isn't it?'

They nod.

The Skipper (*Arse-Hole*) continues: 'So are you telling me you want to get off now, with all of these costs or would you rather finish the trip like men so that you could say you went out there and did it, didn't like it but did your time as an upright partner and finished the trip and unloaded and got paid? Up to you: but if you want to get off now it will cost you.'

The Squall
Beaufort wind scale: 7. Mean wind speed: 29. Limits of wind speed >33. Wind descriptive terms: Near gale. Probable maximum wave height in metres: 5.5. Sea state: heaped. Sea descriptive terms: breaking waves

The Skipper (*Arse-Hole*) had planned to take the shot off and (finally) get some rack, but with a mini mutiny to quell and an early evening squall complete with lightning striking the water all around as the sea heaps up in confusion he continues to man the helm and trawl stern-to the weather until it subsides. He plays his wheel-house stereo loudly, all country with the Red-Headed Stranger and Townes-Van-Sandt. It is not his first rodeo, not even nearly.

He switches off all the radios, satellite phones and any navigational equipment requiring ariels or powered operation for fear of lightning strike. He checked his nav-lights as operational and killed the deck-lights to better enjoy the show as all around him opened up in neon blue sheet flashes. The heavy ozone stench of vaporised seawater permeates.

A congregation of Booby Birds (*Sula leucogaste*) flock around the trawler searching for a safe haven against the storm and they crash-land on the foredeck and huddle against the leeward bulkheads cawing and calling to each other for reassurance. The Skipper (*Arse-Hole*) laughs as their number builds and birds continue to crash-land in explosions of feathers and raucous calls. He braves the squall to shoo at the birds on the bow, screaming their call at them and waving his arms until the congregation, spooked and shooed, take wing; they circle the wheel house in a vortex of dark beating wings and screams.

The Skipper (*Arse-Hole*) laughs and laughs and laughs.

The vessel trawls on, quartering a stern swell, Hauling-the-Trawling until the squall moves on and away with the lightning show disappearing over the horizon line. With the wind's abatement the sea begins to settle with the white caps less frequent and smaller, more orderly, more easily navigated.

A pod of Long-Nosed Dolphins (*Stenella longirostris*) catch air belly slapping, launching themselves at the faces of the swell like torpedos, revelling in flight.

The Skipper (*Arse-Hole*) dozes in the chair as he trawls the shot out to the nor-east, away from the weather and quarter-to the settling swell.

Breakfast

Beaufort wind scale: 0. Mean wind speed: 0. Limits of wind speed >1. Wind descriptive terms: Calm. Probable maximum wave height in metres: –. Sea state: 0. Sea descriptive terms: calm (glassy)

The Skipper (*Arse-Hole*) hauls the trawl through to the crack of dawn and then rouses the crew and begins winch-up. He asks the engineer to operate the winches as the hypnotic roll of the wire on drum is soporific and tired as he is it is unsafe for him to do it. The Skipper (*Arse-Hole*) cat-naps on the wheel-house floor; power-sleeping for 40 minutes as the hydraulics hum and vibrate and the strain runs through the wire and down to the deep where a hungry microcosm, a biomass of predation awaits the next which-up and the gluttony of by-catch.

Haul trawled, The Skipper (*Arse-Hole*) asks the engineer to operate the lazy-line winches; The Skipper (*Arse-Hole*) wants to spill the bags himself, to see if he should seek out fresher pastures where the scab of life is thicker, less trafficked: more profitable.

The shot proves meagre with the weather from the squall held responsible.

The Skipper (*Arse-Hole*) decides to steam south towards Rollie Shoal. He leaves the crew to their duties and sees to the morning meal: bacon and sausage and beans, eggs on toast and coffee. The crew put the meagre shot away quickly and are called in to wash up for breakfast. The engineer leaves the helm to the open miles of empty ocean and descends from the wheel-house via the hatch for his share of the morning meal.

The Skipper (*Arse-Hole*) is tired with a delirium of hilarity and jokes, laughs and joshes with his boys as he serves them breakfast in man-sized serves. They are told, 'Get that into ya' and 'put some meat on your bones' and 'two, four, six, eight, bog in: don't wait!' He jokes with the engineer and they swap tales of school days and compare punishments with expiations and detentions and 'the Cuts'. The youths are horrified and voice their disapproval:

S.L: 'What?'

C.K: 'They hit you?'

D.F: 'And there was nothing you could do about it?'

The Skipper (*Arse-Hole*) is tired with a delirium of hilarity. He jokes and laughs, laughs and jokes and joshes with his boys until tiredness finally takes him to his cabin and sleep. The engineer retakes the helm as the crew clean the galley and the trawler steams south, trailing birds like kites in the morning sun. ●

WJP Newnham's work has been published in *Nocturnal Submissions*, *Overland*, the *Lifted Brow*, *Meanjin*, *Full of Crow* and *Gapped Tooth Madness* among others. His new story 'Merry-Crack-Mass', published by <http://www.inshortpublishing.com>, will be available soon. He lives in Brisbane with his partner and two blue heelers.

SINKING IN THE SUBLIME

The wreck of the SS *Admella* resonated in colonial South Australia's art and soul

Stephen Valambras Graham

THE FINAL RESTING PLACE of Henry Holbrook, a young man of 'most exemplary character' as his obituary in the Adelaide *Advertiser* reported, lies in the shadow of a cypress tree. The address is:

Plot 7W,
Road 1 South,
West Terrace Cemetery,
Adelaide.

The body had been returned by boat to his home city from where it had washed up near Cape Banks, close to the Victorian border. Holbrook was one of 89 victims when the SS *Admella* came to grief on Carpenter Rocks on 6 August 1859. Throngs attended his funeral on 30 November, an occasion for the local community to express its collective sympathy since, as the newspapers of the day pointed out, his remains were the only ones returned to Adelaide from the scene of the wreck, explaining the crowded funeral for one young man and the city's 'unusual interest … in this mournful solemnity'. I knelt down, peering in the eroding light, at the words engraved on Holbrook's headstone.

No marble marks thy couch
of lonely sleep,
But living statues there are
seen to weep.

The lines are from Lord Byron's 'Epitaph on a Beloved Friend', a poem from his early collection *Hours of Idleness*. The couplet was not uncommon on graves of the period, for 'Byromania', the cult of this most seductive literary celebrity, was still in vogue. Byron went on to write *Don Juan* and in the celebrated Canto II we can read a vivid description of shipwreck and the gruesome plight of the crew. Don Juan was the sole survivor; Henry Holbrook did not share his good fortune.

Holbrook boarded the *Admella,* a steamship bound for Melbourne, at Port Adelaide, on the morning of Friday 5 August 1859. A well-educated man of 25, he worked for a firm of wholesale druggists, and was travelling to London via Melbourne on commercial business. Conflicting reports surround the circumstances of Holbrook's death. According to contemporary accounts, he was swept overboard by the heavy rolling of the ship when it rubbed up against the reef early on the morning of 6 August. Ian Mudie, in his account of the disaster, *Wreck of the Admella*, published in 1966, moved the timing of his death to the following Wednesday afternoon. According to the testimony of cabin boy George Ward, Holbrook, in a state of extreme exhaustion and discomfort, was swept out to sea by the 'boiling surf and bounding spray',

The Admella wrecked, Cape Banks, 6th August, 1859, by James Shaw, 1859
Art Gallery of South Australia, Adelaide

as Byron expressed it in *Don Juan*, breaking over the stern deck, while he was trying to adjust his body and momentarily relaxed his hold. The swell carried him off; the crests of the waves like white roses blooming in his wake. He had been holding on for five days and nights.

While shipwrecks accounted for far fewer deaths at sea than disease and sickness, their grip on the popular imagination was strong. Ignorance of the technical capacity of ships increased passengers' sense of vulnerability on long sea voyages. Despite this, the *Admella*, built in the shipyards of Glasgow only two years earlier, had a glowing reputation, especially owing to its coal-fired steam engines and screw-propeller. She was a fast, modern steamer. One local observer admired the ship on her voyage down the Gulf St Vincent the day before she split asunder: 'the *Admella* was rapidly approaching us, with the early morning ray upon her hull and

sails, white funnel, and her peculiarly fresh appearance. I had seldom seen a prettier object. The steamer, trim, buoyant, swift … the triumph of human intelligence.'

Carrying 87 passengers and 26 crew, with a cargo of copper, flour for the Victorian goldfields and three champion racehorses, the sleeping ship ran onto the submerged rocks at five in the morning. Seconds later the swell lifted her up, bringing her down hard on the reef. It is unclear why the steamer was driven off course, running so close to the coast; most probably due to strong currents or magnetic interference with the compasses. Two of the lifeboats that could have been used to ferry passengers to safety were damaged as the masts snapped and the funnel collapsed. Another was swamped and drifted loose. In the tumult, an attempt was made to salvage the boat, but without success. A brave volunteer, the young Danish sailor Soren Holm, managed to reach it. Holm made a sign to the crew on board to pull on the ropes that had been tied to his body and that in turn he attached to the boat. A knot made along its length loosened and he came adrift. The rescue boat, with his lifeless body on board, was washed up on shore days later.

With rollers crashing over the bulwarks in the dawn light and heavy winter fog, the engines stopped, the ship breaking up, the three lifeboats all lost, the scene suddenly turned wretched. Several attempts were made over the next few days to reach the beach and safety. Only Robert Knapman and John Leach made land. After hours at sea battling the currents and backwash, the two accomplished seamen, who had lashed themselves to a makeshift raft cut from the boom with a meat chopper, reached the shore near Cape Northumberland. They dragged themselves 30 kilometres through the night, arriving at the lighthouse manned by Ben Germein as morning broke, three days after the wreck.

The *Admella* disaster held a particular fascination in the colonies of Victoria and South Australia. An intercolonial steamer, it carried passengers between Adelaide and Melbourne. Those departing on the fatal voyage had ties to this region of Australia, through family, friends, business and acquaintances. Moreover, the devastating and protracted nature of the catastrophe supplied content for an uninterrupted stream of telegraph dispatches 'borne on the flashing wire', as George French Angas wrote in his *Admella* poem, feeding a sustained media frenzy in both cities.

The telegraph connecting Adelaide and Melbourne had been completed only a year earlier. For the first time messages could be exchanged between distant centres in the space of minutes. When a messenger on horseback arrived at Mount Gambier from the Cape Northumberland lighthouse with word of the *Admella* disaster, news was sent via telegraph to Adelaide and to Melbourne.

The impact was profound and immediate. The two morning Adelaide papers, the *Advertiser* and *South Australian Register*, brought out extraordinary editions the same day. Business-as-usual came to a standstill. Parliament was adjourned, auctions suspended, trading cancelled. For a week, all interest focused on the agonising events playing out on the broken shell of the *Admella*, still visible from the beaches facing the reef. Regular updates arrived through the week. Necessarily fragmented and often conflicting, telegraphic exchanges nevertheless mediated and united the colonial populace in a collective expression of loss and of sympathy. Like a nineteenth-century Twitter feed, telegrams were dispatched to the two cities day and night: 'Fearful surf around the wreck'; 'Some recognised'; 'No more bodies found'; 'We entertain no hope of saving the few survivors'; 'More in a few minutes'. The public, in a state of lingering uncertainty 'of alternate hope and fear', hungry for each fresh detail regarding the mounting column of dead and the diminishing list of survivors, devoured the breaking news received at the telegraph exchange.

Over eight days the seamen and passengers on the steamer experienced hunger, thirst, constant exposure and extreme fatigue while clinging or tied to the battered stern, the only portion of the *Admella* remaining above the waterline. Many were thrown overboard into the churning seas with no hope of climbing back onto the wreckage; many became delirious, unable to resist the temptation of drinking seawater to drive away their thirst and, like in *Don Juan*:

> leap'd overboard with dreadful yell,
> As eager to anticipate their grave;
> And the sea yawn'd around her like a hell

Others simply let go, slipping quietly into the welcoming white embrace of the ocean, unable to endure the deprivation and the suffering. Of the 113 passengers and crew, only 24 survived. All of the children on board and all of the women, save one, died on the reef. 'The dead and dying side by side recline', wrote James Shaw, 'upon the splintering deck.'

The Sublime and colonial tastemakers

James Frederic Johnstone, who participated in the rescue attempts, gives us a dramatic image of his first glimpse of the survivors marooned on the wreck:

> Huddled together, staring at us with pitiful looks … more like statues than human beings; their eyes fixed; their lips black, for want of water and their limbs bleached white and swollen through exposure to the relentless surf, which roared around like a hungry demon waiting for its prey.

He did more than watch. Johnstone almost shattered his hands trying to fire rockets across to the wreck while balanced, standing up in the Portland lifeboat in the rough seas.

In *Narrative of the Shipwreck of the Admella*, published from public donations to the Melbourne Admella Relief Fund Committee a few months after the tragedy, Samuel Mossman described the scene from the dunes opposite the reef on the final night before the rescue. He meditates on the moonlit backdrop and then assembles two popular images from the Romantic vocabulary—stormy seas and majestic mountains:

> But beyond all in grandeur—approaching sublimity—was the appearance of the dreaded gigantic rollers, when their glittering snowy crests were lit by these lurid lights [the rockets]. Like the lightning's sheen upon the avalanche, they darted fitfully over the surface, whilst the loud reverberating roll of the sea-cataracts upon the shore resounded like thunder among the Alps.

The Sublime was an essential element of the Romantic *Weltanschauung*, or world view, since it epitomised the spiritual and experiential aspects of Romanticism's relationship to nature. The compelling image of the shipwreck was identified within the framework of eighteenth- and nineteenth-century Romantic aesthetics as an ideal subject for evoking the Sublime. Indeed, it became a distinguishing trope: the emotional drama combined with its potential as symbolic narrative contributed to the popularity of the image.

Edmund Burke, in his influential *Philosophical Enquiry into the Origin of Our Ideas of the Sublime and Beautiful* (1757), defined the source of the Sublime as operating 'in a manner analogous to terror' and producing 'the strongest emotion which the mind is capable of feeling'. It is a mode of aesthetic experience that springs from 'an unnatural tension and certain violent emotions of the nerves' that result in sacred awe and sympathy for the distress of others. The Sublime was generally considered the effect of greatness, prompting astonishment, reverence and, as Ruskin put it, 'the elevation of mind'.

The author of an editorial published in the *South Australian Register* two months after the wreck comprehended the sublime nature of this event. The editorial lamented the absence of pictures depicting the *Admella* shipwreck in the current exhibition of the South Australian Society of Arts. Besides providing an opportunity to depict the Sublime, such a work could be conceived as a history painting, therefore launching it into the most respected academic category of art. 'Our art is imitative—not creative,' the critic wrote. 'Our artists can give us landscapes, and portraits, and ideal types of aboriginal forms, but it seems that they do not feel competent to grapple with scenes that awaken the sterner and stormier passions of the soul.' The complaint is directed at descriptive modes of representation and reflects Romantic attitudes of the day, encouraging creative expression over direct imitation.

The critic was proved wrong. Several days after the exhibition opened on 3 October 1859, James Hazel Adamson entered two paintings of the subject of the *Admella*, his work *The Rescue of the Survivors of the Admella by the Portland Lifeboat* winning first prize. The painting's whereabouts are unknown, but from its descriptive title and contemporary articles in the press, we know it represents the morning of the rescue, the survivors saved and the steamer sinking in the distance. By rendering this particular moment, the artist celebrates the courageous efforts of the rescue mission, thus imparting a moral message concordant with its function as a history painting, while maintaining the romantic and emotional frisson evoked by the sinking vessel.

Adamson's painting did, however, cause some controversy. Letters to the press questioned the work's eligibility for the competition: the artist was no longer resident in Adelaide when it was painted (he moved to Melbourne in 1856), and the painting was received after the closing date for entries. The committee of the Society of Arts defended their decision, 'as realising more completely the intention of the Society of Arts' and, no doubt aided by popular sentiment, the work remained the winner.

In the months following the shipwreck, the South Australian Society of Arts also encouraged the production of works of art representing the event by suggesting a prize might be given, of 'a sufficient sum of money', for a painting of the wreck of the *Admella*:

> a painting which, while it embodied truthfully the chief facts of the scene, should also render poetically some of those grief-inspiring episodes which invested the event with extraordinary interest. A picture is wanted adequate to the recollection of those profound sensations which during a week of agonizing suspense thrilled through the whole community. Is such a picture to be obtained? Have we an artist equal to the task?

The subject obviously typified the heroic and expressive possibilities in art—in the spirit of Salvator Rosa and Joseph Vernet—embraced by the Romantic tastes of the press and local societies of art.

Nothing more was heard of this proposal until James Shaw, artist and member of the Society of Arts, organised a Colonial Art Union in June–July 1860, in which a prize of ten guineas would 'be given for the exhibition of the best painting of the Wreck of the Admella, by a resident artist'. A prize was also offered for the best poem, and submissions may have included poems celebrating the shipwreck written by artists George French Angas and James Shaw, poets Philip Barry, Ellie Debney née Turner and Caroline Carleton, who wrote the anthem 'Song of Australia'. A few years later the poet Adam Lindsay Gordon also produced a narrative heavily inspired by the shipwreck.

A number of artists produced paintings of the catastrophe, some of which were exhibited in Shaw's Art Union and in the next Society of Arts exhibition held in April 1861. They included Charles Hill, J.M. Needham and Shaw himself. Other contemporary impressions include sketches by James Fawthrop, who captained the Portland lifeboat in the rescue operation, and H.D. Melville, harbourmaster at Robe at the time of the disaster, as well as a lithograph of the wreck by Adelaide artist Heinrich Berger.

James Shaw and painting the *Admella*

Paintings of the shipwreck by Hill and Shaw are today in the collection of the Art Gallery of South Australia. Hill's work, *Wreck of the*

Admella, 1859, depicts the rescue efforts on the eighth day after the wreck. Boats lowered from the two ships *Lady Bird* and *Ant* in the background, as well as the lifeboat launched from the beach, are seen trying to approach the aft section where 'the unfortunate beings', seen by Captain Greig of the *Lady Bird*, were 'perched like seals on a half-tide rock, moving to and fro, and evidently waving for help'.

The tragedy was still fresh in people's minds, and these works of art petitioned viewers' sympathy, reinforcing the subject's expression of the Sublime. Burke had acknowledged the motivating force historical events had in producing a strong emotional response. In the section 'Of the effects of tragedy' in his *Philosophical Enquiry*, he wrote: 'The nearer it approaches the reality, and the further it removes us from all idea of fiction, the more perfect is its power [to evoke the Sublime].' The subject of the work of art becomes the *source* of the Sublime—not its manifestation; the Sublime is located not in the object itself, but in the viewer's experience of the painting. The editorial quoted earlier demonstrates this commitment to a subject-oriented approach linked to spiritual endeavour: awakening 'the stormier passions of the soul'.

From 1850, the year of his arrival in Adelaide, to 1861, when he devoted himself to his art, James Shaw was employed as a clerk in the Adelaide Post Office. He found himself at a communications epicentre, where news of the disaster reverberated like a seismic shudder across the colony. Eyewitnesses spoke of crowds gathering through the week on the Post Office portico, spilling out along King William Street, eager for reports of the survivors.

Shaw had painted the *Admella* in 1858 when the steamer, 'trim, buoyant, swift', began its run between Melbourne and Adelaide. With black smoke billowing from the funnel, the sleek vessel literally cuts

through the choppy surf and gusty winds, while a sailing ship in the middle ground—creating a visual counterpoint—lists under the heavy weather, tacking bravely in the wind. In *The Admella Wrecked, Cape Banks, 6th August 1859*, painted a year later, tragedy has struck. Dawn breaks and we find the steamer pinned to the saw-tooth spine of Carpenter Rocks, so named by French explorer Nicolas Baudin in 1802 because of the jagged reef's resemblance to a carpenter's saw.

In a spectacular 15 minutes the steamer had broken into three parts along the specially riveted bulkheads designed to prevent flooding of the holds. The fore and aft sections are visible at this stage, as well as the broken side paddle wheel, though by the following day the forepart would begin to

Ode: On an Imprecise Subject
Dugald Williamson

Poetry is a subject as precise as geometry.
—Gustave Flaubert

A garden fence and open field,
Pear trees and bright plums, loaded lines
  In a carousel wind.

Flying sheets we caught by corners,
And I the gist of symmetry,
  Folding into your arms.

Floaters, they call them, sight membranes,
Spreading with their own momentum
  Black rain over iris.

You still can see across the dam
The moorhens dive on washing day,
  Flights and cool synoptics lapse:
  See, as in the mind's eye.

break up and all those who remained at the bow—men, women and children—unable to escape to the stern, would perish. We see passengers, still in nightshirts, rushing to the rails, realising with horror the extent of their plight. In his poem 'The Wreck of the Admella' Shaw describes the very moment he captures in the painting:

The overcrowded foremast now no more
Supported by its overstrained stays gives way
Unable to sustain its living weight,
Gives way and headlong hurls its living load.

Seamen and passengers tumble into Byron's 'dim desolate deep'; the vessel rocks in its cradle, the sharks circle below.

In his *Philosophical Enquiry*, Burke codifies a number of sublime elements that can be described as formal in their application to art, including obscurity, vastness, light and dark, and suddenness. We can observe how Shaw has integrated such devices, using a low-key palette of dark tones set against the bristling white surf and spray, and prompting the bewildering impression of precipitousness as the mast cracks and splits, throwing off 'its living load'. Mossman's description of the heavens that morning could refer equally to Shaw's expressive sky, where 'ruby-tinted clouds floated in the intense blue sky, glowing with the beams of the rising sun'. The midship section is all but submerged, the bow and poop deck swamped, obscuring the ship and rendering it spatially unstable. This reduction of visibility conveys sublime tremors since, according to Burke, clarity and precision scare away the ghosts of our mind, while obscurity is 'dark, uncertain, confused, terrible and sublime to the last degree'.

It is one of Shaw's best paintings. Although our self-trained artist does not exhibit the technical brilliance we find in J.M.W. Turner's fugitive seascapes, inspired by the horror of the events, Shaw has shed his signature 'plodding sincerity', as one critic

has put it, and captures the violence of the pounding surf and the powerlessness of the figures. The artist has transformed the event into an expression of emotional and heroic power and in its strength and grandeur—the painting is distinctly larger in scale than most of his work—reflects constituent elements of the Sublime experience.

For the passengers the drama has but begun. The ship lurches away from the waking sun, predicting the dashed hopes of the passengers: unseeing ships will pass in the night and witnesses, soon gathering to look helplessly on from the beach, will be unable to reach those stranded on the inaccessible wreck. And we, spectators suspended above the carnage, see the glimmer of hope in a sun spreading its wings, yet, 'in alternate hope and fear' we see too the mountainous waves obscuring it from the disoriented passengers reaching the bulwarks and, in the foreground, the blackness of the deep rushing under our feet.

These compositional devices strengthened the status of the shipwreck as a popular motif of Romantic expression. They combine 'the terrible uncertainty of the thing described' (Burke) and a preoccupation with nature's power and destructive force. Such devices allow the artist to re-create the overwhelming and whirling transformations of the sea, and to make accessible an image of terror: an image elevated to the limits of the Sublime. Romanticism is of course much more than a genealogy of the Sublime, but the obvious existence of and yearning for the Sublime in Australian marine painting confirm the transferral and rearticulation of Romantic ideas in their antipodean essence.

The Rescue (c. 1860), attributed to James Shaw, a much smaller painting also in the collection of the Art Gallery of South Australia, is the most enigmatic work exploring the aftermath of the disaster. It re-creates a detail of the rescue operation when one of the lifeboats, most probably the salvaged

Admella lifeboat captained by Ben Germein, the Cape Northumberland lighthouse keeper and the first person alerted to the accident, plunges through the surf. Filling the middle ground like curtains drawn across a stage, the rising, swelling sea distributes its power to the edges of the canvas. The coxswain's outstretched arms and cap echo the profile of the uppermost wave as it reaches its crescendo. One of the rescue ships at the scene, its masts barely visible in the distance, remains enveloped in the mist and spray.

While the sailors struggle to keep the small boat upright, Germein, momentarily unmoved by the turbulence, gazes inscrutably at the man—could it be Soren Holm?—in the foreground, floating, dead, one arm still grasping a fragment of the steamer. Germein himself, suffering later in life from mental illness, would be found dead from suicide, discovered in a mangrove swamp close to the ocean he loved. The young sailor is floating face up, his features clearly distinguishable yet frozen, his soft brown, unseeing eyes wide open—fixed and vacant.

The coxswain steering the boat, perched directly above Germein, waves his arm, looking in the direction of the viewer, his look full of intent. What is he trying to tell us? That he will come back for us? Where are we stationed—with the survivors on the wreck? The floating sailor, almost so close we can lean over and touch him, is a symbolic reminder of a destiny we may have escaped for now, but not forever.

The painting is a poignant tour de force, our eyes drawn persistently to the boat, to the crest of the wave and to the floating body. How ironic is the title, since the young man on his back does not benefit from the rescue. Who *is* rescued in the painting? Ben Germein and his volunteer sailors on the small lifeboat managed to rescue three survivors from the wreck. Here, are they trying to steer the boat around and guide it down towards the wreck—towards us? Or is it just

over the waves, hidden from our view? The melancholic painting raises more questions than it can answer.

Paintings made—like sailcloth—from plain-woven canvas are flotsam washed up on the beaches of history. They are reminders of the way artists imagined events and places and, in the case of the *Admella*, found inspiration in transcending loss. Painters such as Shaw, more often than not busy painting harbours and homesteads, rose to the challenge to produce history painting. In 1859 Adelaide had a population of 120,000, having doubled in just ten years. The colony was a youthful 23 years old—younger even than Henry Holbrook when he joined the cabin passenger list—and its inhabitants held their collective breath, hanging on every telegraph, until the narrative came to an end. Did a colonial consciousness find moral instruction in this desperate struggle for life? Are not creation myths born of struggle? Shaw and his fellow artists' paintings of the *Admella* might be read as vehicles for allegorical intent as much as expressions of Romantic rhetoric.

Walking back along the dry gravel aisles separating the graves, I dwelt on Henry Holbrook's misfortune, a fate shared by 88 men, women and children on the steamer. The lone lifebelt, sweeping out of the picture in the foreground of Shaw's painting of the wreck, was of use to no-one. The sun was now pushing down on the horizon. Shadows spread across the headstones of Adelaide's West Terrace Cemetery, dressing them in black. And the restless, shifting earth of this town made the vertical slabs of stone tilt like mourners stooping over the graves of loved ones, 'living statues there seen to weep'. •

Stephen Valambras Graham studied art history and has worked in communications and the community services sector in France and Australia. He lives in Adelaide.

MUSCLING UP TO THE WORLD

For constrained democratic leaders, foreign policy is another country

Andrew Carr

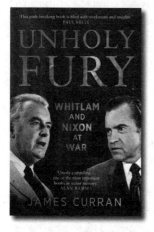

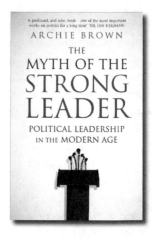

Books reviewed

Unholy Fury: Whitlam and Nixon at War by James Curran

Condemned to Crisis by Ken Ward

The Myth of the Strong Leader: Political Leadership in the Modern Age by Archie Brown

FOREIGN POLICY IS the last refuge of the strong leader. While those who differ too much or dream too big in the domestic sphere are quickly branded 'out of touch', the external affairs of a nation remain a welcoming hearth for 'leaders'. The impact of leaders and public perceptions is at the heart of two recent books on Australian foreign policy: James Curran's *Unholy Fury* and Ken Ward's *Condemned to Crisis*. Their insights are here filtered through a recent work by British scholar Archie Brown, *The Myth of the Strong Leader*.

Together these books suggest a need to rein in foreign-policy leaders and subject their decisions to greater democratic scrutiny. It's most vital this happens through cabinet and parliamentary processes, yet also with a greater sensitivity to domestic opinion and the significant influence it maintains on the way Australia engages with the world. Leadership still matters, but it matters most when it occurs through and with the democratic structures of our society, not as some act of lone genius pointing the way and dragging the nation on its back to get there.

Curran and Ward look at two of Australia's most important relationships: with the United States and Indonesia. Curran is a star academic historian who seeks to shine a light on a nearly forgotten spat. In doing so he helps reveal the internal dynamics of the half-century-long affair between Canberra and Washington. By contrast, Ward, a retired analyst from the Office of National Assessments, has set out to temper enthusiasm for the prospects of the geographically arranged marriage between Australia and Indonesia.

Arguably no other diplomatic relationships are more important to Australia's long-term security and economic needs, yet there is a strange dichotomy in how we talk about these two countries. Each state has its own lobby that seeks the closer ties they regard as both natural and inevitable. But at the same time, these groups assert leadership is absolutely vital to the relationship—whether to cement the bond, in the case of Indonesia, or to preserve it, in the case of the United states. Australia's path is thus argued to be simultaneously unbreakable and inherently fragile.

Combine these attitudes with the general deference we have towards leaders in the foreign-policy sphere and the scope for influence is vast. If a prime minister is seeking to improve either of these relationships, we are told not to complain should they bend national principles to their breaking point. If strengthening these ties requires ignoring or subverting popular will, then so be it. This is just the price we must pay for a vital foreign tie.

Reading Curran and Ward, you realise just how absurd this notion of an unshackled, visionary leader really is. Prime ministers are just as subject to the waves and whimsy of public opinion in foreign affairs as they are in the domestic sphere. Those leaders who try alone to move their society this way or that often risk the whole endeavour. This is not to say leadership is not necessary, but rather we need to rethink just what leadership in the external domain really is.

The popular story of the ANZUS treaty is that Menzies, Holt, Gorton and McMahon defied national interest and public will to go 'all the way' with our 'great and powerful friend'. But as *Unholy Fury* artfully demonstrates, this is both wrong and misses much of the richness of the tale. True, there were real friendships in place. Curran reveals that Robert Menzies and Richard Nixon got on extremely well, while Harold Holt was given the honour of sharing an 'unceremonious sandwich' in the Oval Office with Lyndon B. Johnston.[1]

But it was geopolitics, not personal ties or subservience, that drove these two nations to cooperate. Communism, rightly or wrongly, was seen as a storm that directly threatened Australia and so the public and its leaders looked for help. By the 1960s when this relationship really started to draw attention, it was also the only one of significance that Canberra had left. The British were packing up and leaving Asia, while institutions such as the United Nations and the South-East Asian Treaty Organisation were proving ineffective if not illusory.

Notions of dependency ignore the substantial historical evidence that shows how Australian interests and Australian concerns drove our leaders during this period. Vietnam's fall to communism was far more

---

1   Such was Gorton's desire to repeat this impromptu honour, he cancelled a lunch invitation with the US Secretary of State, just in case. James Curran, *Unholy Fury: Whitlam and Nixon at War*, Melbourne University Press, Melbourne, 2015, p. 90.

significant for Canberra's security than America's, which led the former to be a strong champion of the war, not the reluctant participant of historical memory. In supporting this and other causes, Australia's leaders operated largely in tune with the public.

It was to the misfortune of John Gorton and Billy McMahon that by the time they took office the ground of international geopolitics and domestic opinion had begun to shift. It would continue to do so for the next decade, during which Gough Whitlam would come and go. Personalities would matter during this period but only to the degree they shaped assessments of the United States' changing position. Where those on the right were indulgent, those on the left were indignant.

Curran's deep archival research clearly shows that Richard Nixon and Gough Whitlam were two of the most stubborn men ever to occupy their respective national leadership posts. Yet the differences between them as men were not as significant as those between their two countries. One was a tired nation, stretched thin thanks to a global defence of its ideology. The other was an increasingly proud nation keen to stretch its arms. What they had in common was a sense of paranoia. Washington's fear was that Australia under Whitlam would go feral; that the joint installations would be raided or ripped up, the treaty trashed, and the Soviets emboldened. In Australia Whitlam, his cabinet and large sections of the Australian public feared they were witnessing the end of America's moral authority; that the liberal vision of the founding fathers had been replaced by an authoritarian hegemon, willing to destroy Asia in order to save it.

The circumstances were ripe for misunderstanding and, wilfully, Nixon and Whitlam did just that. Neither was in a mood to accommodate the other, settling in a freeze on the relationship. This inevitably hurt the smaller partner most. Not because of any direct threat, but because the usual rituals of 'strong leadership', namely the stage-managed visit of the Australian prime minister to the president's abode, could not occur. Whitlam was kept out of the Oval Office for many months, while Australian letters went unanswered.

In time the storm would pass, blown away partly because of fears the divide made both sides look like they were not being properly led. Nixon was drowning under his own mortal sin of Watergate and had to accept he could not continue to punish a once-close ally. Likewise, Whitlam had to swallow his pride and use back-door conduits to get his visit to the president and moment in the Oval Office. The exchange between the two men was neither warm nor productive but it did give the image of strong foreign policy leadership that tradition demanded.

The geopolitics that drove the United States and Australia together in the early 1950s would soon push the two nations back together in the late 1970s. They have been glued tight ever since. This was not a pre-destined path. As Curran shows, the alliance really could have broken in 1973—just as happened to New Zealand's with the United States in 1985.[2] But this moment of tension was not the fault of leadership—neither a lack of it, as ran the right's charge against Whitlam, or as the first example of it in Australian foreign policy, as the left celebrated of Whitlam.

Archie Brown's *The Myth of the Strong Leader* unfortunately doesn't cover Australian politics. But Brown would be sure to doubt the view—held on the left and right—that Edward Gough Whitlam was a revolutionary leader. At most, Whitlam fits into Brown's

---

2   A good inside account of New Zealand's decision and the implications can be found in Gerald Hensley *Friendly Fire: Nuclear Politics and the Collapse of ANZUS, 1984–1987*.

'redefining' figure category. This places him alongside Franklin Delano Roosevelt and Lyndon B. Johnson in the United States and Clement Attlee and Margaret Thatcher in Britain.[3] This judgement may seem a slight to Whitlam, but a by-product of Australia's political and economic success is the lack of need for transformational leaders. Brown's catalogue of the leaders who truly mattered, such as Mao Zedong, Mikhail Gorbachev and Nelson Mandela, all presided over societies in great turmoil. The public may wish for 'strong leadership', and leaders may often imagine themselves in such robes. But it is generally only found in situations of great harm and chaos for public and elites alike.

For the lucky country, such situations have not—yet—emerged and thus our leaders are judged on more prosaic grounds: competently managing the daily challenges while having a publicly acceptable sense of the things that need to be changed and those that must be preserved. Times of great flux put stress on both aspects, and diverging perspectives in societies can easily overwhelm leaders—as both McMahon and Whitlam found. These differences of attitude also matter across societies and it is this factor more than any other that explains why Australia and the United States clashed in the early 1970s. What had been tamped down during the last years of the Coalition government had to erupt at some point.

Today the notion of an eruption of popular concern seems as far as possible from occurring. The Australian people could not be happier with the relationship. ANZUS is far and away the most popular foreign policy of Liberal and Labor governments. Those who are seen to challenge 'the alliance' are deemed not fit for office. This, Curran warns, is not a healthy state of affairs. It can lead to absent-minded drift; a lover's silence

that fails to bring into the open potential disruptions. Gaps in perception—such as what Australia would be expected to do in the case of a US–China clash over the East or South China seas—are left unasked and unanswered.

Yet the ground is starting to shift and once more it will not be politicians who decide the future of our ties. Americans may decide they have had enough of Asia in the face of a rising China. Australians may decide they don't want to choose and so seek the safety of isolation in the South Pacific. Leaders may champion or oppose either course, but the relationship's path ultimately depends upon the popular will.

That the public may be in charge of foreign policy is the deepest fear of those pushing for closer ties with Indonesia. Not so for Ken Ward, who cautions that any leaders who get too far ahead of public sentiment and national identity in either country will meet with strife.

Ward's Lowy Penguin paper is something of a strange text. Like others in this series, I suspect he didn't quite have the space to develop his argument. Instead there are warnings about placing too much faith in the relationship with Indonesia and discussions of that country's difficult relationships with Malaysia and Singapore. This concludes with rumination on Indonesia's identity and why it required two Australian drug smugglers to die. Ward is at his best describing the historical grievances and expected future glories that shape the Indonesian world view. A nation—somewhat like China—that has suffered greatly but now presumes a return to greatness is pre-ordained. This can make it a difficult place for a present-oriented society like Australia to engage with.

What Ward's analysis leaves out is how we might escape this pattern. The book

---

3   Archie Brown, *The Myth of the Strong Leader: Political Leadership in the Modern Age*, Vintage, London, 2015, pp. 101–47.

jacket enticingly asks, 'Will the relationship between Australia and Indonesia always be volatile?' The text does not provide an answer. Yet no careful reader could come away from his essay and believe—as many on the left still do—that if only we had another leader like Paul Keating the relationship would be set right.

No Australian leader is more closely associated with the Indonesia relationship than Keating. Yet drawing on Archie Brown's insights, a case can be made that we don't correctly recognise the way this leadership occurred. Indeed, the man himself seems to contribute to this misunderstanding. While still treasurer, Keating famously declared that Australia had never had a truly great leader. This obviously snubbed then PM Bob Hawke, while also dismissing Labor's obsession and celebration of its own history. During his time in the Lodge, Keating was determined to prove leadership mattered and Indonesia was a central test case.

This ambition would lead him to bring the two nations closer than they ever had been before, exemplified by the 1995 Australia–Indonesia Security Agreement signed with then president Suharto. Remarkable as this was, it was also a mirage. Keating had the vision, but the decision to go there was never his alone to make. Without acceptance and advocates in the Australian parliament and wider community to continue the effort, the new space for cooperation with Jakarta he had created went unfilled.

When the East Timor crisis in 1999 shook the core of the relationship—the very circumstances in which a security partnership was necessary—the agreement was cancelled. True, this was a moment of great change and strife with a new democratic Indonesia struggling to appear out of the ashes of its authoritarian past. An agreement with a southern neighbour that now appeared to be an invader was always going to struggle to survive. But more importantly it was an agreement of two men and not two nations. When they left the scene, the ties went with them.

While the dust has long since settled, the relationship has not moved back towards the vision that drove the 1995 agreement. Ward brings a deep and grounded expertise to stress the many ways these two societies divide and continue to divide. Like Whitlam and Nixon 40 years ago, stereotypes and paranoia determine much of the atmosphere of our day. Leaders can embody or defy this, but they cannot ignore it.

Ward is particularly pessimistic about whether the historical and cultural barriers can be overcome. Indeed the take-away message seems to be that it is not even worth bothering.[4] That's an uncomfortable, perhaps even unpalatable idea for those who want to bring an end to these cycles of crisis. And for those who foresee a restructuring of the Asian order over the next half-century, the implications are significant indeed. If the mass of economic and political reports are right that Jakarta is a rising giant while Canberra is an ageing middle power, then to do nothing is potentially to condemn us to a dangerous future.

That so many Australians are uncomfortable about such a poor relationship and have a deep wish to change it is in part evidence of the real leadership of Paul Keating. This leadership did not occur with a signature in a hot Jakarta palace 20 years ago. Instead it happened in office and out, every time Keating fronted a press microphone or an assembled audience and argued for the importance of better relations.

The leadership of Keating's that truly mattered was his use of the democratic

---

4   Ken Ward, *Condemned to Crisis: Will the relationship between Australia and Indonesia always be so volatile?* Penguin Group Australia, Melbourne, 2015, pp. 120–1.

structures and democratic forums to persuade Australians to change their attitudes. No leader before or since has tried to force us to think as seriously about Indonesia and its importance as Keating did. And while we rushed to embrace a political opponent who offered us the chance to be 'relaxed and comfortable' instead, the conversation about Indonesia continues. This legacy can be felt across the country, perhaps most acutely in the words of a then opposition leader who declared in 2013 that we needed 'more Jakarta, less Geneva' as the centrepiece of Australian foreign policy.

Australia and Indonesia will no longer be 'condemned to crisis' when the people of both countries can talk openly and freely about each other. Some may fear what democratic debate about each other would bring but arguably the silence of recent decades has been worse. It has allowed populists a free hand and let rumours and anecdotes serve in place of understanding. Silence keeps businesses unaware of the opportunities today and students oblivious to those of tomorrow.

The best step towards changing Australia's relationship with Indonesia would be for our politicians to debate it openly. What a 'more Jakarta' relationship might look like has never been stated. Likewise, Julia Gillard's three big reports—the National Security Strategy, the 2013 Defence White Paper and the Australia in the Asian Century White Paper—were all full of praise for new forms of regional cooperation. But no real effort has been made by either side of Australian politics to say how these changes might operate, let alone persuade the public that this is the right way forward.

What is needed for the Australia–Indonesia relationship is not a 'leader' who forces the country down a new path, but an open debate that offers the potential for education and persuasion. According to Curran, for all the chaos of the early 1970s, the crisis between Australia and the United States helped usher in a much needed maturity that over time has greatly strengthened the relationship. A similar debate is needed over Indonesia. We need our political parties to be partisan. To declare they truly do want 'more Jakarta' and to mean it.

For the time being, Australia's democratic forces keep any 'leader' from going too far towards Indonesia, just as they punish any who may stray from the United States. These ties make sense, with few obvious costs along our path thus far. Advocates of either relationship may wish for a strong leader to dispel doubt and catapult these relationships into a new era. However, such notions are a myth born of a misreading of history, and one that continues to mislead those with the responsibility for leadership.

This is not to presume the public has the right answer at any time. There is a wisdom of crowds effect, but it's diluted when many aren't paying enough attention.[5] Arguably the public is a little too cosy with the United States, a little too cautious about Indonesia. But the public is also right to say it hasn't been properly asked.[6] Pollsters and politicians seek responses without asking for opinions. Too many scholars and policymakers treat the public as an unfortunate necessity, an irritant to be overcome or ideally sidelined so that the right leader with the right advisers can implement change.

5 James Surowiecki, *The Wisdom of Crowds*, Anchor Books, New York, 2005, p. 266.
6 Fergus Hanson, *Australia and the World: Public Opinion and Foreign Policy*, Lowy Institute for International Policy, Sydney, 2010, p. 9. A larger academic study in 2014 also found foreign and defence policy had some of the lowest congruence between public opinion and government policy. See Aaron Martin, Keith Dowding, Andrew Hindmoor and Andrew Gibbons, 'The Opinion-Policy Link in Australia', *Australian Journal of Political Science* 49, no. 3 (2014), pp. 499–517.

This logic is part of a problematic contradiction at the heart of our thinking about modern foreign-policy leadership, according to Archie Brown. The power and independence of presidents and prime ministers has continued to grow in the management of external affairs. Yet leaders have also looked increasingly helpless in the face of globalisation and an interconnected global community. Thus leaders tell us—some even believe it—that if we elect them they can hold the line at the borders, deciding who and what crosses and in what circumstances. And when they fail at this, and fail they will, we elect someone else who declares they can hold the line. Whether it is stopping immigrants from getting in or key industries from going out, this is the area where one person can do the least, yet the most is expected. And as the tide's pull grows stronger, so does our demand for someone to yell 'halt'—or at least 'slow down'.

Leaders are thus increasingly judged on the one thing they do not control: the interaction of their nation with the world around it. This is not to excuse the failures of current and past leaders of Australian foreign policy. But it does put their actions into context. They have not truly failed nor fully succeeded because neither path was completely open to them. They are not captains of our ship of state but deckhands like the rest of us, with no one person plausibly strong enough to handle the wheel.

The only way to stop that wheel spinning is to stop the ship itself. To drop anchor as North Korea has since the 1950s, Iran since the 1970s, and as Russia seems to be doing in our own time. To halt the nation in one place, tossing the people and their standards of living into the depths. Many leaders have tried to halt the big forces of popular will or economic or geographic change, but only some anchors hold. Whatever enthusiasm parts of the West had for cutting those chains, as was tried by the right and left in places such as Iraq and Libya, has ebbed away. It will be for the people of those countries to embrace the tide of globalisation again. We may cheer their release, but no longer trust our capacity to help.

For those whose nations are happily committed to the rocking sea of a hyperconnected world, our desire for 'strong' leaders is both understandable and unhelpful. In rare moments of strife, we still need quick decisions—perhaps quicker than ever. But that is no way to manage our daily path or long-term journey. Instead, it is to our own spirit level of democracy we must turn.

Loss
Michelle Cahill

Dog otter, forgetful squire, how
long must I wait in this jumble
with my blind, translucent mess?

For the frenzied scent of hounds
rifles our holt, Norse pagans came
after you left—when I broke a little.

Our pups huddled, whined like birds
flummoxed as by the scruff I seized
each one, nudged to a nascent dive.

Baptised in algae, petroleum blooms
they flushed in the lake's oily shallows
to pop like velvet corks. Or lotteries.

Their fingers knot in prayer, suckled,
they dream of snow slides, shooting
weeds, the bladderwrack of your deep.

What have you plucked from mud?
I watch the homeless crows, eagles quiz
your riddle, my proxy, never to return.

Scraps swivelled, crushed fish-bone,
I sniff a little shuck of homecoming.
The wind blows musk into my dreams.

This floating bubble of debate may seem hopelessly susceptible to the merest wave or bump but it is also the only way to find true balance.

That balance in how the nation approaches the wider world begins fundamentally with the restoration of our democratic structures, parliament and cabinet to the decision-making process. If there is one central message in Brown's fascinating tome, it is the importance of collective decision-making. In many cases he suggests, the cabinet or small groups of leaders are the ideal mix of efficiency and balance. Focusing on British and US experience, though also drawing on Germany, China and South Africa, he shows that leaders who disregard their colleagues soon falter. Dominating a cabinet room or spurning its role altogether may seem 'strong', but it is a way to invite poor decision-making and weak policy effect. True leaders, those who either redefined their societies by making the system work better or transformed it by moving it from one form to another, never achieve their success alone. Nor do they try to. The best—both in terms of the success but also the moral merit of their choices—did so in concert with their colleagues and the consent of their society.

To accept this, however, is implicitly to accept the role of politics, and partisan politics. Many would like to keep this idea as far away as possible from policymaking in foreign affairs. But quite why this is so is never made clear. Just like domestic challenges, foreign policy is not something that experts can 'solve'. There are real values that need to be articulated and argued over. Take one of the most divisive recent issues, the 2003 invasion of Iraq by the Coalition of the Willing. On one side were those who wanted to remove a dictator and support an ally; who hoped it would bring democracy to a foreign region and reduce the threat of terrorism closer to home. On the other

were those who worried about the lives that would be lost and the institutions and laws betrayed. They feared the task could not be done, that the leaders did not grasp what they were attempting and were not being honest about the reasons.

Neither Australia nor the United States was harmed by this debate becoming partisan. Indeed, there was a debate precisely because there was a partisan divide. Both sides had the courage to stand up and say what they believed and we are the better for it. While an anger still lingers beneath the surface on both sides, people felt their voice was heard and they had leaders who represented them.

On many issues facing us today, the need to move away from trusting a single leader and towards embracing debate and collective decision-making is absolutely necessary. No one person could or should provide answers to the myriad questions we face in our foreign and defence policy: What is the right way to think about China? What if it goes wrong? How many submarines should we get and where should we build them? What type of relationship should we have with the United States? Do we need to fight in the Middle East to keep the United States in Asia, or does our presence over there distract us and them from the vital issues here? These issues are crying out for genuine public argument.

No longer should a weak leader be able to escape into the foreign-policy sphere as a way to regain their credentials or prove their leadership matters. The stakes are too high to risk by allowing just one person to guess and gamble their way through. It's time to tame that final frontier and return foreign policy and the management of key relationships to the democratic fold. ●

Andrew Carr is a research fellow in the Strategic and Defence Studies Centre at the ANU. His most recent book is *Winning the Peace: Australia's Campaigns to Change the Asia-Pacific* (MUP, 2015).

CAPITALISM AND THE USELESSNESS OF THE POEM

On monetary value and how the arts allow us to recognise other kinds

Martin Langford

CAPITALISM HAS TURNED us all into migrants. Not just geographical ones—though few these days do not travel for the sake of their work—but migrants of capitalist possibility. Many are innocents who walk out of school with neat and poignant folders, and who dream of becoming heroes of the interview, aristocrats of the gun CV—people who intend to *go somewhere*. Not everyone takes such journeys, of course. One can be disqualified before one starts: poverty, disability, lack of education. But the capitalist migration is widely portrayed as the shape of hope in a modern society. The search for the means by which as many people as possible can participate in such journeys is regarded as a central equity issue by all political parties, though they might approach the problem in different ways. It is one of the great matters of unfinished business in our democracies: the fitful, half-hearted attempt to give everyone a chance to participate.

What shape a life might take beyond that is a different question. It is one that gets asked too rarely, largely because our migrations—and the anxieties that accompany them—so dominate our imaginations that we think of it as a secondary matter: *no point in wasting time on hypotheticals.* We have to engage with the circumstances we find ourselves in: we have to survive and to work with the possibilities that present themselves. Ubiquitous as these journeys are, however, the mindsets required to manage them are neither innocent nor straightforward. For all their capacity to engender achievement, they also generate perspectives that are limiting and even self-destructive, and unless we can learn to think past them as well as within them, we will find ourselves trapped in the stagnant paranoias of the status-obsessed.

Central to the problem with capitalist narratives are the enthusiasms that emerge once the issues of survival have been solved. All too rapidly—as if without effort—the needs of security segue into enlargement narratives, conceived primarily in terms of status: stories in which going *somewhere* can only mean *somewhere relative to others*. Once set in motion, this status anxiety is chafed so relentlessly—by one's peers, one's bosses and, not least, by one's own imagination—that it is all but impossible not to surrender to its judgements. By placing the self at the centre of the universe, moreover, the narratives minimise the importance of all those *others*—other selves, other creatures, other ecosystems—that must be set to one side if their goals are to be attained. It is one of the strengths of capitalist democracy that it has put more selves at the centre of 'transformational' stories than any other system we have thought of. But in doing so it has narrowed the perspectives of participants to the point where the individual can be in danger of losing as much through the necessities of focus as can be gained in reward and opportunity.

To maximise the efficiency with which we undertake these migrations, we exclude whatever impedes them. One of the first impediments removed is our engagement with others. Others, seen through the lens of one's needs, only require consideration if they are allies or enemies: in all other respects they are incidental, and ultimately irrelevant. We do need to interact with other parties: we must negotiate, for the sake of our interests. But this is a different matter to those less calculated engagements— underpinned by pleasure and affection—by which our more meaningful relationships are sustained.

The deal does not require us to acknowledge other parties as entities in their own right. As long as the objects of the discussion have been translated into suitable terms, and providing expectations of reliability have been met, we do not need to ask to whom we are talking. What we do have to do is to create a currency in common. We have all become experts at the translation of materialities into terms—a translation so habitual we barely notice ourselves performing it. The shorthand has taken over, and the thing itself has been relegated to a background whisper. From a capitalist point of view, an object hardly exists until it has a price. Without a price, it cannot take its place in the world's numerical conversation—and it is there, increasingly, that the key negotiations occur: the play of words having been relegated to an earnestness on its periphery.

Not everything translates readily into terms. Plants, animals and ecosystems are notoriously difficult to place a value on, unless they can be conceived as tourist dollars, or coefficients of carbon absorption or wellness—unless, that is, a use can be found for them. Nor are the majority of experiences ever translated into currency: most qualia and interiorities still remain sequestered from our markets. Ultimately we value such useless things precisely because they don't have a price, because they speak to that part of us which needs to see the world as itself and untranslatable. Sometimes one's terms of trade can feel like the conditions of one's imprisonment: it is good to know there is a world out there that resists them. It may be our most important freedom, this stubborn wonder—this refusal to translate— at the centre of our imaginations. Capitalist narratives can hardly be avoided when it comes to the articulation and achievement of goals. But by turning everything into the terms of a self-based story, they also quietly steal the world away.

One of the principal counterweights to this process of reification lies in the way the arts maintain an ongoing meditation on the terms of representation. One might say that much of their project nowadays revolves around trying to find some way of representing the world that still allows the world to exist. The arts are not alone in balking at the overwriting that our capitalist efficiencies create: all activities that engage with the world for its own sake share this reticence— science, for instance, and sometimes, even religion—as well as the things that we do just for pleasure. Nor can one say that the arts necessarily operate as counterweights: many films and texts are just practice versions of self-aggrandisement. Thoughtful texts, however, either critique the stories they are shaped by, or turn their attention from, the management of status and look for alternatives.

One could argue that artistic interest begins at the point where the text is not simply an uncritical expression of enlargement: when it begins to resist power rather than embody it. There isn't, however, a simple dichotomy between those texts that are rituals of enlargement and those that aren't: many enactments of enlargement contain layers of critique, and many critiques exhibit an incompletely distanced fascination with enlargement (*Pride and Prejudice* is a romantic fantasy inflected by critiques; *Maldoror* is a critique obsessed by the images of power it denies). Allowing for variations in degree of distancing or embrace, art has nevertheless become one of the main repositories of the useless: of attempts to respond to the thing itself, as opposed to the terms it might yield. And poetry, which tends to look outwards into the moment, rather than towards an ending where status is either achieved or restored, is one of our strongest expressions of this. 'Plum Trees' is by Martin Harrison:

What the plum trees were doing
was loading galaxies of flowers
like night sky's sprawling fire
in the middle of daylight.
Space turned into bloom and fruit.
Soil rose into juice and scent.
Electric, shaken, utterly still,
unpruned wands thirsted for Spring.
Like gluttons, the trees sucked everywhere
from hidden water, seemingly nowhere—
that was the ground inside the dark
as we walked dry earth, dead grass.

Unreasonably, not beyond forgetting,
it's that year's dry light which falls away
as if plum trees flare in unfenced shadow,
momentary as thought, or as a trace of
    thought.[1]

These trees are not being turned into anything useful. Harrison simply wished to make them available to the imagination: for the reader to be able to see how miraculously they dispel the 'dry air', even though they 'flare' only briefly—'momentary as thought, or as a trace of thought'. It is a response sourced in fascination with the tree itself, rather than in an enquiry after advantage. And rather than leading towards the benefits of the deal, it offers only the fragile and unstable communion of the reading.

In JS Harry's 'A Sunlit Morning, Labor Day, Late Twentieth Century', Peter Rabbit watches his friend, a magpie, which has succumbed to the sealing cap on a milk container:

He does not sing
though Peter squats beside him, waiting.
His friend's mouth & tongue
are torn & black; old blood
has set & cracked: the flesh
that'd set in jagged peaks
has been re-opened scarlet.
A white ring
jags into the magpie's flesh
at the back of his beak — too hard & stiff
for him to close it. The ring
nooses his head, burying itself
in the neckfeathers' snowcape.
It's shortening his neck. Peter sees
why, yesterday, when he tried,
his friend
couldn't scoop up drink
from the swimming pool, & why
for days, when he flies
he's been dropping the spiders.[2]

The magpie has no economic value. In economic terms, its death is only an unintended consequence of a useful process—just visible enough to be labelled 'unfortunate'.

---

1   Martin Harrison, *Wild Bees*, UWA Press, 2008.
2   JS Harry, *Not Finding Wittgenstein*, Giramondo, 2007.

Usually, wild animals only participate in the capitalist story when they develop a taste for something that humans also want—at which point they are labelled 'pests', and enter the system as debits. Mostly—as here—when writers engage with such subjects, they are not suggesting that the object of their poem has no value. They are really saying it has an absolute value, one that cannot be translated into human terms: an otherness that invites only the ever-tentative, ever-resisted alternatives of representation—phrases such as 'the neckfeathers' snowcape', which attempt to 'capture' the magpie, without taking anything away from it.

Both of the preceding examples are attempts to make the natural world visible. But poets also try to think past the terms of utility in the human world. If there is one topic that has attracted more tendentious representation than any other, it is female sexuality. In 'Sidonie', Kate Lilley plays with Freud's attempts to translate this most dangerous of qualities into a terminology that can manage it:

Sidonie
A single case not too pronounced
a misfortune like any other
a *cocotte* in the ordinary sense
a severe beauty mature but still youthful
a well-made girl intact unversed
she did not scruple to appear
in the most frequented streets
she was in fact a feminist[3]

Lilley selects phrases from Freud's analyses and uses them to challenge his reading of Sidonie's behaviour. She doesn't have to add a layer of commentary: it is enough to isolate Freud's terms and to give them a space to be visible in, as there is a world of alternative interpretations in the reader's mind that

will do that for her. Her purpose is to make Freud's lugubrious disapproval disintegrate, under the pressure of implied comparison, so that Sidonie might be freed, at least in retrospect, from the judgements that oppress her. Lilley can only do this because she can imagine Sidonie without Freud's oppressive abstractions: without, that is, her being burdened with the uses the male emotional economy has found for her. The poem is an attempt to restore Sidonie to something like her original uselessness—a uselessness that Freud is uncomfortable with. As so often, however, with our most potent and unstable signifiers—death, sex, love—the attempt to manage them is unsuccessful: above all because they rarely fit into the categories we prepare for them. One finds it hard to believe, despite his ponderous relegations, that Freud wasn't as obsessed by her—or figures like her—after his analysis as before. His language might have provided him with a performance of disavowal—a certificate of distancing—but it resolved little for him, and created only damage for Sidonie.

'The Weighing', by South Australian poet Peter Lloyd, is another poem in which object and value are set side by side:

Where, on a stone wharf,
a white shark,
a long red flower in its mouth,
is being weighed and foto-flashed.
Two men, with the air of those who have
returned from a voyage round the world,
or some vast enterprise involving the moon,
stand ankle-deep among fish-blood and guts,
their arms raised in victory.

Sun glitters on chunky male jewelry and the
    universal brotherhood of man …[4]

Lloyd's fishermen are barely aware of the shark, excited as they are by the meaning of

---

3   Kate Lilley, *Ladylike*, UWA Press, 2012.
4   Peter Lloyd, *The Stone Ladder*, Wakefield Press, 2008.

its death. The poet, despairing of this, can only separate the shark from its interpretation, and imply that it did once have a life of its own, independent of what the men's imaginations have done with it. As Lilley did with Sidonie, Lloyd returns us to a point prior to that in which the object of attention was converted into currency. Over and over, in the arts, we see the uninterpreted object being placed against its meaning, and the consequence of its meaning: the cumulative effect is of a long, troubling revelation of the things we have done.

Few, if any, art forms are less seduced by enlargement than poetry. This is not simply because of the distancing effect of its critiques. Most poetry begins in an engagement with an other—a person, situation or idea—rather than in the management of an anxiety towards an advantageous position. In this respect there are radical differences between narrative forms and the lyric poem and its equivalents. Although some poets display an ongoing interest in narrative, most poems are either lyrics or collagist or other attempts to articulate an alternative. Looking outwards into the situation rather than towards an arrival, any interest they may have in the point of arrival is in terms of its meaning, which is quite distinct from the narrative's desire to arrive irrespective of what that might mean. Arrival is the point at which the story loses interest. A little idiosyncratically, one might describe it as the point at which the poem becomes engaged—the point, that is, at which story has paused long enough for the subject to look around.

Enlargement is meaningless in terms of the present and its situations. It can only be defined by the measurement of changes within the story: once one has entered upon one's migration, one must gauge how far one has travelled in order to measure and define success. The anxieties this generates overrule everything else in narrative forms. The author may surround them with critical meditations, but they are the engines that drive the text. The lyric and its alternatives, however, not having invoked such anxieties in the first place, are free to engage with the others the moment presents, as in the examples above. This engagement with the others that story finds problematic marks a key difference between literary or poetic interest, and interest based on the needs of narrative. And it finds a significant echo in the way capitalism—the system based on transformational story—finds it so difficult to maintain a respectful or just engagement with the world it has relegated with its management.

There is much here that has been simplified for the sake of argument. A great number of non-poetic texts obviously share that fascination with the strangeness of things that prompts so much poetry. There are, moreover, many forms that, despite being based in narrative, do not make it their focus: short stories often behave more like poems than stories, meditating on situation rather than pursuing resolution; even novels can be more like poems than novels (David Malouf's *An Imaginary Life*, for example).[5] Memoir too is often as interested in personality and event as it is in the development of narrative—one might cite *Romulus, My Father*, where Raimond Gaita is more concerned with the intractability of the father's sorrow than with the mechanics of story.[6] The key point, however, is that the needs of story can inhibit engagement with the others that lie beyond it, and that this effect is as ubiquitous in real-world behaviours as it is in literature. One implication of this is that we need stories that pay attention to their

---

5   David Malouf, *An Imaginary Life*, Picador, 1980.
6   Raimond Gaita, *Romulus, My Father*, Text, 1998.

others, rather than stories that interpret their others in terms of their narrative needs.

For all the satisfactions they might generate, seeing the world only through the lens of narrative convenience is inadequate and reductive. It cancels the first response, wonder, and casts a mist of valuations in front of it. We have language, we have a need to get things done, and therefore, it seems, we will go on reifying and negotiating until we ourselves are in danger of vanishing into the reductiveness of our energetic careers. In this light, the practical people of the world are actually some of the dreamiest: they are the ones subsumed by their currencies, while the poets—the ones with the reputation for unworldliness—are much more likely to have their imaginative feet on the ground, to be fighting to maintain their engagement with their others. Increasingly, too, those old divisions between science and art look out of date: the writers are closer to the observers of the world—the scientists and clinicians—than they are to the fantasists of status and arrival.

There is a battle going on between the unreified, unsubsumed world and those stories of triumph and enlargement that, while no doubt initiated with the intention of allowing their subjects more opportunities to engage with it, too often only render it invisible. At the moment, the stories are winning. Which is why, just now, it is more important than ever that we keep a space for the uselessness of the poem. •

Martin Langford's recent publications are *The Human Project: New and Selected Poems* (Puncher & Wattmann, 2009) and *Ground* (P&W, 2015). He is the editor of *Harbour City Poems: Sydney in Verse 1788-2008* (P&W, 2009).

Saltpan

Nike Sulway

THEY HAD BEEN seeing each other for several months. He had lost his wife and child in a car accident on their way to a birthday party. He had been across town when it happened, working late. She only knew what had happened because someone else had told her, or perhaps she had read about it in the paper. He had no interest in the past, his own or others', which suited her fine. She had her own secrets and was relieved to be able to keep them.

They were at a party at a friend's house when somebody started talking about the years when they had been at university: the parties, and the drinking and the politics they had shared. He stood and started clearing away the dishes. She caught the expression on his face in a mirror as he stood, his arms full of dishes, and turned towards the kitchen. His face was bereft: a closed and blasted landscape. She stood, collected an armful of plates and followed him. She ran a sink full of hot, soapy water and he found a tea-towel. While they worked, he told her that he no longer wanted a family; that sometimes, late at night, he felt relieved to be free of the burden of being a husband and a father. He would not marry again, he said.

That night they drove back to her house in silence. She was watching the moon follow them, remembering how as a child she had wondered why it was tethered to her. She still couldn't explain the way it sailed alongside the car, peering in the windows, as though it was waiting for her to say something, do something. Its vast face contained a question she could not answer.

They went inside without turning the lights on. She asked him to stay the night. She had never asked him to stay before. They walked over to the bed. He unbuttoned her shirt and slid it back over her shoulders. He eased her pants down over her hips. He folded his own clothes neatly and put them in a small pile by the side of the bed. They lay down without saying a word, and made love.

At midnight he said, 'Come outside,' and in the darkness they saw the sky of September bend down towards them with the stars held in its outstretched hands.

They had a small wedding at the registry office. She and a friend from the office made lavender cupcakes to serve at the reception, which was held at her house. They had two daughters in the first three years.

Lake Ballard, image courtesy Tamsin Slater

In the fourth year of their marriage they travelled to the saltpan of Lake Ballard. They left their hotel in Menzies while it was still dark and drove in unrelieved silence, both of them content that their daughters were safe, back on the east coast with her mother for the holidays. The girls were small and noisy, and would not have appreciated the beauty of the saltpans, or the long drives between country towns. When they reached Lake Ballard they parked and got out of the car. They were wearing hats and sunblock, and had brought bottled water. At first they walked together, but soon they found themselves attracted to the feeling of space between their attenuated bodies, to the sense that their intimacy was being stretched and enlarged as they moved away from each other.

She turned and saw him standing face to face with one of the sculptures that spotted the expanse. The heat of the day had started to shirr the air and it was hard to tell which of the figures was her husband and which was not. She watched as a valley opened in the earth between them and houses appeared, towns scrawled like Braille on the flanks of a white mountain. The moon rose up out of the earth near her husband's feet, its great, round head shouldering aside cakes of salt. She waited a moment, tipped back her head and felt the early sunlight pour down over her face. The sky was so near. Discovery. The end of things.

They found a depression in the brittle earth in which to sit and eat their breakfast. There were still no other visitors to the lake. When he had finished eating he put his head down in her lap and she held the weight of his skull in her hands. They made love, something they had not done for a long time. She fell pregnant with their third child.

Back at home, she found she had missed her daughters more than she had understood while they had been away, and was touched by the urgency with which her husband held them when they were reunited. Both she and her husband looked forward to the birth of another child, and hoped perhaps it would be a boy this time.

There were complications throughout the pregnancy, and finally the child had to be delivered by Caesarean section, under general anaesthetic. The woman and her husband waited in a hospital room for the nurse to bring them their child. The nurse, who had been present at the delivery, and who had been the one to clamp the umbilical cord and wash the child—like a soft, dense plate—in the sink in the delivery room, swaddled him in a blanket and presented him to the parents. The mother looked down at her son's face and made a small, sharp sound. They had been told what to expect. Before the nurse came in, the woman had been determined to love her son in measured scoops. One scoop of her flesh for each year he was expected to survive.

The husband put his hand on her arm. The woman pushed the edge of the blanket away from their son's head so that her husband could see. For the first time in several years she saw that look slide up and over his face: that private hollow into which he curled.

'Hello, little man,' she said to the child in her arms, and he turned his great head towards her chest, his mouth open and urgent.

The little girls came running in from the waiting room, where they had been sitting with their grandmother. They were careful not to clamber up onto the bed, but they were anxious to see their sibling. One of them made her father lift her up, and the other pushed the visitor's chair closer to her mother's bed and stood on it. They were both wearing new, polished shoes bought for them by their grandmother. When they saw their brother's face the older sister frowned and reached out to touch it with the tip of her finger, like an exotic fruit. The other got down from the chair and pushed it over to the window, where she sat throughout that first visit, watching the cars in the car park many floors below.

At first he didn't seem very different to other babies. He attached to the breast easily enough, but had to stop more frequently than was usual. He would fall back from the breast, his small face pink with effort, and take a series of deep, considering breaths. He would look at her as though he knew something she didn't yet understand, and pitied her.

The little boy turned out to be very quiet. When he woke up from a nap he played in his crib without crying until someone noticed he was awake. He would lie on a blanket in the shade while his mother gardened, watching her move from bed to bed with interest. He often appeared to be concentrating. At kindergarten he made a few friends, and enjoyed taking part in the school play each year. He particularly loved to dress up. His mother spent long hours making his costumes, and was always deeply touched by the pleasure her son took in them. One year he was a Christmas beetle, in a costume made of shimmering green organza underlaid with black silk. His father made beetle-legs out of plastic, and sat his son on a stool in the garage to watch while he spray-painted them.

Another year the boy was a bee, with wings that opened and closed all on their own thanks to a special motor his father installed in the striped belly of his costume. One year he arrived home with a note indicating he was to play the moon, but his mother refused to go along with it. They waited until their son was up in his room to call and discuss the matter with Mrs Dempster, who was in charge of the school play. He tried not to raise his voice when he spoke about the bullying, about the school's ineffectual attempts to get the other children to stop calling him Moonface. About the cruelty of casting him in this role, which could only feed the children's cruelty.

While the father was on the phone, sorting things out, the mother went upstairs to check on the children. The girls were each tucked up in their beds. One of them was reading aloud to a small array of paper dolls, pegged on a line she had stretched from the end of her bed to the window. The other girl had fallen asleep on the floor with her colouring-in book scrunched under her cheek and a blue crayon still grasped in her hand. Her mother picked her up and tucked her into bed. Then she went into her son's room. His room was neat as a pin. His light was out, and he had tucked himself in. She sat on his bed. She could tell by the way he was lying that he was upset about something. She had learned how to know that much. She pushed the sweat-damp hair back from his forehead and kissed him good night. He pretended to be comforted, and closed his eyes as if to sleep.

On the day of the school performance the children's mother had to work, but their grandmother had agreed to pick them up from school. One of the girls had a speaking part in the play, and the other was singing a solo. The little boy was to dress up as a polar bear. His costume was made out of synthetic fur with silver threads in it. He had a silver crown to wear, which his father had made, dotted with glass diamonds.

The grandmother had made fresh biscuits to give the children for afternoon

apologia to the converted
Judy Durrant

the bush is absurd with bloom
the air alive with blossoming chinks
my brazen annulling of its
bright revers
chuckle for each   slow rub
smack of the palm

mine for the picking—'off with their heads' i say
moldavian backwoods upstart romanticism—
i sneer at esperanto's *mistletoe imperative*
desperado!
maya—roll me one into many
serve me a sheriff's on a plate—serve me
        carroll's
and i'll spit on it
i finger cold steel—with a clear brain

mine's the expansive picture
i don't touch secateurs myself
but matrices—shrink from my warm
current embalming life on their
grand floor in their
coral castles

how green is my blade?—blood green
i appraise the blooms   prize the splayed
petal's bud-burst above all
my slaver drools beneficence—
into a valley seared of tears
the blown i have disposed of
my kingdom is my bloom!

and what is a poor inflorescence to do
severed from its roots?
i mete out sugar to its water
as surely as it fades
to its grovel—i may show mercy   i own
the power over sight and limb—
but my issue is order
not life

tea, which she served with glasses of chocolate milk. The little boy finished his first. The girls sat at the kitchen table with their grandmother, telling her all about the play, and about how one of the boys at school had wanted to have real kissing in the final scene, and how another of the boys had sprained his wrist rehearsing for the scene in which Joseph and the shepherds perform a rap version of 'Jingle Bells'.

The little boy had gone up to his neat-as-a-pin room. He had plenty of books and toys, but he was too tired to play. His polar bear suit was hanging on the outside of his wardrobe, and his polar bear crown was sitting on his desk. He ran his hand through the fur of the suit. It looked at him reproachfully, as though he had skinned a small animal in order to disguise himself inside its skin. He put on the silver crown, but that didn't feel very good either.

He went downstairs, past the kitchen where his sisters were helping his grandmother with the dishes, and out the back door. It wasn't far to the shops, where his oldest sister sometimes took him to buy lollies or ice-creams with the pocket money they earned for doing chores.

He walked past the shops to the school. It was mostly empty and unlit, but he could see a cleaner working in the grade four classroom, and the doors of the other rooms were still open. He went into a room he had not been in before. It was the staff storeroom. There were aisles of paints and canvasses, coloured and foiled sheets of paper and cardboard, scissors, glues, paint pots, newspapers and egg cartons. One aisle had bins filled with Styrofoam balls: the kind that his class had used to make models of the solar system. Large balls for the outer planets and the sun, smaller ones for the nearby planets. He looked around for the cleaner, but she was vacuuming the classrooms and emptying the bins.

He opened one of the plastic bins of Styrofoam balls and sank his arm into the slithery, squeaking mass. A few of the balls puffed up and fell onto the floor. He took out a few more and arranged them in a series of elliptical orbits on the carpet tiles. It wasn't like a solar system. There were too many large orbs, and they were all the same: enormous, featureless white globes; moons scrubbed clean of their craters and dunes. He was very tired by now, and regretted not wearing the polar bear suit, which would have been warmer than his shorts and T-shirt. He lay down and closed his eyes. His breathing was hushed and irregular, punctuated by a slow hiss like the air escaping from the pinched mouth of a balloon.

The cleaner was about to leave. She had turned out the lights, put the key in the lock of the staffroom door, and was pulling it closed when she heard the little boy's breathing and wondered whether one of the teachers had left something turned on in the storeroom.

When she saw the little boy lying on the floor, she thought at first someone had left a costume behind and she would have to carry it over to the school hall. But then she heard that sound—his peculiar breath—and saw his chest effortfully rise and sink. She knew who it was: she had never seen him before but it was clear to her whose boy she had found.

She called the boy's house, and the mother and father, who had arrived home and were just deciding whether to call the police, came straight to the school. The cleaner stood outside the staffroom and waited. She didn't turn on any of the lights in the staffroom or the storeroom. She left everything just as it was when she had found him. The mother came running across the school playground in bare feet; the father not far behind her. They hurried past the cleaner into the dark storeroom, and held their son close. The father carried him home, the mother's hand stroking their son's wet cheeks as they walked.

At home the mother ran a bath for her son while the father called the boy's doctor to tell him what had happened. Then he made the boy something to eat. A good meal, the kind of thing he had liked to eat as a boy. He took the food up to his son's room on a special tray. His son was washed and clean, his wet hair still clinging to his forehead. He was wearing his polar bear outfit, including the crown, but he didn't want to go to the school play. The mother lay down on the bed beside him and looked out the window at the moon, and told him a story about a tower and a bear and a princess. The father sat on the floor near his son's head. Every now and then, he would add something—some small, practical detail—the kind of thing they both knew their little boy loved.

Outside in the hall, with the door pulled mostly closed and her hand still on the handle, the mother and the father agreed that one of them would stay home with him as the doctor had recommended, and the other would go with the girls to the school performance. They flipped a coin to see who would stay.

When the father came home at midnight, he carried his girls one by one out of the car into their bedrooms. He slipped their shoes and socks off their feet and their costumes up over their sleepily extended arms. He pulled their sheets up over their shoulders and kissed their hot, happy faces. His wife had fallen asleep in front of the television. He kissed her too, and when she roused sleepily he kissed her again. It was the kind of kiss a man gave his wife in the dark, when she was sleep-rumpled and hot-breathed, and they had not yet said a word.

It was dark and quiet in the house. They held hands and went up the stairs to their bedroom, stopping outside their son's door for a moment to listen to him breathing.

By the time they had finished making love, their son was dead. While they were in their room, he had come downstairs and turned on the TV, with the volume turned down very low. He was lying on the lounge with his soft head turned into the cushions. The father had come downstairs to get his wife a glass of water, and when he saw his son lying there, at first he smiled. The boy was still wearing the polar bear suit and the silver crown, but when the father gently shook his son's arm, the boy didn't feel right. He didn't feel *firm* enough. The father turned off the TV. He listened for his son's breath. There was no sound. No sound at all. The father wished he had left the TV on: even that would have been something. He buckled onto the floor beside his son and pulled him close. How long had it been since he had held his son so close? Since he had smelled the milk-hot skin of his head and kissed him? The father stroked his son's silver and white fur, and felt the soft bones underneath the fur. He adjusted the crown on his son's head and cried and cried.

When his wife came down to find him, wondering what had taken so long, the husband felt ashamed and furious. He could not let go of his little boy. His wife knelt beside him on the lounge-room floor and tried to take the weight of them both; tried to steady them and separate them, and make sense of their bodies. So similar, so separate. Her husband; her son.

The moon was outside the window, peering in, still tethered to her, still asking whether she loved him. •

Nike Sulway is a Toowoomba-based writer. Her fifth book, *Dying in the First Person*, will be released by Transit Lounge in 2016.

FROM *THEIR BRILLIANT CAREERS*: MARCUS STEELE (1864–1924)

Ryan O'Neill

1 lb of onions
+ ditto of oranges
don't forget the spuds

(extract from 'The Shopping List', c. 1908. Original held in the Marcus Steele Museum, Canberra)

MARCUS STEELE, widely regarded as Australia's greatest novelist, short-story writer and poet, was born on 1 July 1864 in Newcastle, New South Wales. His father Peter, a carpenter, and mother, Elsie, were Scottish immigrants. Little is known of Steele's early life save that it was a difficult one, marked by dire poverty, and his parents' undemonstrative nature. Steele excelled at reading, writing and mathematics, and at ten years of age he won a scholarship to Sydney Grammar School, where he was in the same class as Banjo Paterson, though the two boys never became friends. The first of Steele's poems, a scrap of juvenilia called 'The Man from the Hunter River' (now sadly lost), dates from this time, as does his short story 'Wife of the Shepherd', which won first prize in a writing competition held by the school. Though the story was printed in the school newspaper, no copies are known to have survived.

Steele left the school in 1880 and spent the next several years travelling around rural New South Wales, gathering material for his first collection of poetry, *Bush, Beer and Ballads*. In 1891 Steele encountered Henry Lawson in a pub in Bourke, and spent the evening regaling him with his poetry. Lawson was entranced, and immediately wrote to J.F. Archibald, editor of the *Bulletin*, extolling Steele's talents. When Archibald asked to see Steele's work, the young man immediately wrote out his collection from memory, and dispatched it to the offices of the journal in Sydney. Sadly the manuscript was lost in transit, but based on Lawson's description, Archibald wrote a glowing review of Steele's work in the yellow pages of the *Bulletin*, praising him as an 'Australian Wordsworth'. Publication of *Bush, Beer and Ballads* was announced several times over the next two decades but it never appeared, with everything from wartime paper shortages to Steele's notorious perfectionism blamed for the endless delays. This has not stopped *Bush, Beer and Ballads* from being voted the nation's favourite poetry collection in every poll held since 1972.

Artwork by Ward O'Neill

Having conquered the world of poetry, Steele turned his hand to writing prose. His first short-story collection, *Charlie Cobb's Cobbers*, was written from 1902 to 1907, with the title story added in 1910. During this time, Steele survived on handouts from a number of wealthy patrons, including, it was rumoured, the governor-general and the prime minister, both of whom professed themselves admirers of Steele's work. Finally, in December 1910, the collection was completed, and submitted to publishers Allenby & Godwin. The editor, Lloyd Allenby, accepted the book immediately, and invited Steele to his home for a celebratory dinner. According to legend, the two men drank long into the night, reading passages of *Charlie Cobb's Cobbers* to each other, and roaring with laughter. Unfortunately, when they awoke the next morning, they found that a maid had thrown the only copy of Steele's manuscript on the fire. Allenby apologised profusely, honoured Steele's payment for his book, and wrote him a handsome letter of recommendation to his friend and fellow publisher Richard Pallister of Longmans, London. Steele sailed to London in 1913, already celebrated as one of Australia's finest writers. Neither Henry Lawson nor Banjo Paterson, whom Steele claimed had stolen ideas from him, were present in the delegation of writers from the *Bulletin* who farewelled Steele at the docks.

Little is known of Steele's activities during the First World War. It appears he began work on his first and only novel, *English Eucalyptus*, in 1914, and finished the book in late 1917 as, shortly afterwards, it was accepted by Longmans. Unfortunately, all two thousand copies of the book were destroyed in a fire caused by a zeppelin raid in March 1918. Steele's work had by then come to the attention of James Joyce, who had read an early version of *English Eucalyptus* (now lost) and described it as a 'masterpiece'. In 1920 Joyce invited Steele to Paris, where Steele gave advice to the Irish writer on the composition of *Ulysses*, then being published in instalments in the *Little Review*. Joyce later said that Steele had helped him reduce the length of the book by half, and many critics have since observed it was unfortunate that Steele did not live to offer his advice to Joyce on *Finnegans Wake*.

Steele was to remain in Paris until his premature and tragic death in 1924. When warned against drinking the Parisian tap water, he replied that he had drunk far worse in Newcastle. He died of cholera six weeks later, and was buried in an unmarked grave, at his own request, in a small cemetery in the northern suburbs of Paris. His life and works are commemorated in the Marcus Steele Museum in Canberra, where tens of thousands of visitors each year wait patiently in line to be admitted to the secure darkened room containing the scrap of paper on which is written his only surviving composition. ●

'Marcus Steele' is taken from **Ryan O'Neill's** new short-story collection *Their Brilliant Careers: The Lives of Sixteen Remarkable Australian Writers*, to be published in 2016 by Black Inc.

Poetry contributors

Trevor Bailey is a middle-aged jury court hack who aspires to writing verse as penance for the hurt he does our language at work.

Michelle Cahill has received prizes in poetry and fiction. Her collection *Vishvarupa* was short-listed in the Victorian Premier's Literary Awards.

Louise Carter's poetry has appeared in *Cordite Poetry Review*, *The Best Australian Poems* 2012 and 2015, *Westerly* and *Seizure*. She is a doctoral candidate at Western Sydney University and a member of the Writing & Society Research Centre.

Benjamin Dodds is the author of *Regulator* (Puncher & Wattmann, 2014). His current project explores the ethical and personal boundaries of scientific research.

Judy Durrant has twice been short-listed in the Newcastle Poetry Prize and tied second in the Judith Wright Poetry Prize; her latest poetry published was in *Prosopisia*.

Russell Erwin operates a farm in the Southern Tablelands of NSW. He has had three collections published.

Christopher Palmer lives in Canberra. He's been published widely since 2002, and his first collection is forthcoming from Ginninderra Press.

Daniel John Pilkington is a poet from Melbourne.

Brian Purcell has been writing and publishing poetry for more than 30 years. He has worked in community literature and founded the Bellingen Readers and Writers Festival.

Erin Shiel is writing a poetry collection about Australian contemporary art and artists. She has recently had poems published in *Cordite* and *Australian Love Poems*.

Nicolette Stasko has published six collections of poetry. She is also a writer of fiction and nonfiction as well as an independent researcher and academic. She is an honorary associate at Sydney University.

Corey Wakeling is the author of *Gargantuan Terrier, Buggy or Dinghy* (Vagabond, 2012) and *Goad Omen* (Giramondo, 2013), and co-editor of *Outcrop: Radical Australian Poetry of Land* (Black Rider, 2013). He lives in Nishinomiya, Japan.

Dugald Williamson lives in Armidale, NSW. He publishes on media and writing, including documentary, and does some university-style administration, at medium altitude.

David Wood was piccolist with the Queensland Symphony Orchestra. He plays the 'soft complaining flute' and reads his poetry at mountain concerts in Springbrook forest.

Meanjin thanks its supporters

Subscription Rates

Subscribe online at
www.meanjin.com.au/subscribe

Within Australia
Individual—regular: $80
Individual—concession: $70
Institutions: $145
CAL members: $70
MTC subscribers: $70

8 issues (individuals only)
Regular: $150
Overseas: $180

Overseas
Individual: $120
Institutions: $185

We also offer joint subscriptions with
Overland ($121), *Griffith Review* ($148),
Island ($119) and *Southerly* ($133.50).

To subscribe or make a donation,
contact the *Meanjin* office on
(03) 9342 0317
or visit our website at
www.meanjin.com.au